CITIZEN KLANSMEN

Citizen Klansmen
The Ku Klux Klan in Indiana, 1921–1928

LEONARD J. MOORE

The University of North Carolina Press *Chapel Hill & London*

© 1991 The University of North Carolina Press
All rights reserved

Library of Congress Cataloging-in-Publication Data
Moore, Leonard Joseph, 1952–
  Citizen klansmen : the Ku Klux Klan in Indiana, 1921–1928 /
by Leonard J. Moore.
    p.   cm.
  Includes bibliographical references and index.
  ISBN 0-8078-1981-6 (cloth: alk. paper)
  ISBN 0-8078-4627-9 (pbk: alk. paper)
  1. Ku Klux Klan (1915–   )—Indiana—History.   I. Title.
  HS2330.K63M66   1991
  322.4′2′0977209042—dc20   91-2602
                                      CIP

The paper in this book meets the guidelines for permanence and
durability of the Committee on Production Guidelines for Book
Longevity of the Council on Library Resources.

Manufactured in the United States of America
09 08 07 06 05   7 6 5 4 3

Extensive excerpts from the *Richmond Evening Item* and the
Richmond Palladium are used with the permission of the
publisher.

THIS BOOK WAS DIGITALLY PRINTED.

FOR MERLE

Contents

Preface, xi

Chapter 1 Introduction: Indiana and the Radical Interpretation of the Ku Klux Klan, 1

Chapter 2 White Protestant Nationalism, 13

Chapter 3 The Klansmen, 44

Chapter 4 Klan and Community, 76

Chapter 5 City, Town, and Village, 107

Chapter 6 Political Power, 151

Chapter 7 Conclusion, 184

Appendix Documentation, 193

Notes, 197

Bibliography, 229

Index, 251

Tables, Maps, and Figures

Tables

2.1	New Klansmen for Selected Weeks, 17
3.1	Klan Membership among Native-born White Men, 48
3.2	Foreign-born Population, 51
3.3	Influence of Southern Counties on Klan Membership, 55
3.4	Klan Membership in Urban Areas, 58
3.5	Influence of Urban and Rural Residence on Klan Membership, 60
3.6	Occupations of Indianapolis Klansmen, 63
3.7	Occupations of Richmond Klansmen, 66
3.8	Occupations of Crown Point Klansmen, 68
3.9	Influence of Wage Earners on Klan Membership, 68
3.10	Influence of Home Owners and Renters on Klan Membership, 69
3.11	Klan Membership within Central Indianapolis Protestant Churches, 71
3.12	Religious Affiliations of Richmond Klansmen, 73
3.13	Religious Affiliations of Crown Point Klansmen, 74
3.14	Influence of Church Membership on Klan Membership, 75
4.1	Native White Composition of Indiana Cities, 83
5.1	Percentage of Voter Turnout, Wayne County and Richmond, 114
5.2	Occupational Differences among Early Klansmen, All Klansmen, and Non-Klansmen in Richmond, 117
5.3	Klan Membership in Incorporated Towns, Wayne County, 134
5.4	Occupations of Klan and Non-Klan Rural Residents, Wayne County, 135

5.5	Residential Distribution of Klan Members and All Males, Indianapolis, 143
6.1	Influence of Klansmen on Votes for Governor and President, 161
6.2	Party Alignment in Vote for Governor, 163
6.3	Influence of Evangelical and Nonevangelical Protestants on Votes for Governor and President, 165
6.4	Influence of Protestant Church Members and Nonchurch Members on Votes for Governor and President, 166
6.5	Influence of Southern Residence on Votes for Governor and President, 166
6.6	Influence of Urban and Rural Residence on Votes for Governor and President, 168
6.7	Influence of Home Owners and Renters on Votes for Governor and President, 169
6.8	Influence of Wage Earners on Votes for Governor and President, 170

Maps

3.1	Klansmen among Native White Men, by County, 54

Figures

4.1	Valparaiso Klan Barbecue Advertisement, 99

Preface

Scholars often study groups and causes with which they feel a certain affinity. This has been particularly true during the last three decades, as historians have delved into the lives of ordinary Americans in attempts to understand their contributions and reactions to the great forces of change that have shaped modern American society. As a result, historians have uncovered a vast amount of new knowledge about African Americans, Native Americans, Mexican Americans, immigrants, women, workers, the poor, and others who have faced the greatest barriers to social and economic opportunity and political equality.

Not surprisingly, historians generally have not felt a similar attraction to the people who joined or supported modern conservative and right-wing movements. These movements, after all, have sought to maintain many of the very barriers that other groups have attempted to tear down. Conservatives have struggled to uphold traditional patterns of authority and ethnocentric cultural values. They have attempted to and at times succeeded in thwarting civil liberties, pluralism, free political and artistic expression, and other freedoms crucial to the integrity of a democratic society.

At the same time, however, not liking conservative and right-wing causes is insufficient reason to ignore them or, more accurately, to be content with pat answers about the social, economic, and political forces that have made these causes so popular in modern American life. Racist, anti-Catholic, anti-Semitic, nativist, anticommunist, antifeminist, and anti–civil rights movements have flourished at different times and places and at different levels throughout American society in the twentieth century. In recent years, religious fundamentalism, antiabortionism, antigovernment attitudes, and other concerns of what has come to be called the New Right have exerted a powerful influence in American politics. The power of these movements demands that historians examine their supporters with the same care that they expend studying more likable social groups. Like other movements, conservative ones cannot be understood by examining leaders and ideology alone. As important as these aspects of any movement may be, it is also crucial to investigate the movement's actual participants, to explore their characteristics and concerns and the reasons they chose to support particular solutions to the various problems they perceived.

During the 1920s perhaps as many as five million Americans joined national Ku Klux Klan organizations that had been created separately for men and women. The men's order appeared first and was much larger than the women's Klan. But taken together, these groups represented a huge segment of American society and one of the largest social movements of any kind in modern American history.

This book examines the largest and politically most powerful state Klan organization of the era. Its basic purpose is to explore the social bases of the movement—the social characteristics of the Klan members, their motives for joining, the conditions in which they lived, and the influence they exerted in state and local politics. Like a number of other recent studies that have analyzed Klan organizations in a variety of communities and states, this book challenges many of the accepted ideas about the Klan movement and offers a new explanation for the order's enormous popularity. It should be noted that this is a book primarily about Klansmen rather than Klanswomen. Few Klan records have survived over the years. Indeed, those that have survived for Indiana are unique in the amount of information they reveal about rank-and-file members. Unfortunately, they reveal almost nothing about Klanswomen, and I have chosen not to speculate in any significant detail about their numbers and characteristics.

One of the great pleasures of completing this book is having a chance to thank some of the people and institutions that were kind enough to offer support, encouragement, or critical insights. The Indiana Historical Society and the Graduate Division of the University of California, Los Angeles, provided critical financial support when this study began as a doctoral dissertation. The Andrew W. Mellon Foundation and the California Institute of Technology (Caltech) supported a great deal of additional research and writing. For that, and much more, I am grateful to have been part of Caltech's Mellon postdoctoral program. In addition to a dissertation fellowship, the Indiana Historical Society also furnished the most important primary resources for this book—the Klan membership documents. I am indebted to the staff of this wonderful organization, particularly Gayle Thornbrough, who directed it during the time when I was conducting the research for this study. Many other libraries and librarians both inside and outside the state of Indiana also contributed to this book. I am grateful to each of them but wish to acknowledge specifically the research staffs of the Indiana Division of the Indiana State Library and the Morrisson-Reeves Library in Richmond, Indiana. My thanks as well to the individuals who agreed to be interviewed.

When I began this project, I knew very little about the use of quantitative methods in historical research. I know a bit more now, thanks to J. Morgan Kousser, Allan J. Lichtman, Lawrence S. Rothenberg, and David L. Waterhouse.

Professors Kousser and Lichtman offered not only their expertise but also their encouragement in the early phase of this study and their critical assessments of the manuscript. William F. Deverell, Otis L. Graham, Jr., Daniel J. Kevles, James H. Madison, Martin Ridge, and Emma Lou Thornbrough read all or part of the manuscript. I am most grateful for their kindnesses and astute perceptions; of course, any errors are mine, not theirs. Friends and former colleagues at Caltech listened to my ideas and responded to presentations and other work related to this project. In addition to those mentioned above, I wish to thank Laird Boswell, Doug Flamming, Gregg Herken, Will Jones, James Lee, Gyan Prakash, and Robert Rosenstone. My special thanks, too, to Morris Schonbach and Richard Kleeberg whose friendship and encouragement helped see this work through its long journey.

My greatest single debt is to Stanley Coben, who guided my interest in the Klan from seminar paper to dissertation to book. His suggestion resulted in my first trip to Indianapolis; his patient insistence that I could do it caused me to overcome my dread of learning quantitative methods; his knowledge and sharp insights helped me discover new questions and, I hope, new answers.

The members of my family—both Northern and Southern California branches—have contributed much more than they probably realize to the completion of this book. I do not tell them enough how much their interest and support help me in my work, so I will take the opportunity to tell them now. I would like to thank specifically my brothers and sisters, Christine, Colleen, Ellen, Frank, John, Karen, and P. J., for their strength and courage during the hard days that surrounded the recent death of our mother, Patricia Nissen Moore. We all miss her, and I especially wish that I could thank her now for being my most dedicated teacher. She was able to read an earlier version of the manuscript, however, and, not surprisingly, found it to be excellent.

I thought writing a book was a daunting, time-consuming challenge until my son, Patrick Moore, appeared two and a half years ago. For that lesson and his smiling face, I thank him. This book is dedicated to my wife, Merle Moore. She knows why it could not possibly be dedicated to anyone else.

CITIZEN KLANSMEN

1. Introduction

Indiana and the Radical Interpretation of the Ku Klux Klan

The image of the robed and hooded Ku Klux Klansman is one of the most vivid and frightening in American history. It is the image of the southern racial terrorist, the midnight raider with the lash or club in hand and the hangman's noose or shotgun within easy reach—the image, in other words, of the Reconstruction-era Klansman and his descendant who emerged during the civil rights movement of the 1950s and 1960s. Most Americans are probably aware that Klan groups made their presence felt at other times between 1865 and 1965, and that isolated pockets of Klansmen continue to exist today. But the popular perception of the Klansmen seems welded securely to those two momentous periods, when reformers pressured the federal government to extend basic civil liberties to black Americans, and when Ku Klux Klansmen acted as the self-appointed shock troops of white supremacy, the most radical and dangerous bigots in American society.[1]

Historians have long maintained that the other major Klan movement in American history—that of the 1920s—did not conform in many respects to the popular images so strongly associated with the Klans of the Reconstruction and civil rights eras.[2] Unlike its earlier and later counterparts, the Klan of the twenties was not primarily southern. Rather, it became popular throughout the nation, enrolling at least three million and perhaps as many as six million members. From its national headquarters in Atlanta, Georgia, the Klan did attract a significant following in southern states, particularly Georgia and Alabama, but it prospered as well in parts of northeastern states such as Pennsylvania, New Jersey, and New York. It built large, extremely influential organizations west of the Mississippi in Texas, Oklahoma, Arkansas, Kansas, Colorado, Montana, California, and Oregon. The largest, most powerful state organizations were those of the Midwest—Ohio, Illinois, Michigan, and especially Indiana, where, by all accounts, the Klan gained its greatest influence and highest level of membership for any state.[3]

While the Reconstruction- and civil rights–era Klans depended exclusively on violence and intimidation, Klansmen in the twenties engaged in a wide range of activities and appeared especially interested in political power. The Democratic National Convention of 1924 provided one example of the Klan's political influence. During a bitter, sixteen-day meeting at New York's Madison Square Garden, Klan supporters and detractors hopelessly divided the convention and the party. In the process, they all but ensured that the presidency would remain in the hands of Calvin Coolidge and the Republicans—who carefully avoided the Klan issue at their convention.[4] Numerous political candidates supported by the Klan won state and local elections throughout the nation, including U.S. Senate races in Alabama, Colorado, Georgia, Indiana, Oklahoma, and Texas, and gubernatorial contests in each of these states except Texas, where an anti-Klan candidate narrowly won. In 1924, a Klan candidate won the governorship in Kansas and another was narrowly defeated in the U.S. Senate race in Montana. Oregon voters elected a Klan-endorsed gubernatorial candidate in 1922 and at the same time passed an anti-Catholic school bill that the secret order sponsored even more enthusiastically than the governor. In many communities—probably many more, in fact, than historians have currently documented—Klan chapters briefly dominated local politics. This was true in major cities such as Denver and Indianapolis, as well as in smaller communities such as Youngstown, Ohio, El Paso, Texas, Canon City, Colorado, and Anaheim, California.[5]

The Klan movement of the twenties stood apart not only because of its national scope and emphasis on politics, but also because of its ideological orientation. While the Klans of the Reconstruction and civil rights eras were driven primarily by the single issue of white supremacy in the South, the Klan of the 1920s espoused, through its many newspapers and widely distributed recruiting pamphlets, a more complex creed of racism, nativism, Americanism; the defense of traditional moral and family values; and support for Prohibition. The popularity of this ideology, historians have generally concluded, could be traced to a sense of national peril, a pervasive fear by native white Protestants that rural, small-town culture had lost its place at the center of American life, that the nation had been delivered into the hands of urbanites, anarchists, and immigrants.[6]

Although historians have noted these distinct characteristics of the Ku Klux Klan in the 1920s, the accepted interpretation of this mass movement still remains tied to the radical image of its counterparts during Reconstruction and the civil rights period—and not without reason. The Klan of the twenties, after all, drew its inspiration from the mysterious Reconstruction-era vigilantes romanticized in Thomas Dixon's best-selling novels and D. W. Griffith's controversial, but immensely popular film, *The Birth of a Nation*, which Klan agents used as a recruiting tool.[7] The ideology of the Klan in the twenties, though more elaborate, in its own way seemed no less extreme than the ideas of the vigilante Klans. To some degree, the Klan of the twenties may have appeared even more threatening precisely because its list of enemies was so long, including, in addition to blacks, Catholics, Jews, immigrants, political radicals, feminists, intellectuals, gamblers, bootleggers, thrill-seeking teenagers, motion picture producers, and many others. Moreover, it clearly contained extremist elements and during its early stages, many individual incidents of vigilante violence—both mild and severe—were associated with the movement, particularly in the South and the Southwest. Indeed, in a decade that witnessed a frightening wave of race riots, the Red Scare, the onset of national Prohibition, blatantly racist and discriminatory immigration restrictions, Sacco and Vanzetti, and the Scopes trial, the Klan in many ways appeared to be at the forefront of a national wave of dangerous intolerance, confusion, and fear. Like the southern Klansmen of other eras who were unwilling to accept the idea of racial integration, those who participated in the Klan movement in the twenties seemed unable to adjust to the wider notion of pluralism in an urban-based society.[8]

The radical image of the Klan and the volatile climate of the 1920s also led historians to conclude that those who joined the order or supported it with their votes represented disaffected fringe groups in society. One persistent view was that the Klan of the twenties attracted a particularly strong following in small towns and villages. The residents of these communities, historians believed, were the victims of provincial isolation and ignorance. Almost all of them were thought to be fundamentalists, drawn to the Klan as a result of their deep resentment of what, by that time, had become the obvious dominance of cities and cosmopolitan values in American life.[9] Other scholars placed less emphasis on the idea of urban-rural conflict, claiming that the Klan movement was equally popular in major cities. According to this interpretation, large numbers of Klansmen could be found in lower middle-class white and blue-collar neighborhoods. Badly paid and poorly educated, residents of these areas were thought to have joined the Klan largely out of resentment at being trapped in economic and residential competition with the growing populations of blacks and immigrants nearby.[10]

Historians' just contempt for the Klan's intolerance certainly contributed to many of these conclusions. Much of the history of the Ku Klux Klan was written during the late 1950s and 1960s by a generation of scholars that had witnessed the horrific consequences of European fascism, the anticommunist hysteria of the 1950s, and the hard-fought battles of the civil rights movement. Many of the most well-known works on the Klan of the 1920s, in fact, were written at the same time that new, extremely violent Klan groups were being linked with the bombings of black homes and churches, the widely publicized execution-style murder of civil rights workers, and numerous other crimes. In such an atmosphere, it may have been inevitable that the condemnation of bigotry would be the first priority in any writing about the Klan. Historians, like many other Americans who were confronted by these deep and disturbing divisions in American society, ultimately concluded that Klan organizations, regardless of the era in which they appeared, represented aberrant outbursts of hatred, ignorance, and anxiety over lost status.[11]

Yet to whatever degree one may sympathize with these ideas, the fact remains that it has been much easier to damn the Klan of the 1920s than to explain convincingly the reasons for its extraordinary popularity and influence. This book, supported by a number of recent studies of Klan organizations throughout the nation, asserts that the traditional interpretation contains basic flaws and ultimately does not divorce strongly enough the Klan movement of the twenties from the infamous traditions of the southern vigilante Klans.[12]

One weakness in the radical interpretation has been its reliance on an extremely small body of evidence. Klan documents have always been scarce. For the most part, historians have interpreted the movement by examining Klan newspapers, pamphlets, and other writings, and by following the activities of Klan leaders through local newspapers and national publications. As a result, historians have uncovered relatively little reliable information about the social characteristics of the rank-and-file Klansmen, their motives for joining the order, and the activities in which they engaged. Were Klansmen religious fundamentalists, small-town bumpkins, and ignorant, economically marginal individuals? Did they come together primarily to initiate a campaign of intimidation against threatening foreigners and the loathsome city? The authors of the radical interpretation have made these assumptions because they viewed the Klan's ideology as backward and militant and its leaders as corrupt. But without membership documents, close inspection of local circumstances and events, or analysis of the basis for Klan political victories, such generalizations cannot be substantiated.

The radical interpretation has also suffered from a narrow focus on the idea that the Klan movement of the twenties resulted primarily from increased conflict between white Protestants and other ethnic groups in American society. The Klan's white supremacist, anti-Catholic, and anti-Semitic ideology certainly played an important role in the success of the movement, but exactly what role? If the Klan existed to persecute ethnic minority groups, why did it become most popular in states such as Indiana, Colorado, and Oregon where members of these groups constituted only a tiny fraction of the population and no serious threat to white Protestant hegemony? When Klans assumed political power in these and other areas, why did they all but ignore the small communities of Catholics, Jews, and blacks that did reside within their domains? With millions of members assumed to be overwhelmed by resentment of the foreign born, why, despite some claims to the contrary, did the Klan engage in so little violence, especially in cities like Chicago and Detroit where the Klansmen and their perceived enemies both lived in huge numbers?[13] According to the traditional argument, these aspects of the movement could be explained by the fact that the Klan's fixation on ethnic minorities was primarily symbolic. Catholics, Jews, and immigrants—proximate or not—represented convenient targets for the anger of white Protestants whose values and traditions had been displaced by ascendant modernism.[14] It is possible, however, that people joined the Klan not merely to express their rage at immigrants and all that they symbolized, but also, or perhaps primarily, to address other, real concerns that historians have overlooked— concerns that grew out of social conditions in the communities and states in which the largest concentrations of Klansmen actually lived.

The traditional interpretation of the Klan of the 1920s contains another flaw as well. In general, it underestimates the importance of the movement by viewing it as a temporary outburst against modern culture that was sparked by "post-war excitement," the Red Scare, renewed immigration, and other events of the early 1920s. In this view, the Klan was of fleeting significance, an irrational last gasp of nineteenth-century nativism that appeared as white Protestants went through a process of adjustment to their declining ability to shape the nation according to their values and traditions. Yet the ethnic nationalism of white Protestant Americans was not rendered insignificant during the twenties, as this interpretation implies. Instead, it has formed the basis for many conservative social and political movements of the twentieth century. These movements, including Prohibition, fundamentalism, anticommunism, antievolutionism, antifeminism, and, in recent years, the various campaigns of the New Right, have been far from insignificant. As one of the outstanding examples of white Protestant ethnic nationalism and, indeed, as one of the largest social movements in modern American history, the Klan of the twenties may not have been a backward-looking aberration as much as it was an important example of one of the powerful popular responses to social conditions in twentieth-century America.[15]

Perhaps the most fertile ground for testing any theory about the Ku Klux Klan of the 1920s is the state of Indiana. Between 1922 and

1925, Indiana was the epicenter of the national Klan movement, the state that produced the Klan's largest, most enthusiastic membership, its greatest political victories, and its most powerful, well-known leaders outside of Atlanta. By any standard, Klan membership in Indiana was enormous. Between one-quarter and one-third of all native-born white men in the state paid ten dollars to become Klansmen during the 1920s; in some communities, the figure was as high as 40 or 50 percent. As astonishing as these figures may seem, they do not even include the thousands of women who joined the auxiliary order, Women of the Ku Klux Klan, or the Junior Klan for children.[16] Hardly a fringe group, the Klan became the largest organization of any kind in the state. It was many times larger, for instance, than any of the veterans' organizations that flourished in Indiana at the same time and even larger than the Methodist church, the state's leading Protestant denomination.[17]

With its massive following, the Klan temporarily transformed Indiana politics, assuming control of the state Republican party in 1924 and electing a governor and an entire slate of candidates for state government, a majority in both houses of the state legislature, and nearly all of the state's thirteen congressmen. In local politics, the Klan stunned established leaders in both parties, capturing city and county offices throughout the state and, for a time, controlling local party organizations.[18] The great popularity of the Indiana Klan made its leaders powerful figures, both within the Klan's national organization and in state politics, as well as the focus of a great deal of national publicity. David Curtis (D. C.) Stephenson, who stood at the head of the Indiana Klan, at least in its early stages, rivaled the order's national leader, Hiram Wesley Evans, as the most prominent Klansman of the period. Stephenson's influence in state politics led him to boast in 1924 that he was "the law" in Indiana. Moreover, the scandal surrounding his downfall played a critical role in undermining the national Klan movement.[19]

Recently uncovered membership documents make the case of the Indiana Klan even more consequential. One document, a report on conditions in local chapters prepared at the state Klan headquarters in Indianapolis during the summer of 1925, discloses membership figures for all but three of Indiana's ninety-two counties. This information opens the door to the kind of analysis that has been missing in studies of the 1920s' Klan: reliable estimates of statewide membership; regional membership variations, especially in regard to the urban-rural question; the social characteristics of Klansmen on a broad scale; and the dynamics of the Klan's electoral victories. Individual membership lists for several communities have also survived, making it possible to examine local trends and circumstances. One document contains the names and addresses of the first twelve thousand men to join the Indianapolis Klan; another lists all the Klansmen in the city of Richmond and the other communities of Wayne County. By happy coincidence, the state with the most powerful Klan appears to provide the best opportunity to examine the movement from the perspective of the Klansmen themselves.[20]

Traditionally, the Indiana Klan has been interpreted as a prime example of the hooded order's radical nature in the 1920s. Previous assessments have emphasized Indiana's particularly strong connection with the traditions of preindustrial America, the eruption of powerful antiurban, antiimmigrant—particularly anti-Catholic—attitudes in the state during the twenties, and the ability of opportunistic Klan leaders and ambitious politicians to mold these forces into a powerful movement. Most often, these accounts have focused on D. C. Stephenson, whose career has often been interpreted as a near-complete embodiment of the Indiana Klan movement.[21]

Typically, Stephenson has been depicted as a cunning opportunist who used his oratorical skills to manipulate multitudes of Indiana's citizens while he gathered Republican politicians into his hip pocket and used a fortune in membership fees to support a reckless lifestyle given to plush offices, expensive automobiles, women, and alcohol. Stephenson made the Klan a success, it has been asserted, by playing on the elevated prejudices of Indiana's overwhelmingly white, native-born population, convincing its citizens that only the Klan could protect America from crooked politicians, immigrant bootleggers, Jewish bankers, and the pope's legions. In politics, Stephenson has been credited with masterminding the Klan's domination of the state election in 1924 and, in the process, installing himself as the boss of Indiana's Republican party. Stephenson also has personified the Klan's reputedly inherent criminal nature. In 1925, he sexually assaulted an Indianapolis woman during an overnight train ride to Chicago; then, after she took poison, he kept her sequestered until it was too late for doctors to save her life. Following a sensational trial, Stephenson was convicted of second-degree murder and sentenced to life in prison.[22]

The story of Stephenson's rapid rise and lurid downfall was a notorious episode in Indiana history, and certainly it helps explain the course of the Klan movement. At the same time, however, its importance has been greatly exaggerated and has served generally as a substitute for a more comprehensive examination of the reasons for the Klan's great popularity and the bases of its political power. As we shall see, Stephenson did symbolize important aspects of the Klan movement but not the Klan movement itself. He did not, as it has been assumed, exercise tight control over an army of lieutenants and loyal Klan foot soldiers; he exploited, rather than controlled, a movement that was essentially decentralized and community-oriented. He was not "the law" in Indiana and did not control lawmaking in the Klan-dominated legislative session of 1925. His only major legislative effort, which had nothing to do with the Klan, was, in fact, defeated. Furthermore, Stephenson's crimes, and those of other Klan leaders and politicians in Indiana, did not represent a general lawlessness in the Klan movement. On the contrary, they discredited the order in the eyes of its members, distressing and angering ordinary Klansmen who had joined the organization to support law enforcement and traditional morality.

In general, the radical interpretation of the Indiana Klan is almost completely inadequate. The exaggerated emphasis on Stephenson implies that the movement was an aberration, that it succeeded because a medicine-show huckster had beguiled unwashed members of society—uneducated blue-collar workers and unsophisticated inhabitants of villages and small towns. Klan membership documents demonstrate that these narrow, Mencken-like assumptions are invalid. Indiana's Klansmen represented a wide cross section of society: they were not disproportionately urban or rural, nor were they significantly more or less likely than other members of society to be from the working class, middle class, or professional ranks. Klansmen were Protestants, of course, but they cannot be described exclusively or even predominately as fundamentalists. In reality, their religious affiliations mirrored the whole of white Protestant society, including those who did not belong to any church.[23]

Not only is it incorrect to identify the Ku Klux Klan as representative of a disaffected fringe group, it also is wrong to assume that the Klan movement was wholly defined by issues relating to a sense of conflict between Indiana's native white Protestants and ethnic minority groups either local or distant. These groups posed little if any threat to white Protestant hegemony in Indiana. Blacks accounted for less than 3 percent of the state's population in 1920, and the figure increased only slightly in the following decade. Foreign-born residents made up only 5 percent of the population in 1920, a figure that had declined since 1910 and would continue to do so. The number of Catholic church members did grow—from approximately 10 to 20 percent of all church members between 1916 and 1926. Like the black and foreign-born populations in general, however, this increase affected only a handful of Indiana's largest industrial centers, whereas the Klan was popular throughout the state. Jews represented less than 2 percent of Indiana's church members during the 1920s. In reality, the vast majority of the state's Klansmen lived in communities that were overwhelmingly, if not exclusively, native born, Protestant, and white.[24]

The ethnic conflict argument for Indiana is made even weaker by the fact that, despite its massive membership and great political power, the Klan did not carry out a campaign of persecution against ethnic minority groups. Large-scale, violent battles between Klan and anti-Klan groups, such as those that occurred in both Ohio and Illinois, never took place in Indiana, and there were no lynchings in the state during the Klan era. On the whole, the Indiana Klan did not employ violence and usually went out of its way to avoid confrontations in Catholic, Jewish, or black neighborhoods.[25] A similar tendency to avoid conflict with ethnic minorities could be seen in politics. A number of anti-Catholic laws were proposed in the Klan-dominated state legislature in 1925, but they were not passed. For the most part, Klan politicians ignored Indiana's black and Jewish citizens.[26]

None of this, of course, suggests that the Klan's ideology was not bigoted, that popular resentment of the growing influence of ethnic minorities in American life did not play a crucial role in the Klan movement, or that Indiana's Catholics, Jews, and blacks did not view the Klan with considerable alarm. All of these things were certainly true. At the same time, however, it is apparent that the role of ethnocentric ideas and values in the Klan movement must be viewed in a broader context, and that, alone, the ethnic conflict argument does not explain the Klan's great popularity.

The thesis presented in this book is that the largest state Klan of the 1920s is best understood not as a nativist organization, at least as nativism is usually defined by historians, but rather as a populist organization. This term, it should be noted, is not used here to suggest any connection with nineteenth-century agrarian radicalism. It is meant to describe a movement that was united by a temporary, but powerful outpouring of ethnic nationalism, and that concerned itself primarily not with persecuting ethnic minorities but with promoting the ability of average citizens to influence the workings of society and government.[27]

A close examination of Indiana's Klansmen and their activities reveals that they were not marginal men who were concerned solely with the idea that they had been displaced in American life by ethnic minorities and the distant metropolis. It shows that they represented a wide cross section of white Protestant society and that their concerns could be traced to a complex array of social pressures and changes, the consequences of which they could see in their own communities and feel in their own lives. Indiana's Klansmen were concerned first and foremost with Prohibition enforcement and crime, with state and local political corruption, and with a wide range of other issues that affected individual towns and cities. In the process of dealing with these issues, the Klansmen also sought to revitalize a sense of social and civic unity in community life and uphold traditional religious and moral values. These concerns were all related to the fact that by 1920 American society had been fundamentally altered by decades of industrial growth and economic concentration. The forces of consolidation had eroded established patterns in community life, undermined traditional, commonly held values, and diminished the ability of the average citizen to exert a strong influence in public affairs.[28]

Perhaps the best indication of the Klan's true nature is that once its members had been brought together in a celebration, of sorts, of their ethnocentric vision of what it meant to be an American, they all but ignored the distant and symbolic enemy of white Protestant

America—the urban immigrant. Instead, they found themselves embroiled in a series of battles with the real antagonists of traditional values and popular control in community life: political and economic elites. Community business leaders stood nearly alone as a white Protestant social group that was generally unwilling to support the Ku Klux Klan. In fact, in their opposition to the secret society they rivaled Indiana's Catholic, Jewish, and black communities. As Klan chapters grew powerful in individual communities around the state and as they threatened to assume political control, their most powerful adversaries were businessmen's organizations such as the Rotary club and the Chamber of Commerce, not the relatively powerless or, in many communities, nearly nonexistent ethnic minorities. And when the Indiana Klan swept the state election in 1924, the real victims were the members of the Republican (and in some areas, the Democratic) political establishment, who, in the wake of Ku Klux Klan populism, found themselves temporarily removed from power.

2. White Protestant Nationalism

The excitement began in Evansville. Agents of the national Ku Klux Klan organization entered the Ohio River city during the fall of 1920 and began promoting the mysterious new fraternal order among church groups, social clubs, and civic organizations. For the first eighteen months of its existence, Evansville Klan No. 1 represented little more than a curiosity, a small but steadily growing brotherhood of superpatriots distinguished by its unusual costume and the occasional cross burnings it conducted in the hills outside the city. Between the summer of 1922 and the fall of 1924, however, the Klan became much more than just another men's fraternity—both in Evansville and throughout the state. Suddenly, thousands of Vanderburgh County men began flocking to the organization, making it a local sensation and a political force that was powerful enough to unseat the district's anti-Klan Democratic congressman. Eventually, more than 5,400 men—or 23 percent of all native white men in the county—joined the Evansville Klan.[1]

To organize and preside over Indiana's first klavern, the Klan sent Joseph M. (Joe) Huffington, a native of Houston, Texas, who had been working as a Klan recruiter in his home state and in Oklahoma. The twenty-seven-year-old Huffington probably acquired the new territory as a result of his association with fellow Texan Hiram Evans, the high Klan official who later became the Klan's Imperial Wizard—the leader of the national movement. Little is known about Huffington's activities or the progress of recruitment in the Klan's early stages. It does seem that Huffington was somewhat less ambitious than other Klan leaders, content with his 25 percent share of the ten-dollar initiation fee paid by local members. He remained in Evansville throughout the Klan era, never sought public office himself, and moved up in rank in the state organization only after the movement was in decline. Although other Indiana Klan leaders became more prominent, Huffington was significant nonetheless. Under his direction, the Evansville klavern became the largest and most powerful in southern Indiana, and among all leaders in the state Klan, Huffington maintained the closest ties to Hiram Evans and the national organization.[2]

One of Huffington's noteworthy contributions was to bring D. C. Stephenson into the Klan's inner circle. It is not clear when or how the two men met, when Stephenson began working as a Klan agent, or when he became acquainted with Hiram Evans. Perhaps Stephenson first encountered Huffington as the Klan representative circulated among groups of Evansville veterans; Stephenson often socialized with veterans, and they were a natural target for Klan recruiters. However Huffington and Stephenson came to know one another, their common background surely promoted their relationship. Like Huffington, Stephenson had grown up in Houston and had lived for a time in Oklahoma before moving north. Perhaps even more important, both were young men on the make, new in town, and seeking to increase their prospects any way they could. But Stephenson did differ from Huffington in one important respect. "Steve," as he liked to be called, was extremely ambitious, and the Klan came to represent the opportunity of his lifetime.[3]

Before settling in Evansville, Stephenson had meandered through a number of towns and occupations and was said to have married and abandoned at least two wives. He had been a typesetter and a socialist in Oklahoma before World War I and, during the conflict, had completed officers' training (although he did not go overseas). Just before moving to Indiana, he had worked as a salesman and may have lived in Akron, Ohio. When he arrived in Evansville, at age twenty-nine, Stephenson worked in some capacity for a newly formed retail coal company. In the spring of 1922, shortly after becoming involved in the Klan, he made a hopeless run at winning the Democratic nomination for Congress.[4]

Stephenson's ascent to the leadership of the Indiana Klan came quickly. At the time of his failed congressional campaign, he had lived in Evansville for a little more than a year. Just months later, he took charge of the state Klan organization and soon would be a powerful figure in the national movement. Part of his success can be explained by his shameless pretension and guile, his shrewd understanding of the Klan's potential, his forceful personality, and his fascination with military hierarchy and organization, which he put to good use in marshaling the recruitment campaign. Yet, while Stephenson contributed much to his own advancement, he probably would have remained little more than a roguish drifter and con man had he not stumbled into the Klan and Evansville at precisely the right time.

For five years before the founding of the Evansville chapter, the Klan movement had been an inconsequential southern phenomenon, the creation of a floundering itinerant preacher and fraternal organizer, William Joseph Simmons of Atlanta, Georgia. Simmons had witnessed with great interest the enthusiastic reception to D. W. Griffith's film, *The Birth of a Nation*, in cities throughout the country and hoped that its Atlanta showing in December 1915 might be a springboard for a new superfraternity based on the mystique of the old Reconstruction-era vigilantes. The film—and the tumult surrounding the Leo Frank episode, which had gripped Atlanta for much of that year—did indeed stimulate interest in a new Ku Klux Klan. In the next few years, Simmons was able to scratch out a living by attracting several thousand men from Georgia and Alabama to his secret society. Although the order had no particular goals, its ideals were racism, religious bigotry, and hidebound patriotism, and on a number of occasions it was linked to violent vigilante activities. Wartime passions helped sustain the new Klan and even gave it a measure of legitimacy. Still, it remained small and probably would not have survived the passing of the Red Scare had Simmons not been persuaded to try a new means of promoting his organization.[5]

In the spring of 1920, Simmons engaged an obscure Atlanta public relations firm run by a former newspaperman, Edward Young

Clarke, and his partner, Mrs. Elizabeth Tyler.[6] Clarke and Tyler concocted a plan to hire a small army of recruiters who would work on commission to promote the Klan nationwide as a law-abiding, patriotic organization. The marketing scheme worked wonders for Simmons's struggling fraternity, transforming it into a national sensation with chapters in nearly every state and making it the subject of countless newspaper stories and the focus, in October 1921, of a congressional investigation. At the same time, the scheme brought hundreds of thousands—and eventually millions—of dollars into the Klan's Atlanta headquarters, making Simmons, Clarke, and Tyler wealthier perhaps than they had imagined possible.[7]

The Evansville chapter was created as part of this national expansion and, initially, represented just another outpost in the Klan's rapidly growing network. As the movement began to gain momentum in Indiana and throughout the Midwest, however, Evansville's founding Klansmen were in a unique position to assume control of the state organization and become leaders in the national movement. During the summer of 1922, with interest in the Klan already running high in many parts of the state, Stephenson moved to establish himself as Indiana's leading Klansman.

Leaving Evansville in the hands of Joe Huffington, Stephenson set up an office in Indianapolis, helped organize the Klan's state newspaper, the *Fiery Cross*, and hired associates and recruiting agents to assist in spreading the Klan gospel. That summer Stephenson and his men crisscrossed the state, doing everything they could to stimulate public interest in their organization. They spoke and distributed Klan literature at church meetings and men's clubs, they displayed their goodwill and honorable intentions with offers of free membership to Protestant ministers and other community leaders who might be sympathetic, and they acted quickly to appoint leaders who would establish local chapters, plan future community activities, and receive themselves a small percentage of future initiation fees. While the new Klan chapters were ostensibly secret, Stephenson and his fellow recruiters were actually eager to draw as much attention as possible to their membership campaign. The *Fiery Cross* heralded the growth of klaverns at every opportunity, and individual chapters often took out ads in local newspapers to promote upcoming Klan parades, picnics, and holiday celebrations. These highly

Table 2.1
*New Klansmen for Selected Weeks,
July 2, 1922–July 27, 1923*

Week	Paid	Honorary	Total
July 2, 1922	445	0	445
September 23	1,434	15	1,449
December 2	1,726	0	1,726
March 10, 1923	2,162	25	2,187
April 21	2,263	21	2,284
May 26	3,525	32	3,557
June 2	3,399	35	3,434
June 9	3,590	24	3,614
June 16	5,600	33	5,633
June 23	5,323	21	5,344
June 30	9,580	41	9,621
July 7	6,873	32	6,905
July 14	2,281	15	2,296
July 21	1,586	8	1,594
Total for All Weeks	117,245	724	117,969

Source: "Ernst and Ernst Report," D. C. Stephenson Collection, Indiana Historical Society.

publicized social events, in fact, proved particularly useful in attracting new members.[8] An audit of Stephenson's recruitment campaign from July 1922 to July 1923 revealed its astonishing success. Each week during this period, an average of more than 2,000 Indiana men joined the Klan—for a total of nearly 118,000 members (see Table 2.1).[9]

As Stephenson assumed control of the state organization, it is not clear how much direction, if any, he was receiving from Atlanta. Surely he could not have appointed himself leader of the Indiana Klan without at least tacit approval from the national leadership. At the same time, however, Stephenson, like other state Klan leaders, appears to have been in complete control of the recruitment campaign and other matters involving the Indiana organization. Such autonomy was possible because state leaders were not financially dependent on Atlanta, funding their operations out of a portion of local membership fees. In addition, the Klan's top leaders—Simmons, Clarke, and Tyler—were preoccupied with spending and investing the large amounts of money that were flowing into Atlanta, not with monitoring day-to-day affairs in the many states where Klan membership was booming.[10]

In fact, Simmons and his public relations advisers became so detached from state leaders and local operations and so enraptured by their sudden wealth that, by the end of 1922, they lost control of the organization to Hiram Evans. Evans, the Dallas dentist who had left his post as overseer of the successful membership campaign in Texas to take charge of the national recruitment drive, wanted the Klan to be more than just a moneymaking scheme. In November, at the Klan's annual convention in Atlanta, Evans gained control of the national organization with the hope that he could make the hooded order a force in national politics. The details of Evans's insurrection have never been clear. What is known for certain is that Simmons agreed to relinquish the position of Imperial Wizard to Evans and accept the ceremonial title of Emperor, and that, within weeks, both Simmons and Clarke were removed altogether from the Klan organization. The deposed leaders failed to regain their positions through a series of lawsuits.[11]

Whether Simmons was duped, blackmailed, threatened, or simply the victim of his own intoxication (a condition that was evidently common for the Klan's founder), Evans's success ultimately relied on his relationship with the state Klan leaders. Whereas Simmons, Clarke, and Tyler had failed to maintain close ties with the state organizations, Evans spent much of 1921 and 1922 traveling the nation and building a high profile among state leaders—many of whom he had appointed or approved for their positions. First among these men was D. C. Stephenson. Since he headed the Klan's largest state organization, Stephenson's support of Evans was crucial, and since Evans had almost certainly selected Stephenson for his exalted position, Indiana's Klan leader was quite willing to cooperate. Indeed, Stephenson seems to have helped orchestrate the takeover and probably did so in return for the promise of an even greater share of power in the national movement.[12]

On the Fourth of July, 1923, at a massive Klan rally in Kokomo, one that symbolized both the growing national importance of the Klan and Indiana's place at the center of the movement, D. C. Stephenson received his compensation. In front of more than 100,000 Klansmen and their families from throughout the Midwest, Evans officially declared Stephenson to be the Grand Dragon of the Indiana Klan; at the same time, he privately agreed to make Stephenson the head of recruitment in seven other northern states east of the Mississippi. This second part of the reward—more specifically, the share of membership fees that was to accompany it—never materialized, and within weeks Stephenson and Evans became embroiled in a bitter dispute over money.[13] Still, the Kokomo rally represented a personal triumph for Stephenson. Just a little more than a year earlier he had been an obscure figure trying to make a name for himself in a small Midwestern city. Now he was an acknowledged leader in a national movement with millions of members, a man with considerable fame, newfound wealth, and growing political power.

What were Stephenson and his fellow Klan salesmen offering that so many Americans—and, in particular, so many Hoosiers—were eager to buy? On one level, obviously, their commodity was racial and religious hatred. Bigoted rhetoric and literature accompanied Klan recruiters wherever they went, and a good deal of their success resulted from their ability to stir the anti-Catholic, antiforeign, and racist attitudes of native white Protestants.

American Catholics were the most frequent targets of the Klan's ethnocentric propaganda. Stories of alleged Catholic conspiracies appeared in nearly every issue of the *Fiery Cross*, and the many recruiting pamphlets that circulated in Indiana nearly boiled over with warnings about the Catholic "menace" and the need to "reestablish and maintain" the United States as a "Protestant country."[14] American anti-Catholicism, of course, was as old as the nation itself, and the Klan hurled no accusations that had not been standard since the great Irish immigration of the 1840s and 1850s. Klan literature focused most often on the traditional charge that the Catholic church was authoritarian, corrupt, and intent on taking over the United States. "Rome has no right," one Klan pamphlet proclaimed, "to try to force upon Christian America her pagan ideals and propositions." Another circular, a lengthy essay by Hiram Evans, gave a detailed account of how the Catholic church "assumed the right of control over states" and was therefore incompatible with America's democratic institutions. American Catholics, Evans warned, must be made to learn that "our government is on the banks of the Potomac and not on the Tiber in Rome."[15] Catholic schools and their alleged threat to public education represented another fixation of the Klan's anti-Catholic propaganda. Recruiting pamphlets repeatedly made the time-honored assertion that Catholic schools undermined Americanization. One pamphlet warned that "in many of the largest cities in this country the parochial schools outnumber our own American public schools," thus allowing countless immigrant children to avoid the "surest process of assimilation." Klan literature also accused Catholics of exerting undue influence on public education. The *Fiery Cross*, for example, frequently claimed that, at the direction of the church, Catholic members of the Indianapolis school board were working to undermine improvements in the city's schools.[16]

While anti-Catholic ideas were the most common in Klan literature, racism and anti-Semitism were also part of the order's ideology. Recruiting pamphlets declared that a central purpose of the Klan was to ensure white supremacy. One circular maintained that the United States was "established by White Men . . . for White Men" and was never intended to "fall into the hands of an inferior race." Mixing of the races was "biologically disastrous" and sharing political power with blacks represented "an invasion of our sacred Constitutional prerogatives and a violation of divinely established laws."[17] Rhetorical attacks on American Jews were equally harsh. "America was founded upon the principles enunciated by Jesus Christ," according to one piece of Klan literature. "No one who denies these principles can be a true Klansman, neither can he be a true American." Hiram Evans made a similar assessment in an essay that was actually designed to refute the idea that the Klan was anti-Semitic. While asserting that Jews did not threaten America like Catholics and that they possessed qualities that "all men respect and admire," Evans argued that Jews had benefited from American institutions without contributing to them: "It was only after the white, Gentile Christian had won the American continent by conflict and sacrifice that the Jew began to view America as his Mecca." Jews, he observed in another essay, lacked public spirit, were submissive and materialistic, and, because of their "Jewish Nationalism," would "ever remain a people apart" in the United States.[18]

The Klan's message of white Protestant hegemony in America naturally extended to immigrants as well. Klan recruiting literature, in fact, reserved some of its more acrid rhetoric for America's foreign born. Another of Evans's essays, this one concentrating specifically on immigrants, avoided even the pretense of objectivity. "America must close the door to the diseased minds and bodies and souls of the peoples of foreign lands," Evans declared. The "present horde of immigrant invaders" are composed of "Italian anarchists, Irish Catholic malcontents, Russian Jews," and other undesirable groups. They are "ignorant and unskilled, covetous and greedy"; they maintain "loyalty to the lands of their birth . . . they preach their own religions—mostly Roman Catholic or Jewish; they read their own newspapers, printed in foreign tongues; they deride America and its ideals." Capital and labor were equally threatened by the foreigner, according to Evans. Immigration brought "red agitators" as well as swarms of men "weak in mind, but strong in back," willing to undercut current wages and "live with their families in filth far below any possible American standards." America, he concluded, was essentially surrounded by foreigners who were eager to emigrate and further debase American society: "thousands of Mexicans, many of them communists, are waiting a chance to cross the Rio Grande . . . thousands of Chinamen wait in Cuba . . . on the Pacific Slope the yellow peril is a reality. . . . In Ireland discontented Republican rebels wait passage across the Atlantic . . . hundreds of thousands of pauper undesirables [from nearly every country in southern and eastern Europe] await the opportunity to come here."[19]

To Catholics, Jews, immigrants, and blacks in Indiana and throughout the country, such rhetoric was offensive indeed. The antiforeign climate of the war years, as well as the Red Scare and the race riots in the war's aftermath, were still fresh in the minds of the nation's ethnic minorities, and they could rightly assume that the Klan's "100 percent Americanism" represented on one level an attempt to rebuild the fires of suspicion and fear that had marked those days. Indiana's leading Catholic newspaper, the *Indiana Catholic and*

Record, reacted with alarm and anger to the Klan's appearance in the state, calling for Catholic solidarity against the order's "absurd" ideology and warning that Klan political power would threaten the lives and property of all Americans. The editors of the *Indiana Jewish Chronicle* and the *Indianapolis Freeman* also viewed the Klan's growth with great concern. The *Chronicle* followed the Klan's activities closely, characterizing the secret fraternity as bigoted, undemocratic, un-American, and a threat to the political rights of ethnic minorities. The *Freeman*, Indiana's most important black newspaper, made similar arguments, reminding its readers of the violent history of the Reconstruction-era Klan and cautioning that this new Klan might further segregate Indianapolis.[20]

While the Klan's diatribes against papist conspirators and inferior races provoked understandable outrage among ethnic minorities, as well as many white Protestants who also disapproved of such bigotry, it would be a mistake to conclude that prejudice alone defined the Klan's ideology or, for that matter, that its central's message was irrational, pathological, or radical. Klan recruiting pamphlets and other literature also focused on such issues as law enforcement, especially of Prohibition, problems of vice and public morality, political corruption, the decline of public involvement in civic affairs, the erosion of traditional family values, waning church attendance, and the need for better public schools. These issues amounted to more than just window dressing designed to help make the Klan's prejudice more respectable—even if, as one might suspect, that was the original intention of its profit-minded ideologues. To a huge portion of Indiana's white Protestant society, these concerns were just as powerful as those involving ethnic minorities. They may, in fact, have been more compelling, since Indiana Klansmen acted on many of these issues while they all but ignored the state's Catholics, Jews, and blacks. Furthermore, in the Klan's ideology, there was nothing incompatible about prejudice and civic activism. The Klan's views on ethnic minorities were widely shared or at least tolerated in society; and in Indiana especially, public affairs and political movements had always been interwoven with a deeply rooted white Protestant cultural hegemony.

The Klan salesman's real commodity was a defensive form of ethnic nationalism—white Protestant nationalism—and it was defined not by bigotry alone, but by a broader, more complex set of concerns about the place of the white Protestant majority in American society. The order's basic message was that average white Protestants were under attack: their values and traditions were being undermined, their vision of America's national purpose and social order appeared to be threatened, and their ability to shape the course of public affairs seemed to have diminished. The easiest way to articulate this message was to focus on traditional ethnic scapegoats. These groups *had* changed the nature of American life, and blaming them for unwanted social conditions represented a gut-level means of enhancing the ethnic identities of white Protestants. At the same time, however, the actual threat posed by ethnic minorities, in Indiana and other states where the Klan flourished, was too small to have been, by itself, the catalyst for these ethnocentric concerns. The problems associated with Prohibition, on the other hand, were immediate and real and provided disturbing, almost daily evidence that the values of white Protestant Americans could not easily be made dominant in society. This issue, and others embraced by many white Protestants throughout Indiana, provided the substance that racial and religious bigotry by itself could not.

Together, symbolic fears about distant ethnic minorities and more tangible concerns over social and political conditions that shaped everyday life forged the basis for a powerful populist ideology. White Protestant nationalism defiantly asserted that the nation's chosen people had lost their place at the center of American life and, therefore, that the power of the "average citizen" had been diminished. While many Americans were disturbed at the ethnocentric dimensions of such an ideology, or amused, perhaps, by its provincialism, more than 200,000 residents of Indiana saw in white Protestant nationalism a means through which they could express a wide array of social and political grievances. Ultimately, the Klan's ethnic nationalism appealed to the mainstream of white Protestant society—not its radical fringe elements—and succeeded in overwhelmingly white Protestant Indiana because it gave average citizens more influence over public affairs.

The Klan's attitude toward violence and the role of violence in the

Indiana movement provide important evidence that the order appealed primarily to mainstream elements in society. Klan recruiting pamphlets claimed that the organization opposed violence as a tactic and condemned acts of violence by its members. Indiana's Klansmen generally complied. Large-scale confrontations between Klan and anti-Klan groups, such as those in Herrin, Illinois, and Niles, Ohio, never occurred in Indiana.[21] The state Klan organization did not employ violence as a strategy, and only a tiny fraction of the order's membership ever engaged in violent or threatening acts. Indiana's anti-Klan newspapers, such as the *Indianapolis Times* and the *Muncie Post Democrat*, which took every opportunity to condemn the Klan, especially its association in any part of the country with crime or vigilantism, did not characterize the Indiana Klan as a violent organization. The *Indiana Catholic and Record*, the *Indiana Jewish Chronicle*, and the *Indianapolis Freeman*, which certainly had no reason to ignore it, uncovered no significant instances of Klan-inspired violence in the state. Like other anti-Klan publications, their main concern related to the consequences of the Klan's political victories.[22]

The lack of overt violence did not mean that the Indiana Klan failed to convey an ominous image. The vigilante reputation of the Klan, its aggressive racial and religious bigotry, its secretive nature, and its obvious popularity were by themselves enough to intimidate and cause alarm. Murders, beatings, bombings, and riots may not have characterized the Indiana Klan, but its militant self-righteousness periodically unleashed overtly threatening behavior. When George R. Durgan, the anti-Klan mayor of Lafayette, announced his candidacy for governor in 1924, hundreds of angry Klansmen descended on the Indianapolis hall where he was speaking, nearly causing a riot. Trouble also occurred in the mining districts of southwestern Indiana. Mine owners evidently complained to Governor Warren T. McCray in 1923 that Klan miners were harassing non-Klan workers. In the small town of Mitchell in southern Indiana, a group of Klansmen led a raid on a gambling and bootlegging operation. The lawyer of a black sharecropper in Vincennes claimed that Klansmen had forced his client to sign a confession to a charge of assault with intent to rape.[23] On two known occasions, Klansmen persuaded Catholic public school employees to seek jobs in other communities. And in Shelby County, the Klan was rumored to have been responsible for a fire that destroyed a Catholic church.[24]

Yet, if the Indiana Klan stimulated fear among many of the state's citizens, it also provoked anger and was itself the victim of violent attack. On several occasions, the *Fiery Cross* reported that its salesmen had been threatened and beaten on streetcorners in a number of cities. The Klan publication also complained that Klanswomen in one town had been attacked with rocks and bricks after attending a church meeting, and that bottles, bricks, and tire irons had been thrown through the windows of homes belonging to "Protestant businessmen" after their names appeared on a published list of Klan members in Indianapolis. In South Bend, one Indiana city with a large Catholic population, local Klansmen were assaulted on a number of occasions. University of Notre Dame students broke up one Klan rally in March 1924. Two months later, a group of Catholic men attacked two Klansmen as they stood guard outside a Klan meeting. In October, the South Bend Klan canceled a scheduled meeting after a rumor circulated that it would be the target of gunmen. The Terre Haute Klan faced even more violent resistance. Early in 1924 two local Klansmen were murdered, and in November an arsonist destroyed the Vigo County Klan headquarters.[25]

Reactions to the Klan's growth by Indiana newspapers, church groups, politicians, and others also suggest that the order appealed to prevailing rather than extremist views. This does not mean that Catholic, Jewish, and black organizations were alone in their opposition to the Klan. Courageous Protestant ministers, politicians, and newspaper editors spoke out against the Klan, even though to do so could damage their community standing and careers. Two Disciples of Christ ministers in Indianapolis, for example, resisted Klan recruitment and later condemned the order from the pulpit. Both dissenting clergymen were released by their congregations. The Indianapolis Diocese of the Protestant Episcopal church soundly denounced the Klan as it rose to power; so did one regional Methodist newspaper, even though it was clear that thousands of its readers were members. Other politicians, in addition to Mayor Durgan of Lafayette, were bold enough to reject Klan political support or to campaign on openly anti-Klan platforms. Noted anti-Klan politicians included Mayor Lew Shank of Indianapolis and congressional candidates William E. Wilson of Evansville, Arthur Greenwood of Washington, Joseph P. Turk of Indianapolis, and James W. Hill of Franklin.[26]

Strong, open opposition to the Klan in Indiana, however—except from Catholics, Jews, and blacks—was far less common than passive acceptance or outright approval of the organization. Newspapers that openly criticized the Klan, such as the *South Bend Tribune, Muncie Post Democrat,* and *Indianapolis Times,* represented only a small minority of the state's papers. Some publications did offer mild resistance by refusing to print stories about the Klan despite its obvious importance. Most newspapers, however, chose the safest course of refusing to offer either approval or condemnation, and others, such as the *Kokomo Daily Tribune,* the *Richmond Evening Item,* and the *Franklin Evening Star,* openly gushed enthusiasm for the Klan's appearance in their communities, especially when Klansmen spoke in support of law enforcement or worked on behalf of local charities.[27]

Numerous civic, political, and religious groups chose to remain quiet while the Klan gained momentum. The silence was particularly telling among Indiana's major Protestant churches. The three largest denominations—Methodist, Disciples of Christ, and Baptist—which together accounted for over half of all Protestant church members in the state, never openly broached the Klan issue at state conventions. The reticence of these churches did not signify hushed approval of the Klan; rather, by ignoring the hooded order, churches avoided the prospect of bitter internal disputes between the Klan's enthusiastic supporters and those who opposed it with equal passion. Yet, while the major Protestant bodies conferred no sanction on the Indiana Klan, hundreds of its clergymen were deeply involved in Klan affairs. For instance, thirteen Methodist pastors were among the first to join the Indianapolis Klan, along with eleven ministers from Baptist, Disciples, and Presbyterian churches and over thirty more from other denominations.[28]

Other groups displayed a similar tolerance of the Klan's growth. The Indiana American Legion voted down an anti-Klan resolution at its 1924 annual meeting. Influential organizations such as the Anti-Saloon League and the Woman's Christian Temperance Union (WCTU), which, unlike the American Legion, did not have strong contingents of Catholic members to offer the suggestion, also failed to denounce the Klan. The temperance groups in particular supported many Klan candidates for political office and undoubtedly supplied numerous members to the Klan's ranks.[29]

The Klan's ability to influence state politics may have been the best single indication of the degree to which it was sanctioned by the social mainstream. In 1924, the state Republican party was almost powerless to stop its takeover by Klan-supported political candidates at every level. Those Republicans who opposed the Ku Klux Klan were swept out of office in the spring primary; the only safe Republicans were those who agreed to accept Klan support or, at the very least, remain neutral. Indiana's Democratic party was also reluctant to oppose the Klan. The Democratic machine, under the direction of Thomas Taggart, realizing that many Democrats had also become Klansmen, had hoped to avoid making the Klan an issue in the state election of 1924. Taggart and the party's gubernatorial candidate, Carleton B. McCulloch, agreed to change this strategy only after strong voter support for several minor anti-Klan candidates in the primary made it necessary to place an anti-Klan plank in the platform. The condemnation, however, did not mention the Klan by name and was as mild as the party machine could make it and still satisfy anti-Klan elements. Taggart remained convinced that a neutral stand on the Klan would be in McCulloch's best interests; the party boss also planned to promote Indiana senator Samuel Ralston as a compromise presidential candidate at the 1924 Democratic National Convention and wanted Indiana Democrats not to be viewed as strongly anti-Klan.[30]

Even when the Klan did encounter criticism, often it was mixed with admiration for the order's ideals. One Disciples of Christ publication rebuked the Klan only because it was unnecessarily militant and disruptive, not because its goals were misguided. An editorial in 1923 argued that the churches could achieve the aims of the Klan without its divisive interference. "Does the Klan stand for one hundred percent Americanism? So do I, not a Klansmen," its author pointed out. "Is it against the encroachment of the Roman hierarchy? So am I . . . there is nothing it champions that I do not champion, though I wear no mask." The Klan's popularity, he was forced to admit, was not at all mysterious:

There are those who affirm that in its protests against lawlessness, against Roman Catholic domination, against Jewish monopolies here and there, against a divided allegiance to our country, it is doing a great and needed work; that it is the savior of Protestantism; that it is the defender of the Constitution; that it is a help to morals and religion; that its masks are but legitimate appeals to the dramatic within all of us; . . . that it has "cleaned up" villages, towns and cities; that its record is high pitched. There can be no doubt but that thousands and tens of thousands of good people feel just this way about it and are fervent in its advocacy.[31]

This assessment of the Klan revealed a particularly important reason for its wide acceptance: although some aspects of the movement were strident and controversial, the thrust of its ideology—including its Protestant chauvinism and its intolerance of ethnic minorities—conformed to views that were prevalent among Indiana's white Protestants. One did not have to look far, for example, to find spokespersons who echoed the Klan's adamant belief that Protestant values should be dominant in society, clearly demonstrating that the Klan had no monopoly on dogmatic religious ideas. One primary concern was that traditional Protestant values were in decline. Religious and community leaders throughout the state charged that the Bible was being ignored in homes and schools and that the results threatened disaster. Community newspapers claimed that people broke the law primarily because they had not learned reverence for authority through religion. They also warned that the future leadership of the nation would be dangerously weakened by a lack of spiritual training in America's colleges.[32] One paper, inspired by a local Billy Sunday revival meeting, proclaimed in a front-page headline: "If You Don't Believe in the Bible You're a Fool!" The expression of such views caused little controversy in most Indiana communities. The average citizen had been conditioned to see Christianity as the foundation for ethical behavior and to accept Protestant evangelism as a traditional force for public good. Robert and Helen Lynd's *Middletown* confirmed how deeply these assumptions were rooted among the people of Muncie. As part of their survey of the attitudes of high school students, the Lynds reported that 83 percent of the boys and

92 percent of the girls agreed with the statement: "Christianity is the one true religion and all peoples should be converted to it."[33]

Protestant ideals were transmitted in public affairs in numerous, often subtle ways and with a powerful effect. In many community newspapers, especially outside the large cities, religious news could be elevated to front-page importance. In one instance during a week in January 1924, a series of lectures on the Bible monopolized the front page of the *Greensburg Daily News*. "Do not fail to hear the recital tonight," one article advised. Some publications, such as the *Vincennes Sun*, ran daily Bible verses as a public service; in some papers, Christmas and Easter editorials read as if they could have been delivered from the pulpit. In a front-page editorial during the spring of 1922, the *Richmond Evening Item* proclaimed that after nineteen centuries of human turmoil, the only hope for the world "still lies in the truth of the divine miracle of Easter morn."[34] Religious values were also imparted through social and benevolent organizations such as the YMCA and the Salvation Army, as well as by local politicians. Even the anti-Klan mayor of Indianapolis, Lew Shank, recognized the importance of being associated with conservative Protestant ideas. In one campaign, he told an audience that unlike Darwin, who "didn't know what he was talking about [,] . . . I believe every word in the Bible."[35]

If the Klan's zealous Protestantism was common rather than exceptional, so too was its anti-Catholicism. Indiana's largest Protestant churches may have been disinclined to take a position on the Klan, but they showed no such reluctance when it came to criticizing the Catholic church. Much of their rhetoric was indistinguishable from the Klan's. Like the Klan, church leaders believed that Protestants were locked in competition with American Catholics and that the Catholics were winning. Protestant ministers and church publications warned that Catholics were becoming more powerful than Protestants because they were better organized and because Catholic children received more religious training. A report presented at the Indiana Baptist Convention of 1920 concluded that Catholic youths received over eight times more religious instruction than Protestants and that churches must work to increase Sunday School attendance. In 1925, the *Baptist Observer* supported a bill proposed by Klan legislators that would allow early release from public schools for the purpose of religious instruction. Such a law, the *Observer* maintained, would "prove whether Protestants care as much about the religious education of their children as do the Catholics." Protestant publications naturally blamed the Catholics' competitive edge on the parochial schools and frequently criticized their place in American society. The Methodist *Indianapolis Area Herald* claimed that parochial schools made children narrow-minded, prejudiced, and poor citizens of democracy and that they put out the fire under the melting pot. To rekindle the fire, the *Area Herald* suggested compulsory public school attendance, an idea that was popular with the Klan nationwide. Catholics, the paper said, should "either melt or get out."[36]

On occasions when American Catholics stood up against anti-Catholicism, some Protestant spokespersons became furious. When a 1921 Knights of Columbus convention in Chicago denounced the Klan as un-American and offered to assist in a congressional investigation of its activities, one Midwestern Disciples of Christ publication, which circulated in Indiana, could not contain its anger. "We hold no brief for the Ku Klux Klan," said the editors of the *Christian Standard*, but "this is the limit. A Roman Catholic organization branding another organization as 'un-American' and resolving to cooperate with the Federal Government in an effort to locate something un-American in a Protestant organization!" If Congress investigated the Klan, the *Standard* suggested, it should also investigate the Knights of Columbus.[37]

Like the Klan, other supporters of Protestant anti-Catholicism routinely argued that their views were not bigoted or incompatible with America's tradition of religious freedom. They believed just the opposite: they were fighting to protect the separation of church and state by working against the Catholic desire for political control of the nation. Such rationalizations were as transparent in church newspapers as they were in the Klan press. "The political, religious, social and industrial life of the country is the result of Protestant dominance," asserted an editorial in the *Western Christian Advocate*, even as it attempted to explain its respect for the religious rights of Catholics. Roman Catholicism, the Methodist newspaper claimed in another editorial, simply did not mix with American traditions: "We do not believe in popery. History does not believe in it.

Progress does not believe in it. Liberty does not believe in it. Free institutions do not believe in it. Democracy does not believe in it. The light of Christian truth does not believe in it. The freedom of assemblage does not believe in it. Freedom of religious conviction does not believe in it. Freedom of religious conscience does not believe in it."[38]

Like anti-Catholicism, antiforeign attitudes were common enough in Indiana to make it difficult to distinguish the Klan's prejudicial views from mainstream ideas. A rash of xenophobic opinion, for example, appeared in Indiana newspapers as Congress debated the merits of what eventually became the National Origins Act of 1924. Except for the Indianapolis papers, which wondered about the diplomatic consequences of immigration restrictions directed squarely against Japan and the nations of southern and eastern Europe, most state publications agreed that such restrictions were necessary. The *Muncie Morning Star* said that Japanese leaders would just have to accept the fact that their people were unfit to be Americans. Even the *Gary Post-Tribune*, which operated under the control of U.S. Steel and usually sought to avoid antagonizing Gary's many foreign-born and black workers, concluded that the discriminatory restrictions were needed to "save the white civilization."[39]

The striking parallel between the Klan's ethnocentric rhetoric and that of more conventional spokespersons should not be taken as an indication that racial and religious bigotry epitomized white Protestant culture in Indiana. It does suggest, however, that such ideas were an accepted part of that culture, that white Protestant society itself was awash with defensive ethnocentric concerns in the early 1920s, and that the Klan's ideology stood as a particularly important example of white Protestant attitudes, not a deviant exception to mainstream thinking. In fact, much of the ethnocentric rhetoric— whether it came from Klan recruiting pamphlets, Protestant journals, politicians, or newspaper editors—was little more than hyperbole. Few white Protestants actually believed that "white civilization" was on the brink of collapse or that the pope was about to destroy Indianapolis's public schools. At the same time, doomsday predictions and conspiratorial accusations, however incredible, captured the attention of white Protestants and heightened their identification with the cause of defending ethnic values and traditions. Spokespersons for other ethnic groups, it should be noted, were also willing to employ ethnic "campaign rhetoric." In 1923, for instance, the editor of the *Indiana Catholic and Record* arrived at the rather unlikely conclusion that the Ku Klux Klan was part of a British conspiracy to "destroy the unity of the people of the United States."[40]

The connection between the Klan's ideology and mainstream ideas and concerns is even more apparent when one considers Klan attitudes toward more immediate social issues. By far, the most important of these was Prohibition enforcement. Klan recruiters, backed by editorial support from the *Fiery Cross*, endorsed the liquor laws, condemned those who violated them, and called upon Klansmen to do what they could to support enforcement. "When the government of the United States crushed out the saloon with the Eighteenth Amendment," one Klan pamphlet proclaimed, "one of the greatest evils that threatened our homes was conquered forever. It is our duty to see that [any attempt to change the existing law] is unsuccessful and that the wedge is not driven into our Constitution. There is only one way to protect our homes and our nation, and that is to enforce the law without fear or favor." To ensure that Prohibition succeeded, Klansmen, according to another pamphlet, stood ready to "help, aid and assist the duly constituted authorities of the law in the proper performance of their legal duties." The Klan's literature urged members not to break any laws themselves in the process. For the most part, Klansmen obeyed, doing their part by putting political pressure on local government officials or by supporting "law enforcement" candidates to replace city councilmen, sheriffs, or district attorneys who failed to respond to demands for better enforcement.[41]

Spokesmen for the Klan blamed immigrants and organized crime for much of the liquor problem. The *Fiery Cross* pointed to Chicago as the source of a large percentage of Indiana's illegal alcohol and on more than one occasion identified the small Italian neighborhood in Indianapolis as a center of Prohibition-related crime. The Klan did not use the Prohibition issue solely as another means to attack the foreign born, however. A great deal of its rhetoric was directed at corrupt politicians and law enforcement officials who allowed Prohibition violations to continue, as well as citizens who purchased liquor or condoned the breaking of the law by their apathy. In seeking to bolster support for Prohibition enforcement, the Klan turned frequently to the traditional argument that an end to alcohol consumption would uplift society. Crime, the Klan argued, would practically disappear if only citizens would obey the liquor laws. This applied not only to organized criminal syndicates, but also to street crime, domestic violence, and public dangers such as drunk driving. The drunk driver, according to one Klan writer, was "like a dog with rabies." Judges, he declared, should give the maximum penalty to anyone "who drives an automobile, swinging from curb to curb . . . while he's drunk and seeing double."[42] In essence, the Klan endorsed the entire argument for prohibiting alcohol as a means of reforming society. Prohibition would erase adult illiteracy and promote the Americanization of the immigrant, good citizenship, public health, and greater economic productivity.[43]

The Klan's rhetoric regarding Prohibition—its aggressive antiforeign tendencies as well as its reformist leanings—was very much a part of Indiana's dry tradition. The same arguments had been made when the state first outlawed liquor in the 1850s, when it nearly passed another prohibition law in 1882, when remonstrance laws and local option elections drove saloons out of individual communities in the late nineteenth and early twentieth centuries, and when statewide Prohibition was enacted for the second time in 1917.[44] The passage of the 1917 statute, followed by the Eighteenth Amendment and the Volstead Act in 1919, if anything, led to an intensification of prohibitionist rhetoric, much of it indistinguishable from the Klan's. Faced with the problem of widespread violation of the liquor laws, Indiana newspaper editors, Protestant churches, and dry organizations were more than willing to blame the foreign born, corrupt politicians, and an apathetic public.

Immigrants were an easy and traditional target for prohibitionist frustrations. A newspaper editor in Richmond, though not a Klansman himself, produced one assessment of the law enforcement problem that could easily have appeared in the *Fiery Cross*:

> The police have clues that are leading them straight to the dens of the worst outscourings of Europe. . . . They have the best chance in ten years to rid this country of its most desperate and dangerous criminals. It will be the biggest service to this country

since the "Red" raids two years ago.... The great bulk of bootlegging is done by foreigners, so there should be no problem with the proposed law in Congress to kick out foreigners caught bootlegging. The foreign bootlegger is not just a criminal. He is an unpatriotic criminal because he is violating the Constitution. Putting him in jail is just a waste. Shipping him to his foreign land is wiser, more economical, and patriotic.[45]

The Indiana Woman's Christian Temperance Union advised Americanization rather than deportation but conveyed the same basic criticism of the foreigner. According to WCTU leaders, 75 percent of the law enforcement problem was due to the immigrants, and a major task of the organization would be "to teach both native and foreign born total abstinence, Prohibition and respect for the law."[46]

Apathy and corruption were particularly disturbing to those who had fought to enact Prohibition and wanted to see it succeed. One Baptist newspaper in Indiana pleaded with the public to support the ban on alcohol and be alert to the fact that powerful forces were working to end the Noble Experiment: "Millions of dollars are being spent and many newspapers are being subsidized by the liquor interests. Those who have fought so hard to make the nation dry must not go to sleep and allow the hard won victory to turn into defeat. If one-half the money and effort spent in attempting to nullify the Eighteenth Amendment were used in the enforcement of the Prohibition laws, we would soon hear the last of the bootleggers and illicit stills." An editorial in the *Kokomo Daily Tribune* chastised average citizens, citing their half-hearted support for Prohibition as the main obstacle to its success and warning the public that "[e]ither the U.S. will give Prohibition to the world in this generation, or it will by its failure, hold back the world from its benefits for a century or more."[47]

In their effort to weed out corrupt politicians, dry forces in Indiana were willing to support the Klan's "law enforcement" political slates. The Indiana Anti-Saloon League and its president, Edward Shumaker, endorsed numerous Klan candidates in the state election of 1924 and worked closely with the Klan-dominated legislature to strengthen state liquor laws in 1925. Spokespersons for the Indiana Baptist church also made it known that Baptists did not oppose the

Klan's entry into politics on the side of the drys. In fact, the *Baptist Observer* came close to an outright endorsement of the Klan slate in the 1924 spring primary. One editorial, which duplicated almost word for word the Klan's political rhetoric, declared: "The biggest issue before the voters, irrespective of party affiliation, is the authority of the national Constitution, respect for the law and its proper enforcement." The only issue of the campaign, the Klan had repeatedly argued, was whether "real Americans" would vote to uphold the law. The *Baptist Observer* saw it no differently: "Our nation was founded on Christian principles. The writing of the Eighteenth Amendment into the Constitution was the crystallization of nation-wide Christian sentiment. The enemy liquor gang—angry, vindictive, unpatriotic—is seeking the overthrow of the highest authority in the land—the Constitution. They can count on the hoodlums, the crooks, the vice-joints, the whiskey-loving aliens, and the indifferent citizen to help them win at the coming primary and subsequent elections. Can they count on you?"[48]

Reaction in Indiana to the Klan riot in Herrin, Illinois, demonstrates that for some, the Klan's reputation as a vigilante organization carried positive connotations when applied to the liquor problem. In Herrin, a liquor raid by Klansmen in January 1924 degenerated into a minor war with Klansmen on one side and local police and bootleggers on the other. After several days of gun battle, the governor of Illinois was forced to call in troops to restore order. In Indiana, the Klan applauded the shooting war against the bootleggers. The blame for the bloodshed, according to the *Fiery Cross*, rested with the police, which had ignored citizens' demands that it clean up the county's liquor problem. Indiana newspapers followed the events in Herrin closely; while all deplored the violence, few blamed the Klan directly, believing the bootleggers and local officials to be more culpable. One newspaper in Richmond was willing to place the responsibility almost anywhere rather than on the Klan. The editor offered the rather hysterical explanation that Herrin's bootleggers were "spending the Soviet's money in conspiring [to start] a revolution." But he expressed the more typical view of many citizens when he said: "The booze runner of today deserves no sympathy whatever. He and his fellows are recruited from the most desperate and reckless dope fiends of the United States!" The gangs, he noted in another article, "are organized like never before. They operate in high powered motor cars and have no scruples, even against murder."[49]

After Prohibition enforcement, education was the next most important social issue in the Klan's ideology. Parochial schools, as we have seen, occupied much of the Klan's attention in this area. Recruiting pamphlets, the *Fiery Cross*, and other Klan publications presented a seemingly endless string of charges against the parochial schools, blaming them for a long list of social problems and attacking the Catholic church for attempting to undermine public education. But just as the Klan's interest in Prohibition could not be explained by antiforeign concerns alone, its ideas about public education could not be reduced simply to anti-Catholicism.

In addition to the ever-present worry that Catholic schools were becoming too powerful, the Klan expressed concern that public education itself was in a deplorable state. In a recruiting pamphlet, *The Public School Problem in America*, by Hiram Evans, and in an essay entitled "Our Educational Duty," which appeared in the *Fiery Cross* and other Klan newspapers throughout the country, the secret order declared that conditions in the public schools were "positively appalling." The most obvious failure of public education, according to Evans, was the high illiteracy rate. As evidence, the Imperial Wizard accurately cited a recent census estimate of a 6 percent overall illiteracy rate and a U.S. Army report disclosing that more than 20 percent of the soldiers drafted during World War I had been unable to read and write.[50] Illiteracy, the Klan argued, could be traced to the nation's weak commitment to public education. Teachers were undertrained, and their salaries failed to "command the best obtainable talents and character." School facilities and equipment, particularly in poor and rural communities, were inadequate. Insufficient child labor laws allowed too many children to be drawn into the work force before they had completed a basic education. Restricted access to high school and higher education was an especially disturbing problem. "Four-fifths of the children in primary school never reach the high school," Evans asserted. "They must be saved and their education completed." "It is time," he concluded, "to expunge the disgrace of illiteracy. It is time to provide superb school facilities for every citizen and every child. It is time to train the rising generation in elementary public schools and give them ready access to high schools, colleges and universities pulsating with the spirit of America."[51]

The Klan's interest in these issues could not easily be separated from its prejudice toward the foreign born or its fear that Catholic schools were overshadowing public ones. Evans's ideas about improving public education were in every instance accompanied by dire warnings about the "tide of debased aliens" pouring into the United States, exhortations on the importance of building a "great and patriotic education system" to Americanize the foreigners, and predictions regarding the threat that parochial schools represented to the process of assimilation. Compulsory public school attendance, as noted earlier, was also a part of the Klan's program for educational reform.[52]

At the same time, however, Klan ideologues were not alone in their belief that a central purpose of public education should be to make good American citizens out of immigrant children. The Klan's ideas about Americanization were only slightly more aggressive than those that were actually put in place by educational reformers in Indiana and nationwide in the first decades of the twentieth century.[53] Furthermore, the Klan's wider concerns about public education were in general agreement with activists who wanted to modernize the nation's educational system. Educators and school administrators were working during this period to institute exactly what the Klan said it wanted: more professionally trained teachers, improved school facilities, and wider access to high schools and higher education.[54] One goal of educational reformers during the 1920s—to create a federal Department of Education—received particularly strong support from the Klan. Evans called it the "fundamental, all-important part" of the Klan's educational program and made support for the proposed Cabinet-level department a major theme of his writings on education. The Klan's assertion that the Catholic church represented a primary obstacle to its establishment was correct. The church adamantly opposed the idea of a nationally administered system of public education and worked to defeat congressional efforts on behalf of the new department.[55]

The Klan's concerns about public education had particular relevance in Indiana. During the early twenties, a series of highly publicized reports by the state government indicated that Indiana's rural schools were alarmingly backward. One study found that more than 4,500 one-teacher schools still existed, that 93 percent of rural elementary schoolteachers had not graduated from high school, that 77 percent of rural teachers had less than five years' experience, and that rural children had short school terms and attended class in dilapidated, unhealthy buildings. Indiana's leading educators blamed the deplorable conditions on the system of township control over rural schools and supported legislative efforts to develop state educational standards and consolidate township schools into more efficient countywide districts.[56] While rural schools attracted the greatest attention, problems existed in urban schools as well. In Indianapolis, for example, parents, civic groups, and local newspapers complained that classrooms were overcrowded; that heating, ventilation, and plumbing systems were inadequate; and that school buildings were in disrepair. The public outcry led to a protracted political battle and a series of bond issues to finance repairs, new elementary schools, and a new high school.[57]

The *Fiery Cross* did not become deeply involved in the school consolidation debate, and Klan politicians apparently believed that urban and rural Klansmen might be divided over the issue. The Indianapolis school building program, however, received the Klan's full support. Like other Indianapolis newspapers, the *Fiery Cross* condemned the conditions in city schools, went on to remind Klansmen that the state tax commission had blocked an approved school bond in 1921, and asked them to vote for the bond issue in the city election in March 1923. When the bond passed, the Klan newspaper declared its approval in a front-page editorial. Later, when the school board delayed start-up of the building program, the *Fiery Cross* blamed Catholic board members and the Klan nominated its own slate of candidates, all of whom were elected in 1925.[58]

In 1923, the Indiana Klan directed itself to the issue of higher education by attempting to buy financially troubled Valparaiso University. During the summer, D. C. Stephenson reached an agreement with the institution's trustees but was unable to complete his part of the contract when the Klan's national organization refused at the last minute to provide financial backing. Before the deal fell through, however, the *Fiery Cross* had been ecstatic. The Indiana Klan, it claimed, would make Valparaiso the "poor man's Harvard" and continue the university's traditional course offerings. Klan leaders even promised the university's administration that Catholic faculty members would not lose their jobs.[59]

In addition to Prohibition enforcement and public education, the Klan took on a wide variety of issues that reflected popular rather than radical concerns. Much of its recruitment literature discussed America's political system, the responsibilities of citizenship, and the "problems" of modern government. Bureaucracy, the Klan argued in one pamphlet, stood in the way of self-government; it represented "government by political appointees rather than a government by elected representatives." Political machines and corruption also weakened democratic institutions, according to recruiting literature. The secret order was "working toward the elimination of professional political bosses.... We propose government by the people which pre-supposes an educated, informed, active electorate, not a government by political machines that are corrupted by shyster politicians, by cliques and by crowds." Moreover, too many Americans were ignoring their responsibilities as voters. A circular asserted: "The Ku Klux Klan teaches a pure and undying patriotism toward our country; and no citizen is a patriot unless he votes." "It is hardly possible to over estimate the value of government," stated another recruiting pamphlet. "Yet it must be sadly admitted that Americans, probably more than any other first-rate power on earth, ignore their responsibility to government."[60]

Recruiting literature also referred with considerable frequency to a crisis in traditional values and claimed that one reason for the Klan's existence was to pull America back from "the brink of moral bankruptcy." In the Klan's view, Prohibition violations, gambling, and political corruption provided ample evidence of moral decline. By supporting law enforcement, clean government, and particularly an improved system of public education that, among other things, would inculcate traditional values and citizenship, the secret order was helping to restore decency in public life.

At the same time, it pledged to combat the "forces of evil which attack the American home." Part of this could be accomplished, Klan writers argued on numerous occasions, by protecting the "purity of womanhood" and defending the traditional role of women in the home. The *Fiery Cross* criticized businessmen who threatened the family and contributed to immoral behavior by employing women in their offices: "Every girl that works in an office is the potential mistress of an American home and the potential mother of a future generation of Americans." "Everyone knows of instances," the editorial continued, "where businessmen insist on dating secretaries and imply that should they refuse, their jobs are in danger." One recent study of the Klan in Athens, Georgia, underscores the Klan's emphasis on preserving traditional gender roles and suggests that this has been an overlooked dimension of the Klan's appeal.[61]

Another threat to the home, the Klan maintained, was the increasing power of the youth culture. Social activities and clubs in high schools drew children away from the family and the control of their parents and led in too many instances to "petting parties" and the often disturbing results of unchaperoned "automobile dates." Films and magazines that reflected "cosmopolitan" themes further endangered traditional values. One recruiting pamphlet declared that "real Americans must regain control of the press and motion pictures, and see to it that the American public opinion is never more misled."[62]

The Klan's concerns about immoral behavior, along with its devotion to Protestantism, led, not surprisingly, to an insistence on church attendance and respect for the Bible. Lack of devotion to religion helped explain, in the Klan's view, the erosion of traditional values. One way of reversing the process was to strengthen Protestant churches as institutions. "To keep his character unclouded and his honor unstained," a recruiting pamphlet instructed, "every honest-to-God Klansman should be a backer of some American Protestant church." The Bible represented another means of making society more moral: it is "our guide of conduct both in our private and our public life." Recruiting literature stated that spiritual values should be restored in public schools by daily Bible reading. "Klansmen," one pamphlet admonished, "it is our obligation to God that we place the open Bible in the public schools of America."[63]

Indiana's Klansmen were not the only Hoosiers who were concerned about the family, the youth culture, and declining devotion to religion. When the Lynds investigated Muncie, they found that traditional values were indeed under siege and that apprehension about their demise was common. Divorce occurred more often as a result of women's refusal to accept tightly circumscribed roles as wife and mother. Many of Muncie's parents confessed that they had great difficulty in exercising authority over teenage children, whose elaborate social life emphasized early sophistication and independence. "We try to make home as much a center [for social activities] as possible," one mother said, "but it isn't of much use any more. There is always some party or dance going on in a hotel or some other public place." Numerous voices lamented that church attendance was declining and that churches themselves were becoming hollow shells of religious spirit. Ministers throughout the state complained that young people did not care about religion and that many of their parents seemingly went to church only to fulfill a social obligation. One pastor of a large Protestant church in Muncie told the Lynds: "My people seem to sit through the sermon in a kind of dazed, comatose state. They don't seem to be wrestling with my thought."[64]

It has often been assumed that the Ku Klux Klan and Protestant fundamentalism were closely linked. The Klan's attention to the perceived problems of moral decline and waning religious zeal, perhaps, made it appear likely that the Klan and fundamentalists had overlapping ideas and goals. In fact, the two movements had little in common beyond a shared belief that society had become corrupt. Klan recruiting literature made no reference to the fundamentalist's central concern—the problem of "modernism" in Protestant churches. And while the Klan pointed frequently to the need for increased devotion to the Bible, it generally ignored the issue of whether the Bible should be interpreted literally. The theory of evolution also failed to appear on the Klan's extensive list of social and religious interests.[65]

In Indiana, fundamentalism made little headway during the 1920s. Unlike in a number of other states, there was no serious attempt to outlaw Darwin's theories—either by Klan politicians or other forces. And although fundamentalist agitation did disrupt Indiana's large Protestant churches, as it did throughout the country, the major churches generally attempted to moderate between modernist and fundamentalist attitudes. The Baptist church, for example, occasionally chastised modernist ideas but also criticized fundamentalists for distracting from the main work of the church. The *Baptist Observer* rejected the idea of separate conferences on fundamentals, which occurred in other states. The churches, said the *Observer*, should support programs agreed upon in general meetings, not those proposed by special interests. "Stick to the main line," it advised its readers. The leaders of Indiana's Methodist groups opposed fundamentalism even more adamantly, showing greater interest in their traditional work for social reform than in questioning their basic theology. While the Methodists launched no campaign on behalf of modernism, they tended to see fundamentalist agitation as disruptive and unnecessary. During the Scopes trial in 1925, the *Indianapolis Area Herald*, a Methodist newspaper, asked: "Is Bryan an Elephant?" William Jennings Bryan, the editors said, was destroying confidence in the Bible by trying to force his personal theories on the minds of youth. "Let us remember," one editorial advised, "that the Bible is not a book of science, but a book of religion."[66]

The great difference between Indiana's mainstream Protestant churches and the Klan on the one hand, and its most determined fundamentalists on the other, is that the fundamentalists were essentially isolationists. The Klan and the large Protestant churches wanted to reform society; the fundamentalists looked inward, seeking to purify themselves, not the decadent environment that surrounded them. In the records of its meetings, Indiana's fastest growing fundamentalist denomination, the Church of the Nazarene, made clear that it had little use for civic activism. The concerns of church representatives in 1924 lay in the "great danger of the world creeping into our beloved churches." This meant that the membership should reject such obvious evils as alcohol, dancing, smoking, motion pictures, immodest clothing, and the wearing of gold or jewelry; it also meant that members should not become involved in social or political crusades or join organizations outside the church. The "worldliness" displayed by large Protestant denominations, through an organization such as the Anti-Saloon League, for example, represented exactly what the Church of the Nazarene hoped to eliminate from its sanctified enclave. To save its members from becoming "sinners by world conformity," church representatives also issued a thinly veiled condemnation of the Ku Klux Klan just as the secret order was rising to power: "We heartily commend the church for the stand it takes against secret societies and worldly organizations of every nature, and would insist that we as a people . . . continue to keep our churches free from members of such societies and organizations."[67]

The chasm between the Klan's ideology and fundamentalism in Indiana gave further evidence that when D. C. Stephenson's band of recruiting agents scoured the state in 1922 and 1923, it was dispensing ideas that appealed to average citizens, not disaffected fringe groups. The Klan wanted America's white Protestants to unite, to form a massive organization that could address a long list of perceived social and political problems. Subjecting Protestant churches to a set of theological acid tests was never a part of this program. Narrow religious solutions were not enough.

3. The Klansmen

It has not been easy for historians to look beneath the Klansman's mask, to discover which segments of society made up the vast membership of the hooded order. The greatest obstacle, of course, has been the scarcity of membership documents. Scattered lists for a number of towns and cities have surfaced over the years and have revealed significant findings. However, the most important records—those of the national organization—disappeared from the Klan's Atlanta headquarters sometime before the end of 1925 and have never been recovered.[1] As a result, larger questions about the social basis of the Klan movement remain unanswered and scholars have been forced into a great deal of speculation about the true size of the Klan and the characteristics of its members. Kenneth Jackson's *Ku Klux Klan in the City* provides an important example of the problem. His oft-cited membership figures for every state and major city in the nation are, as he clearly states, "personal estimates" based on the figures claimed by the Klan's newspapers and the opinions of journalists who followed the Klan's activities.[2] Jackson's estimates are conservative and in many instances may be accurate, but there is no way to be certain of their validity. His urban thesis is nearly impossible to confirm without state or at least regional membership information. The idea that conditions in large cities stimulated especially strong support for the Klan cannot be tested unless there is some way of determining the Klan's strength in smaller outlying communities.[3]

The traditional interpretation of the Klan has added to the difficulty in assessing the social basis of the movement. Because scholars have viewed it as an extremist organization, they have assumed that its members must have come from backward or deviant social groups. Often the Klansmen are seen as having had marginal economic status. Jackson's urban thesis supports this perspective, as does Seymour Martin Lipset and Earl Raab's characterization of the Klan as a "low status backlash" by lower middle-class and working-class white Protestants. One recent appraisal of the secret order concludes that, like other "repressive" movements such as Prohibition and fundamentalism, the Klan was strongest in the sections of the country that had been "left behind" by the economic boom of the 1920s.[4] Some have thought that Klansmen were plagued even more profoundly by a kind of cultural poverty, manifested by ignorance, continued attachment to dying small-town traditions, fear of the city, and support for fundamentalism. Another recent assessment of the movement argues that the Klan was extraordinarily popular in Indiana primarily because of the state's "backwardness." According to this study, Indiana had been settled by the "displaced Southern rustic" and over the years had more than earned its reputation for being "insulated, proud, and belligerent." During the 1920s, the "simplicity" and "narrow-minded arrogance" of Indiana's people became "the weakness that the Ku Klux Klan would exploit to the hilt."[5]

Klan membership documents for Indiana demonstrate that much of this speculation about the state's Klansmen has been incorrect. Those who joined the Klan came from the mainstream of white Protestant society. They represented in significant numbers every region of the state, every type of community, and virtually the entire socioeconomic spectrum. Evangelical Protestants naturally joined the Klan with great frequency, but so, too, did members of "liturgical" churches and those who did not belong to any church. The Klan was more popular in some regions of the state than others, and some identifiable social groups seemingly rejected the order while others embraced it. These different levels of support for the Klan do not conform to the sweeping generalizations about backward rustics, benighted denizens of small towns, or embattled urban workers. The Klansmen came from all walks of life. They were average citizens.

▰ Size and Geographic Distribution of Membership

In 1925, Harold Feightner, an Indianapolis newspaper reporter who worked as Indiana correspondent for the *New York Times*, obtained a copy of a Klan report that listed the names of local leaders and the current number of members for Klan chapters in all but three counties in Indiana.[6] The unusual document, obviously intended as an assessment of the current status of the movement, probably had been prompted by the concern of state leaders that the Klan's popularity had begun to decline.

D. C. Stephenson's arrest and conviction for second-degree murder in the spring of 1925 had given Klan leaders good cause to worry. At the time, Stephenson was no longer the Grand Dragon of the Indiana Klan. He had quarreled bitterly with Hiram Evans beginning almost immediately after the great 1923 rally in Kokomo. In the spring of 1924, Evans had replaced Stephenson with Walter Bossert, an ambitious Republican party politician. Soon afterward Evans ordered Joe Huffington to banish Stephenson from his home klavern in Evansville.[7] But due to his close connection with the Klan governor, Edward Jackson, Stephenson had remained a prominent political figure and in the mind of the public was still closely associated with the Klan movement. His trial generated a barrage of negative publicity for the Indiana Klan. Newspapers across the country revealed the gruesome details of Stephenson's sexual assault on Madge Oberholtzer, her attempted suicide, and her slow, painful death due in part to infected human bite wounds inflicted by Stephenson. When Bossert asked local chapters to report their current membership levels in 1925, surely his first interest was to see how badly the Stephenson scandal had hurt the movement.[8]

For this reason, and because the total membership figure was much lower than the one-half million members the state Klan had once claimed, it is safe to assume that the head count was as accurate as Klan leaders could obtain. The report showed an active membership in 1925 of just under 166,000.[9]

What percentage of all those who joined the Indiana Klan in the twenties was represented by the 1925 figure? A complete set of membership records for the Wayne County chapter provides a partial answer.[10] The 1925 report shows just over 2,400 members in Wayne County. This represented only 62 percent of the total membership from 1921 to 1926. Further evidence concerning the Delaware County Klan suggests that by 1925, a decline of 30 to 40 percent in membership may have occurred statewide. In a civil suit against D. C. Stephenson, Muncie Klan leaders testified that Delaware County had enlisted at least 6,800 members.[11] The 1925 report showed that there were only 4,478 active Klansmen in Delaware County—approximately 66 percent of the number claimed by Muncie's Klan leaders. If by 1925 membership had declined by 30 percent, Indiana Klan membership peaked at approximately 262,000; if the nearly 40 percent decline in Wayne County was typical, the total would have been as high as 278,000. There is no way of knowing how many women were members of Indiana's Women of the Ku Klux Klan and how many children belonged to its Junior Klan. These auxiliary groups appear to have been quite active in many communities, but there are no membership documents to indicate the extent of their popularity. It is likely that the Indiana Klan numbered close to 300,000 male and female members.[12]

Whatever the actual total, the 1925 figure of 166,000 by itself revealed the enormity of the movement, especially when viewed on a county-by-county basis. As shown in Table 3.1, 21 percent of all native-born white men over the age of twenty-one belonged to the Klan. In thirty-one of Indiana's ninety-two counties, at least 25 percent of them could be counted as members; in another fourteen counties, 20 percent or more had joined the secret order.[13]

This estimate of the Klan's total strength is conservative not only because membership had declined significantly by 1925, but also because of the method used in calculating the percentage of Klansmen among native-born white men. The above figures are based on census totals not only for native white men with native-born parents, but also for native white men with at least one foreign-born parent. Therefore, this definition of "native white" includes native-born Catholics and Jews as well as a significant number of second-generation immigrants.[14]

On the surface, it may seem inappropriate to include large numbers of second-generation immigrants in a group designed to identify the pool of potential members for an organization such as the

Table 3.1

Klan Membership among Native-born White Men, by County, 1925

County	Number	Percent
Adams	181	3.5
Allen	2,150	7.0
Bartholomew	1,400	19.8
Benton	1,053	31.4
Blackford	550	14.1
Boone	2,200	30.5
Brown	320	16.7
Carroll	1,524	30.4
Cass	2,846	25.1
Clark	1,160	14.6
Clay	2,107	26.2
Clinton	2,300	27.3
Crawford	243	7.6
Daviess	1,591	22.0
Dearborn	945	15.9
Decatur	925	17.0
De Kalb	1,715	22.6
Delaware	4,478	27.0
Dubois	437	8.2
Elkhart	4,300	25.9
Fayette	1,725	33.3
Floyd	369	4.4
Fountain*	—	—
Franklin	775	18.1
Fulton	580	11.7
Gibson	1,791	22.4
Grant	2,329	15.1
Greene	1,700	17.3
Hamilton	2,611	35.4
Hancock	1,300	23.7
Harrison	40	.7
Hendricks	2,057	34.7

Table 3.1 continued

County	Number	Percent
Henry	2,675	24.5
Howard	3,998	30.5
Huntington	1,025	11.0
Jackson	821	12.3
Jasper	900	24.6
Jay	781	11.4
Jefferson	445	7.5
Jennings*	—	—
Johnson	1,600	25.4
Knox	2,241	18.7
Kosciusko	587	7.3
Lagrange	50	1.2
Lake	5,000	20.0
La Porte	2,555	21.4
Lawrence	1,392	18.1
Madison	6,637	33.2
Marion	25,000	26.8
Marshall	641	9.5
Martin	340	10.6
Miami	1,656	19.3
Monroe	1,589	23.8
Montgomery	1,939	22.1
Morgan	1,600	26.8
Newton	610	22.0
Noble	775	11.6
Ohio	212	16.8
Orange	350	7.3
Owen*	—	—
Parke	1,046	19.2
Perry	116	2.7
Pike	1,250	24.2
Porter	1,100	21.7
Posey	800	14.5
Pulaski	1,002	31.2

Table 3.1 continued

County	Number	Percent
Putnam	1,091	18.1
Randolph	1,350	16.9
Ripley	813	15.3
Rush	1,900	32.8
St. Joseph	4,200	18.8
Scott	270	12.9
Shelby	2,467	32.2
Spencer	745	14.7
Starke	725	31.8
Steuben	480	11.5
Sullivan	2,200	25.6
Switzerland	397	13.9
Tippecanoe	2,500	20.8
Tipton	1,622	34.3
Union	516	27.8
Vanderburgh	5,455	22.3
Vermillion	1,800	29.8
Vigo	8,240	31.1
Wabash	2,242	27.5
Warren	951	32.7
Warrick	740	13.7
Washington	386	7.9
Wayne	2,410	16.8
Wells	597	10.1
White	1,853	37.7
Whitley	1,256	26.8
Total	165,641	20.8

Sources: Local Officers of the Ku Klux Klan, Indiana Historical Society; U.S. Bureau of the Census, *Fourteenth Census: Indiana Compendium*, pp. 34–41.

*Klan membership figure not reported.

Table 3.2
Foreign-born Population, by Country, 1920

County	Number	Percent All Foreign Born
Germany	37,377	24.7
Poland	17,791	11.8
Hungary	9,351	6.2
Austria	9,100	6.0
England	8,528	5.6
Russia	7,673	5.1
Ireland	7,271	4.8
Italy	6,712	4.4
Canada	5,147	3.4
Sweden	4,942	3.3
Yugoslavia	4,471	3.0
Greece	4,182	2.8
Czechoslovakia	3,941	2.6
Scotland	3,707	2.4
France	3,247	2.1
Rumania	2,731	1.8
Belgium	2,530	1.7
Switzerland	2,334	1.5
Netherlands	2,018	1.3
All other countries	8,275	5.5
Total	151,328	100.00

Source: U.S. Bureau of the Census, *Fourteenth Census: Indiana Compendium*, pp. 49–50.

Ku Klux Klan. This was necessary, however, due to the nature of Indiana's foreign-born population and evidence that members of certain foreign groups joined the Klan with great frequency. In 1920, nearly 40 percent of the state's immigrant population came from northern and western European nations with predominantly Protestant religious traditions (see Table 3.2).[15] By far, Germans represented the largest immigrant group, accounting for approximately one-quarter of Indiana's foreign-born population. Catholic and Jewish immigrants from Poland, Hungary, Austria, Russia, Italy, and other nations constituted a bare majority of the foreign born in 1920. In general, these immigrants were concentrated in the state's largest cities. In the majority of counties, the small foreign-born populations tended to be of white Protestant ethnic background; most often they were German.

The available evidence also indicates that members of Indiana's white Protestant ethnic groups joined the Klan whether or not they were of recent immigrant or native stock. In the small town of Crown Point, just south of Gary, 42 percent of the men who joined the local Klan chapter had at least one parent who was born in a foreign country. The majority were from Germany, with a smaller number born in Norway, Scotland, Holland, and England. The religious affiliation of Klansmen also seems to confirm this pattern. In every city where membership data are currently available, Lutherans joined the Klan in proportions comparable with Methodists, Baptists, or Disciples of Christ.[16]

Though used here to describe only minimum levels of Klan popularity, the county figures for 1925 are still useful in assessing geographic patterns of Klan membership.[17] Speculation concerning the geographic distribution of Indiana's Klansmen has generally centered on two questions: first, was the Klan strongest in southern Indiana, where most residents could trace their roots to states south of the Ohio River? and second, was the Klan primarily an urban or a rural phenomenon?[18]

Most contemporary observers of the movement assumed that it was strongest in the southern part of the state. This seemed likely because of the popular image of the Klan as a peculiarly southern organization. Romantic concepts about the Reconstruction-era Klan, transmitted by historians and novelists and with particular force by D. W. Griffith's film, *The Birth of a Nation*, provided a basis for thinking that those with the thickest southern drawls would have been most likely to join the Klan. Apologists for the organization's success in Indiana found this a convenient explanation. One observer blamed the strength of the movement on its appeal to "hillbillies" and the "Great Unteachables"—euphemisms for the supposedly backward rural folk and small-town inhabitants of southern Indiana's hill country.[19]

Many who fought the Klan also assumed, not without some justification, that its strength could be measured by the distance from the Klan's national headquarters in Atlanta. After all, the hooded order had spread north from Evansville, its original state leaders were themselves transplanted southerners, and the Klan's national leaders appeared to exert great influence over local affairs. By 1924, Catholics in the Democratic party expressed a fear that Democrats in southern Indiana had deserted the party to support the Klan. To some leaders of the black community in Indianapolis, the growth of the Klan, along with the recent establishment of officially segregated schools and streetcars, symbolized the northward march of Jim Crow. After the Klan seized control of the state Republican party in the 1924 primary election, the *Indianapolis Freeman* reminded blacks that the Klan of the "old days" had helped disenfranchise southern blacks so they could be "lynched with impunity." While it pointed to no immediate threat, the *Freeman* warned that the same fate might await Indiana blacks if the Republicans were not defeated in November.[20]

Despite the belief that the Indiana Klan was an aberration emanating from the South, the Klan was actually strongest in the state's central and northern counties. The counties with the highest levels of Klan membership—at least 25 percent of all native white men—were located north of a line extending from Sullivan County in the west to Union County in the east (see Map 3.1). In many of these counties, particularly those surrounding Marion County and Indianapolis, active Klansmen still represented approximately one-third of all native white men in 1925. The same high levels could also be found along the state's western border from Terre Haute northward to Boone County, then east to White, Pulaski, and Starke counties.[21] Most of the counties with the lowest levels of Klan membership—less than 10 percent of all native white men—were located in a band along Indiana's southern border. The only areas in the southern part of the state that approached the membership levels of the north were the mining counties of the southwest.

Another means of assessing the Klan's strength in southern counties is through the statistical technique of ecological regression.[22] In

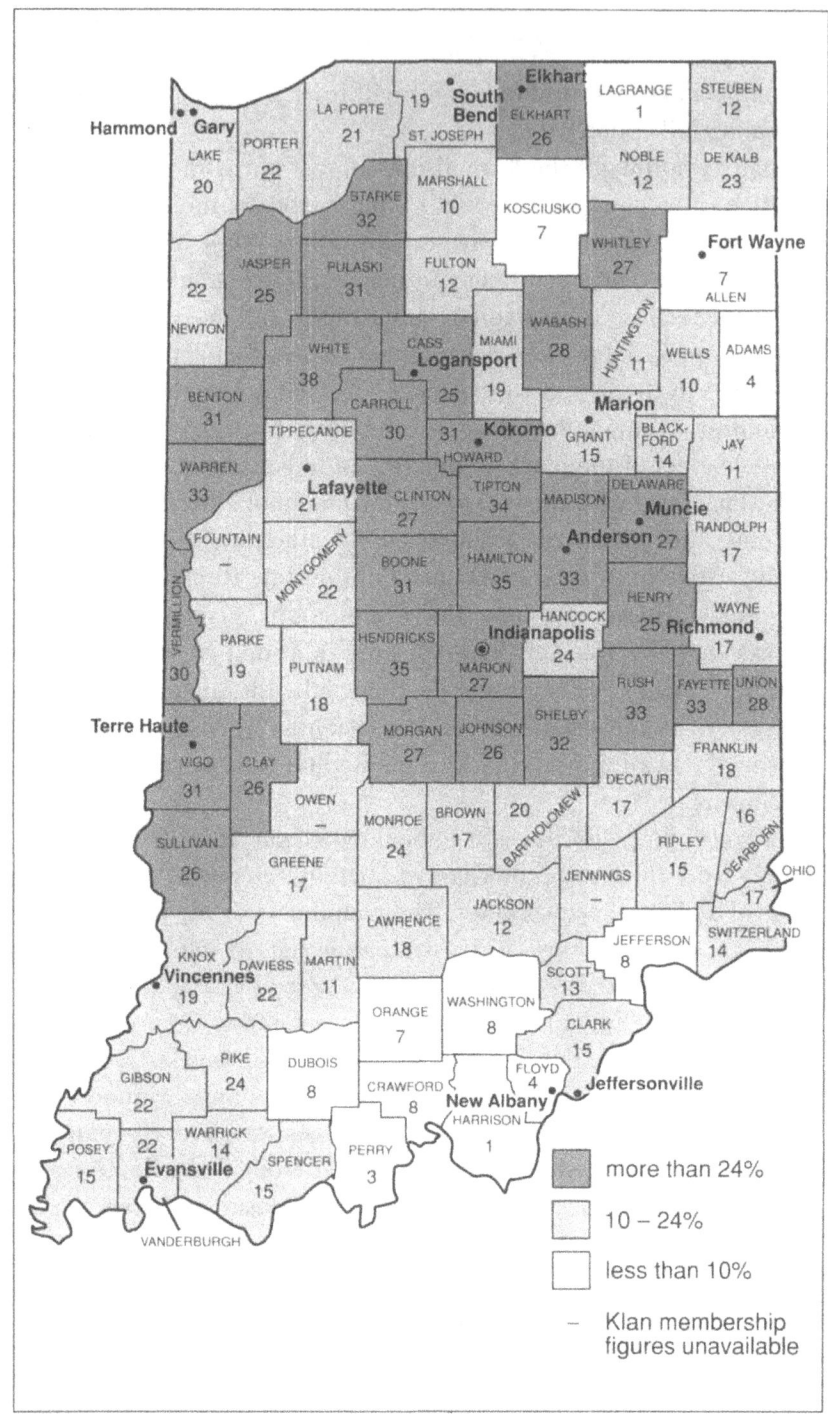

Map 3.1
Klansmen among Native White Men, by County, 1925

Table 3.3
*Influence of Southern Counties on Klan Membership, 1925**

	Regression Coefficient b	Standard Error	R^2
South	−.04	.01	.21

*Controlling for percentage urban, owners, Protestant, and Catholic.

Table 3.3, the regression coefficient b indicates that the variable "South" (southern counties) had a slightly negative influence on the size of the Klan's membership in 1925. The amount of the standard error shows that the b coefficient in this case is statistically significant—for a b coefficient to be significant, it must be greater than 1.96 times the size of the standard error. Table 3.3 also reflects the results of a multiple regression equation. Multiple regression makes it possible to control for other factors that might exert some influence on the variable in question.[23] Results for the variable "South," therefore, exclude the influence of the percentage of urban residents, home owners, and Protestant and Catholic church members in Indiana counties. Put more simply, the table shows that men in southern counties were slightly less likely to join the Klan regardless of whether they were members at the same time as any of the other social groups considered.[24]

Ironically, the "southern" characteristics of Indiana's southern counties probably accounted most for the geographic disparity in Klan strength. One reason for the lower levels of Klan popularity in the South was the regional differences in traditional political loyalties. The strength of the Democratic party in southern counties, combined with the Klan's strong identification with the state Republican party, probably alienated many potential Klansmen. Polarization over the Klan issue within the Democratic party apparently also turned southern Democrats against the Klan.

The impact of these political factors can be seen in the results of the 1924 election. In southern counties, Klan candidates—almost all

Republicans—either lost or won only by narrow margins. In northern and central counties, they were more likely to win by wide margins.[25] Politicians in the south who spoke openly against the Klan depended on traditional Democratic loyalties to preserve their political careers. Incumbent congressman Arthur Greenwood, the only blatantly anti-Klan candidate to win an Indiana congressional seat in 1924, barely overcame strong support for the Klan in his district, winning by just 617 votes out of nearly 90,000 cast.[26] One Democratic leader in the state senate, who had represented Ohio, Jefferson, Clark, and Switzerland counties since 1902, was shocked when the Klan candidate in his home district almost defeated him in the gubernatorial primary of 1924. The experience made Joseph M. (Uncle Joe) Craven an instant opponent of the hooded order; he led the Democratic opposition to the Klan in the 1925 legislative session.[27]

Resistance to the Prohibition movement also appeared to take away from the Klan's popularity in southern counties. Democrats from southern Indiana, joined eventually by German and Irish immigrants, had struggled against Republican efforts to outlaw or restrict liquor sales since the mid-nineteenth century. During Prohibition, the area rivaled the large cities in the flow of illegal alcohol. During the 1920s, much of Indiana's liquor supply filtered through southern counties from Kentucky. Locally produced moonshine from the southern hill country also entered the underground market. One brand, known as Dubois County Dew, was favored throughout the state.[28] The results of remonstrance and county option elections between 1906 and 1915 clearly demonstrated weaker support for the dry crusade in southern counties. During this period, when individual counties voted to permit or outlaw local liquor sales, ten of the twelve predominantly rural counties that consistently voted wet were located in southern Indiana.[29] Of course, some southern counties also voted for Prohibition, but they were outnumbered two to one by southern counties that voted wet. Central and northern counties that consistently voted wet or dry were more evenly divided.[30]

Neither the liquor question nor traditional fealty to the Democratic party were acid tests of anti-Klan sentiment. Many residents of southern counties who disapproved of the Klan's dry Republican politics doubtless found other justifications for joining the secret order. Furthermore, not all prohibitionists automatically enlisted in the Klan. But the strength of a wet, Democratic political tradition in southern Indiana surely kept thousands of potential members estranged from the Klan.

Diminished levels of Klan membership in southern counties were also related to the great social and economic differences between north and south. The rapid growth of industry between 1880 and 1920 had created in central and northern Indiana a network of large and medium-sized cities that were tied to heavy industry, manufacturing, and large-scale commercial agriculture. In general, southern Indiana was less affected by industrialization. With the exception of Evansville, which continued to prosper due to abundant coal reserves in surrounding counties, the early industrial cities along the Ohio River stagnated and by 1920 were isolated from Indiana's economic mainstream.[31]

The Klan was strongest in areas of Indiana that had been most altered by the process of industrial development. Its membership, for example, reached high levels in almost every major urban area; most of these cities were located in the northern and central parts of the state (see Map 3.1). Table 3.4 demonstrates the strength of the Klan in these areas in 1925.

Only two cities, New Albany and Fort Wayne, deviated conspicuously from this pattern. In addition to the factors that influenced Klan membership in southern counties, New Albany's chapter seemed to suffer from its proximity to Louisville, Kentucky. Unlike most other southern cities, Louisville was remarkably inhospitable to the Klan movement. Its mayor, George W. Smith, began a vigorous anti-Klan campaign as soon as organizers arrived in 1921. Smith refused to allow the appearance of a Klan speaker and outlawed the sale of Klan literature. He hired detectives to monitor the activities of the order's leaders and threatened to arrest anyone who attended its meetings.[32] New Albany's city officials also opposed the Klan, and the size of the local chapter reflected the unfriendly atmosphere. By 1925, when the population of Floyd County approached 40,000, only 369 men still participated in the Klan. Some New Albany residents may have traveled to nearby Jeffersonville in Clark County to take part in Klan activities. Louisville Klansmen met in Jeffersonville to escape Smith's jurisdiction, and Klan membership in Clark County

Table 3.4

Klan Membership in Urban Areas, 1925

City	Population	County	Percent Klan
Indianapolis	314,000	Marion	27
Gary, Hammond, East Chicago	128,000	Lake	20
Fort Wayne	86,000	Allen	7
Evansville	85,000	Vanderburgh	22
South Bend	70,000	St. Joseph	19
Terre Haute	66,000	Vigo	31
Muncie	36,000	Delaware	27
Kokomo	30,000	Howard	31
Anderson	30,000	Madison	33
Richmond	27,000	Wayne	17
Elkhart	24,000	Elkhart	26
Marion	24,000	Grant	15
New Albany	23,000	Floyd	4
Lafayette	23,000	Tippecanoe	21
Logansport	22,000	Cass	25

Sources: Local Officers of the Ku Klux Klan, Indiana Historical Society; U.S. Bureau of the Census, *Fourteenth Census: Indiana Compendium*, pp. 34–45.

was significantly larger than in surrounding counties (see Map 3.1).[33] Still, if Jeffersonville acted as a magnet for Klansmen throughout the Louisville area, its pull was relatively weak. In 1925, there were only 1,160 members in Jeffersonville and the rest of Clark County. Urban areas in northern Indiana that were much smaller than Louisville had twice as many Klansmen.[34]

Comparatively low levels of Klan membership in Fort Wayne in the same period are more difficult to explain. As in New Albany, a strong anti-Klan political climate probably helped counter support for the local chapter. The mayor in 1925 was Catholic and was supported by a county judge who strongly opposed the Klan.[35] At the same time, however, the Klan was a force in local politics. In 1924, the order had astonished the Republican establishment in Allen County by winning the party's nomination for every county office in the May primary election.[36] This suggests that the actual strength of the Allen County Klan was not represented accurately in the 1925 membership figures, or that the number of Klansmen in Fort Wayne simply had declined with particular speed by 1925. Without detailed membership records, there can be no definitive answer.

Whatever the reasons for these two exceptions, the cities unquestionably played an important part in the Indiana Klan movement. In 1925, half of the state's Klansmen lived in the fifteen largest urban counties listed in Table 3.4.[37] Of the Klansmen distributed among the remaining seventy-seven counties, many lived in towns with populations greater than 10,000. Counties that contained towns such as La Porte (population in 1920, 15,158), Michigan City (19,457), New Castle (14,458), Peru (12,410), and Vincennes (17,160) represented an additional 11 percent of the total Klan membership in 1925.[38] The membership in Indianapolis dwarfed that of other cities. More than 12,000 had already joined the Indianapolis chapter by the beginning of 1923, over a year before the movement reached its peak.[39] In 1925, Marion County Klan officials counted approximately 25,000 active members, suggesting that total membership for the period may have reached 40,000.[40]

Did its strength in the cities mean that the Indiana Klan movement was primarily an urban phenomenon?[41] A brief examination of Map 3.1 indicates that this was not the case. Many rural counties could be counted among those with the highest percentage of Klansmen in 1925. White County provides an excellent example. According to the 1920 census, White County was 86 percent rural; its largest town had a population of only 3,604. Still, 38 percent of all native white men in the county were Klan members in 1925, the highest percentage of any county in Indiana.[42]

Regression analysis confirms that the size of the Indiana Klan in 1925 was not influenced by either the urban or rural status of potential members. Table 3.5 shows that the percentage of urban residents in a given county had essentially no influence on the size of the Klan in that county. The b coefficient is small and the standard error is large enough to make the b coefficient statistically insignificant. A similar regression of the *Rural* variable reveals the same finding.[43]

Table 3.5

*Influence of Urban and Rural Residence on Klan Membership, 1925**

	Regression Coefficient b	Standard Error	R^2
Urban	−.01	.03	.23
Rural	.02	.04	.21

*Controlling for Southern residence and percentage owners, Protestant, Catholic, and foreign born.

In light of this evidence, there can be little support for Kenneth Jackson's conclusion that the Indiana Klan, like other Klans of the period, was associated primarily with the cities. Nor would it be correct to return to the earlier interpretation that Jackson sought to overturn: that the Klan was essentially an outcry by rural America against the wicked city. The case of Indiana shows clearly that the hooded order found enthusiastic support in *both* rural and urban areas. The more significant pattern in the geographic distribution of Klan members can be seen in a division not between city and country, but between north and south. Enthusiasm for the Klan was greater in the northern and central counties, both urban and rural, than in the counties of southern Indiana. This suggests that support for the Klan was more strongly tied to the Republican dry tradition, which had a larger following in the northern and central parts of the state, as well as to the social changes associated with industrial growth and highly commercialized agriculture, characteristics that also distinguished north from south.

Occupation

The officers of Terre Haute Klan No. 7 presided over an organization that was enormous by community standards. With more than 7,000 members in 1925—almost one-third of all native white men in Vigo County—and bolstered by separate associations for women and children, the Klan became by far the largest community organization in this city of 68,000. Despite the significance of their chapter, however, the leaders of the Terre Haute Klan were remarkably unassuming in their lives outside the Invisible Empire. The Exalted Cyclops, master of the klavern, operated an automobile repair shop. His supporting officers included two grocers, a physician, a bank teller, an insurance agent, a tinner, a carpenter, a truck driver, a blacksmith, the pastor of a United Brethren church, the owner of a clothing store, and a coal miner.[44]

The occupations of these thirteen members of the Terre Haute chapter were typical of those held by Indiana Klansmen. The available evidence indicates that the Ku Klux Klan represented a wide cross section of Indiana's occupational spectrum—a circumstance that should not be surprising given the order's vast following. Skilled and unskilled workers, clerks and other low-level white-collar workers, struggling and prosperous independent small businessmen, civil servants, and professionals all joined the Klan in proportions roughly equivalent to their distribution in the rest of the state's white Protestant society. Yet the Klan did not represent a pure cross section. Those in low white-collar occupations, for example, joined with slightly greater frequency than those in other occupational groups. Workers in semiskilled and unskilled jobs, on the other hand, were less likely to join the Klan. Perhaps most significant, as can be seen in the case of Terre Haute's Klan officials, the secret order did not attract the elite members of society; only rarely did it draw support from the most powerful owners and managers in the community.

These conclusions are based on an investigation of Klan occupations in three Indiana communities where detailed membership lists are available: Indianapolis, Richmond, and Crown Point. While these communities were selected only because membership records exist, they still can be viewed as representative sites of Klan chapters across the state. Each community is located in central or northern Indiana, where the movement was strongest, and each represents a different type of town or city. Centrally located, Indianapolis was the largest city in the state, the center of government, industry, and the Klan movement. Richmond characterized the small industrial city of central Indiana that welcomed the Klan with fervent enthusiasm. Crown Point was a small town in the extreme northwest that primarily served the needs of nearby farmers.

The three locations, while they represent a fortunate variety of communities, also present different research problems. The availability and usefulness of records varies for each community, as well as the type of information provided in each set of Klan records. The smallest Klan, for example, left the most complete record. The leader of the Crown Point chapter saved the detailed membership applications filled out by each of the 128 members who enrolled during the 1920s. The records for Richmond and the rest of Wayne County contain a complete list of all 3,850 members but offer little other useful information. Unlike the Crown Point and Richmond records, those for Indianapolis are not the actual documents of the Klan chapter; rather, they are included in a list of members that was stolen from the Indianapolis Klan headquarters in early 1923 and printed in the Chicago-based anti-Klan newspaper, *Tolerance*. The document's authenticity was challenged by Klan leaders at the time, but some of those whose names appeared admitted they had joined. The primary drawback of this list is that it gives only the first 12,000 members—probably less than one-third of the total.[45]

More than three times larger than any other city in Indiana in 1920, Indianapolis was the economic, political, and cultural center of the state, the home of its most diverse population and largest Klan chapter. The economy of Indianapolis depended on a variety of industries; the most important were automobiles, food processing, and metal casting and cutting, which together employed 40 percent of the city's labor force in 1920. The production of furniture, railroad cars, clothing, and electrical machines also contributed to the economy, as did the railroads (although their importance declined in the twenties), the grain storage business, and state government.[46]

The first 12,000 Indianapolis Klansmen worked throughout these industries and in the network of supporting enterprises. Two random samples—one of 500 Indianapolis men, the other of 500 Klansmen—show that the occupations of Klansmen paralleled those of the city's workers in general (see Table 3.6). But some important differences did exist. First, more Klansmen were employed in low-

Table 3.6
Occupations of Indianapolis Klansmen, 1923

	Klan Number	Klan Percent	Indianapolis Number	Indianapolis Percent
High white collar	45	9.2	46	9.2
Low white collar	187	37.4	155	31.0
Skilled	115	22.9	79	15.8
Lower manual	132	26.5	161	32.2
No occupation	21	4.2	59	11.8
Total	500		500	

Chi-square (4 dof) = 3.06 $P \leq .001$

Source: See Appendix.

level white-collar and skilled occupations than those in the population at large. Sixty percent of all Klansmen sampled fell into these categories, as opposed to 46 percent of men in the general population. Second, fewer Klansmen worked in lower manual occupations (semiskilled and unskilled) and fewer Klansmen were without occupations.

The tendency for Indianapolis Klansmen to be in the middle of the economic spectrum slightly more often probably occurred for two reasons. First, skilled and low-level white-collar workers doubtless found it easier than individuals with lower-paid jobs to pay the ten-dollar initiation fee, in addition to monthly dues and expenses for robes and other Klan paraphernalia. At a time when ten dollars could easily represent a quarter, half, or even more of the weekly income of an average worker, these costs represented a significant sum indeed.[47] The ethnic composition of Indianapolis's work force also helps explain why smaller numbers of lower manual workers appeared in the Klan sample. By 1923, blacks comprised over 11 percent of the population of Indianapolis and worked primarily in low manual occupations. Since blacks and smaller numbers of recent Catholic and Jewish immigrants obviously were not candidates for Klan membership, their presence in the work force makes it less reasonable to conclude that the Klan was significantly underrepresented among white Protestants at the lower end of the economic spectrum.[48]

Second, as noted earlier, the Indiana Klan failed to attract the economic elite of a community. While differences between the Klan and Indianapolis samples in the middle and lower occupational categories may not have been as important as they seem on the surface, a difference of greater consequence can be seen at the high end of the spectrum. Here, the percentage of workers found in each sample is identical, but a closer examination of the occupations in this category reveals that Klansmen identified as high-level white-collar workers tended to be professionals, high-level government employees, or successful owners of small or medium-sized businesses—not the owners or executives of Indianapolis's large businesses. Lawyers, dentists, physicians, and other professionals made up 42 percent of high-level white-collar workers in the Klan sample, compared with only 26 percent of those in the Indianapolis sample. Forty-two percent of the high-level white-collar workers in the Indianapolis sample can be identified as high-level business executives—for example, president of a company that manufactured saw blades, treasurer of an engineering firm, advertising manager, owner of a fire insurance company, or manager of a wholesale meat company. Only 13 percent of the high-level white-collar workers in the Klan sample held similar positions.[49]

Klan membership within specific occupations demonstrated the same pattern. Almost 9 percent of all Indianapolis dentists, for instance, were Klan members by early 1923; more than 5 percent of the city's physicians had also joined. At the same time, none of the presidents of major banks were Klansmen; nor could any Klan members be located among the presidents of the fifty-two largest incorporated companies in Indianapolis.[50]

Customary social barriers doubtless contributed to the distance between the Klan and the economic elite. Despite shared ethnocentric prejudices and the reasonable assumption that some members of the upper class may have believed that the Klan performed a necessary function, the hooded order was still sensational, even ominous, a world away from the lives of the elite. To the wealthy, the leaders of the Klan likely were vulgar politicians, crude salesmen who gave wild speeches at steamy summer night rallies. Many of the Klansmen themselves seemed threatening—some were poor, others were rough blue-collar laborers.

Social customs alone, however, could not account for all of the separation. There were indications that the leading businessmen of Indianapolis fundamentally opposed the Klan as a reckless, disruptive organization. Social and professional organizations representing the wealthy were among the few to openly adopt anti-Klan positions. The Indiana Bar Association and the Indianapolis Diocese of the Protestant Episcopal church, for example, officially condemned the Klan when the strength of the hooded order became apparent in Indianapolis. Corporate executives in particular saw no profit in stirring up overt racial and religious hostilities. Any large companies tainted by the Klan might face protests from blacks and Catholics. The desire of the city's top business leaders to avoid such negative publicity was evident in 1923, when the names of two bank employees appeared on the roster of Indianapolis Klansmen that was published in *Tolerance*. After the *Indiana Catholic and Record* publicized the fact that Brant C. Downey and Chester A. James of Commercial National Bank were Klansmen, both men explained to the newspaper that they had made a "donation" to the Klan in 1921 but did not consider themselves official members. Apparently, their explanation did not satisfy the bank's board of directors, which ordered an investigation. Both men were employed in other occupations by the end of the year.[51]

The social stratification of the first 12,000 Indianapolis Klansmen, as it can be measured by occupation, may have been altered as more people joined the order after early 1923. Robert Goldberg's study of the Klan in Denver, Colorado, found that those who became members in the early phase of the movement had a greater tendency to be from the middle class.[52] In general, however, occupational patterns among the original Indianapolis Klansmen did not differ markedly from those appearing on the complete membership lists for Richmond and Crown Point. In these communities, as in Indianapolis, the Klan represented a wide cross section of the white Protestant population, attracting middle-class individuals slightly more often than blue-collar workers and the wealthiest citizens almost not at all.

Richmond of the 1920s, with its growing population of just under

30,000, its strong manufacturing base, its commanding position in relation to surrounding agricultural areas, and its avid support for the Klan, was much like Muncie, Anderson, Kokomo, and the other small industrial cities of central Indiana. Local businessmen liked to think that Richmond's economic diversity made it "panic proof." A large Pennsylvania Railroad switching yard employed hundreds of workers. Several companies manufactured farm machinery. Richmond also produced a variety of other manufactured goods. When the Klan entered the city, it attracted a huge following. A total of 3,183 joined the Richmond chapter between 1921 and 1926. Approximately 14 percent of the men on the membership list lived outside the city limits, but those who lived in the city represented more than 35 percent of all native-born white men.[53]

An occupational sample of Richmond Klan members—compared, in this case, with an equal sample of non-Klansmen—disclosed patterns very similar to those found in Indianapolis (see Table 3.7). Individuals in low-level white-collar occupations joined the Klan with slightly greater frequency, while lower-level manual workers were somewhat less likely to be members. As in Indianapolis, this pat-

Table 3.7

Occupations of Richmond Klansmen, 1924

	Klan		Non-Klan*	
	Number	Percent	Number	Percent
High white collar	46	9.2	56	11.2
Low white collar	151	30.2	103	20.6
Skilled	176	35.2	162	32.4
Lower manual	116	23.2	156	31.2
No occupation	11	2.2	23	4.6
Total	500		500	
Chi-square (4 dof) = 20.75 $P \leq .01$				

Source: See Appendix.

*Because a complete membership list is available for Richmond, it is possible to compare the occupations of Klansmen directly with those of men who did not join the Klan.

tern can be attributed to the high cost of Klan membership and the large number of those at the low end of the economic spectrum who were not potential members. Workers from Richmond's small black, Italian, and Hungarian neighborhoods held jobs almost exclusively in the semiskilled and unskilled categories. In the high-level white-collar category, again, Klansmen tended to be professionals, moderately successful merchants, and high-level officials of the county and city governments, not members of Richmond's business elite. Thirty percent of Richmond's physicians and 26 percent of its attorneys joined the Klan, while no Klansmen could be located among the city's bank executives or the owners of its most important businesses.[54]

The small town of Crown Point in Lake County also appeared to confirm the Klan's broad appeal within the white Protestant community. While overshadowed by the industrial cities of Gary, Hammond, and East Chicago farther to the north, Crown Point was the historic center of what had traditionally been a rural county prior to 1900; in the 1920s, it retained some political importance as the seat of county government. Some small-scale manufacturing took place in Crown Point, but with only slightly more than 3,000 residents in 1920, the town served primarily as a center for Lake County farmers. The Crown Point Klan was not large compared with other areas of the state or even with the rest of Lake County. With 128 members, it represented less than 9 percent of the native-born white men in the township.[55]

Without a city directory for Crown Point, it is difficult to say with certainty whether Klansmen were representative of the community as a whole; there are indications, however, that this was the case. The percentages of those employed in both white- and blue-collar occupations do not appear out of proportion to those for Richmond and Indianapolis (see Table 3.8). The fact that more than one-quarter of Crown Point's Klansmen were farmers reflects the importance of agriculture to the community. The large number of low-level white-collar workers can be traced to high levels of participation by clerks and other employees of the county government—another dominant aspect of life in this county seat. Crown Point's wealthiest citizens do not appear to have played any role in the Klan. The eight members who fell into the high-level white-collar category included

Table 3.8

Occupations of Crown Point Klansmen, 1921–1927

	Number	Percent
High white collar	8	6.8
Low white collar	38	30.9
Skilled	18	14.6
Lower manual	23	18.7
Farmer*	35	28.5
Retired	1	0.8

Source: See Appendix.

*All those who listed farming as their occupation, whether self-employed or employed by another.

Table 3.9

*Influence of Wage Earners on Klan Membership, 1925**

	Regression Coefficient b	Standard Error	R^2
Wage earner	−.05	.06	.37

*Controlling for southern residence and percentage urban, renters, Protestant, and Catholic.

two city engineers, two lawyers, two supervisors of county departments, one physician, and one dentist.[56]

Beyond these three communities, it is difficult to generalize about the occupational status of Indiana Klansmen. The 1920 census reports do not include occupational breakdowns for individual counties; state economic reports also fail to include this kind of information. The census, however, does give the average number of "wage earners" in each county, so for this one important occupational category it is possible to estimate the level of support for the Klan. Table 3.9 demonstrates that the percentage of wage earners in a given county had no discernible influence on the level of Klan membership. The *b* coefficient indicates a slightly negative relationship; the standard error, however, is so large that the coefficient should be regarded essentially as zero. This is generally consistent with the findings for Indianapolis, Richmond, and Crown Point. Just as blue-collar workers in these communities did not appear extraordinarily more attracted to the Klan than white-collar workers, wage earners employed by manufacturing and industrial firms in Indiana did not show particularly strong or weak support for the Klan in 1925.

While these findings regarding the occupations of Klansmen generally suggest that the movement cut a wide path across Indiana's class structure, it would be unwise to conclude that economic status played no role in the popularity of the hooded order. As we have seen, low-level white-collar workers and skilled blue-collar workers joined the Klan slightly more often than members of other occupational groups. Wealth, measured by the percentage of home owners and renters in each county, also seems to have had an impact on the size of the Klan in 1925. As Table 3.10 indicates, home ownership had no discernible influence on Klan membership. On the other hand, renting rather than owning a home appears to have increased the likelihood of being a Klan member by a significant degree. In this case, the *b* coefficient estimates that, for any given county in Indiana, an increase of 10 percent in the number of renters could be expected to increase the size of the Klan by 3.7 percent.

This relationship between renters and Klan members indicates

Table 3.10

Influence of Home Owners and Renters on Klan Membership, 1925*

	Regression Coefficient *b*	Standard Error	R^2
Owners	−.02	.15	.21
Renters	.37	.09	.37

*Controlling for southern residence and percentage urban, wage earners, Protestant, and Catholic.

that economic status does explain part of the Klan's appeal. At the same time, however, it should not be interpreted as proof that the movement was powered primarily by "low status" individuals. First, the Klan had declined significantly by 1925; by this time, the characteristics of the membership may have shifted somewhat toward the lower end of the economic spectrum. More affluent Klansmen may have been particularly disturbed by the revelations about D. C. Stephenson and may have been among the first to discontinue paying dues. There is some evidence, in fact, that more affluent individuals tended to be early joiners of the movement, whereas the less affluent more often were late joiners. Robert Goldberg discovered this pattern among Denver Klansmen. As we shall see, the same observation can be made about the Richmond Klan.[57] Second, home owner and renter designations provide only a crude measure of economic status, dividing the population roughly in half and leaving room for a great deal of diversity in the economic status of individuals on both sides of this one dividing line. Regression analysis, for example, shows that one cannot automatically assume that wage earners were renters. Residents of the generally less affluent southern counties were also more likely to be home owners than renters.[58]

Religion

Just as the Indiana Klan movement crossed geographic and class boundaries, it also transcended the denominational lines between Protestant church members. During the 1920s, leaders of the state's chief Protestant churches often expressed their concerns about social, moral, and political issues that corresponded to the Klan's view of a besieged white Protestant America. On the issue of the Klan itself, they usually remained silent; only the Indianapolis Diocese of the Protestant Episcopal church and the fundamentalist Church of the Nazarene took noted stands against the secret order.[59] This general acceptance of the Klan by Indiana's Protestant churches takes on even greater significance when the religious affiliations of Klansmen are considered. "Pietist" and "liturgical" Protestants showed comparable enthusiasm for the Klan.[60] Of the major denominations, only the most radically fundamentalist could not count large numbers of Klansmen within their congregations.

These conclusions are supported first by a sample of 2,638 members of Protestant churches in central Indianapolis in the early 1920s (see Table 3.11).[61] For the purposes of this sample, the Protestant denominations were divided into three groups: fundamentalist, which included the relatively new, avidly fundamentalist churches of the period; evangelical, the large Protestant churches that also ex-

Table 3.11

Klan Membership within Central Indianapolis Protestant Churches, 1923

	Church Members	Klan Number	Klan Percent
Nonevangelical			
Lutheran	190	12	6.3
Episcopal	95	4	4.2
Quaker	47	3	6.4
Total	332	19	5.7
Evangelical			
Methodist	807	51	6.3
Disciples of Christ	569	44	7.7
Presbyterian	307	18	5.9
Baptist	284	14	4.9
United Brethren	95	10	10.5
Total	2,062	137	6.6
Fundamentalist			
Church of the Nazarene	210	3	1.4
Church of Christ	34	0	0
Total	244	3	1.2
All denominations	2,638	159	6.0
Chi-square (subtotals only, 2 dof) = 15.9 $P \leq .01$			

Source: See Appendix.

perienced fundamentalist influences during the twenties; and nonevangelical, the churches that usually were perceived as distinct from the evangelical tradition and that, on the whole, were not influenced by fundamentalism.[62] When the names of the church members in this sample are compared with the list of Indianapolis's first 12,000 Klansmen, it becomes clear that in the early phase of the movement, members of nonevangelical and evangelical churches displayed similar interest in the Klan. By 1923, 5.7 percent of the nonevangelicals in the sample and 6.6 percent of the evangelicals belonged to the order.[63] Only 1.2 percent of the fundamentalist church members—three of the 244 sampled—had joined the Klan by the same time.

The religious affiliations of Richmond Klansmen, who were sampled using a different method, also show the organization's wide appeal across denominational lines. The case of Richmond, in fact, provides an example of the Klan representing a near–mirror image of the city's Protestant denominational spectrum. The information in Table 3.12 was compiled using a random sample of 242 Richmond Klansmen whose obituaries appeared in local newspapers between 1922 and 1982. Of the 242 sampled, no religious affiliations were listed for 110 (45.5 percent).[64] The percentage of Klansmen in each Protestant denomination was then compared with a general distribution of Richmond Protestants according to the 1926 census of religious bodies.[65] Given the traditional belief that Klansmen were primarily religious extremists, it is remarkable how closely the Klan followed the contours of Protestantism in Richmond's churches. The Klan's strong representation in Lutheran and United Brethren congregations reflects both traditional and evangelical influences within the city's sizable German population. Richmond's large Quaker community, one of the oldest and most influential in the state, showed no special immunity to the Klan.[66] Episcopal and Baptist church members joined the Klan in rates proportional to their small numbers. Methodists were slightly underrepresented in the Klan, whereas Presbyterians and Disciples of Christ showed particularly strong support. Fundamentalist churches were insignificant in both the Klan and the city of Richmond.

Religious data for Crown Point Klansmen, provided by the members themselves on their applications to the chapter, again demon-

Table 3.12

Religious Affiliations of Richmond Klansmen, 1921–1926

	Klan Sample		Percent Protestant Church Members	
	Number	Percent	Klan	Richmond
Nonevangelical				
Lutheran	30	12.4	22.9	29.3
Quaker	16	6.6	12.2	14.9
Episcopal	6	2.5	4.6	3.0
Evangelical				
Methodist	16	6.6	12.2	19.0
Disciples of Christ	18	7.4	13.7	9.8
Presbyterian	26	10.7	19.8	9.8
Baptist	4	1.7	3.1	2.9
United Brethren	12	5.0	9.2	4.5
Fundamentalist				
Nazarene	1	0.4	0.8	0.4
Adventist	1	0.4	0.8	0.3
Other	2	0.8	0.7	6.1
No affiliation	110	45.5		
Total	242			

Source: See Appendix.

strate the strength of the Klan within the major denominations (see Table 3.13). The great majority of churchgoing Klansmen in Crown Point were Lutherans, Methodists, Disciples of Christ, and Presbyterians. Other denominations, including the fundamentalist Church of Christ, were much less significant. As in Richmond, a large percentage of Crown Point's Klansmen did not belong to any church. It is notable, however, that virtually all members who gave no church affiliation indicated that they were "Protestant" as opposed to having "No religion."

Table 3.13

Religious Affiliations of Crown Point Klansmen, 1921–1926

	Number	Percent
Nonevangelical		
Lutheran	13	10.7
Evangelical		
Methodist	29	24.0
Disciples of Christ	11	9.0
Presbyterian	16	13.2
Evangelical Lutheran	5	4.0
Baptist	2	1.6
Congregational	1	0.8
United Brethren	1	0.8
Fundamentalist		
Church of Christ	1	0.8
Other		
Universalist	2	1.6
Protestant (no affiliation)*	37	30.6
No religion**	2	1.6
Total	120	

Source: See Appendix.

*Members listed religion as "Protestant" but gave no church affiliation.
**Members specified "No religion."

The Klan's ability to cross Protestant denominational lines in Indianapolis, Richmond, and Crown Point can be confirmed on a statewide basis by regression analysis. Evangelical Protestant church membership (Methodist, Disciples of Christ, Presbyterian, Baptist, and United Brethren) had a moderately positive, but clearly significant influence on Klan membership (see Table 3.14). At the same

Table 3.14

Influence of Church Membership on Klan Membership, 1925*

	Regression Coefficient b	Standard Error	R^2
Nonevangelical Protestants	.01	.01	.21
Evangelical Protestants	.07	.03	.26
All Protestants	.03	.01	.21
Nonchurch members	.002	.01	.19

*Controlling for southern residence and percentage urban, owners, and Catholic.

time, nonevangelical church membership (Lutheran, Quaker, and Episcopal) had neither a positive nor a negative impact of any significance. Members of Indiana's evangelical Protestant churches, therefore, were somewhat more likely than members of nonevangelical churches to be Klansmen in 1925. That likelihood, however, was not overwhelming, and nonevangelicals as a group did not strongly oppose the Klan. Fundamentalist church membership in Indiana during the mid-1920s was too small to be analyzed by the regression technique. This fact alone offers some evidence that fundamentalist church membership explains little of the Klan's popularity.

If the Klan appealed to nonevangelical as well as evangelical church members, it also seems to have received support across the state in 1925 from both Protestant church members and nonchurch members. Regression analysis shows some distinction in the manner in which these two groups influenced Klan membership. As a group, Protestant church members had a slightly positive, but significant influence on Klan membership, while nonchurch members demonstrated no influence. But, again, the difference is not great enough to support any conclusion that an individual's status as either a church member or a nonchurch member played a particularly important part in his decision to join the Klan. In general, the order appears to have appealed to all types of white Protestants in Indiana: German Lutherans and Quakers as well as Methodists and Baptists and those who were not active church members, identifying themselves as Protestants only in a broad cultural sense.[67]

4. Klan and Community

On the Fourth of July, 1923, Kokomo, Indiana, played host to perhaps the most famous Ku Klux Klan convention of the 1920s.[1] Klan leaders organized the gathering to demonstrate the secret order's immense popularity in the Midwest and hoped the publicity would entice even more dues-paying recruits. A crowd of more than 100,000 Klansmen, their families, and spectators descended on Kokomo from throughout Indiana and surrounding states; some Klan loyalists journeyed from as far away as Florida and California. The small industrial city of 30,000 had never experienced such commotion. Traffic hopelessly constricted the highways and downtown streets for most of the day, while many store owners quickly sold out their stocks. The entertainment, which was open to the public, created the excitement of a state fair, and thousands of Kokomo's residents turned out for the massive nighttime parade that culminated the celebration.[2]

Despite the notoriety of the 1923 convention, the real impact of the Klan movement on the city of Kokomo could be seen more clearly in the events that followed a year later. By that time, the state Klan organization had become too bitterly divided to sponsor a single gathering for the Fourth of July. Kokomo's Klan leaders, while they had hoped to repeat the excitement of the previous year, were forced to settle for a smaller event for their members, local citizens, and residents of nearby towns. Far from being a disappointment, however, the 1924 Fourth of

July was a great success. It may not have been as sensational as the year before, but it was nonetheless the largest, most galvanizing community event of the year.

In preparation for the festivities, Kokomo's evening newspaper, the *Daily Tribune*, reminded its readers of the previous year's "overwhelming celebration," provided publicity and information for the public, and relayed official instructions to members of the Klan. In an effort to circumvent the expected traffic problem, the *Tribune* informed Kokomo Klansmen of an order to leave their automobiles at home; it also printed traffic control assignments for the three companies of Klansmen who would be on duty the night before the event. Later, the *Tribune* announced last-minute program changes, additional streetcar schedules, parade route information, and parade assignments for Klansmen.[3]

The Klan held the celebration at Exposition Park, which accommodated more people than its usual meeting place. Throughout the day, thousands of spectators and Klansmen milled about the park, setting out their picnic dinners and enjoying the entertainment. A six-round boxing match turned out to be especially popular, as did the Klan's boys' singing quartet. The order also arranged for circus performers, an evening motion picture, and a procession by its new motorcycle brigade. To raise money for the county hospital fund, the Klan's women's auxiliary, the Disabled American Veterans, and a number of church groups sponsored a tag sale. In the evening, the parade again attracted thousands of curious citizens—fully as many as the year before, according to the *Tribune*. The parade featured the Kokomo Klan's thirty-piece band, followed by nearly a thousand Klansmen from Kokomo, Muncie, Anderson, and other communities. The procession also included thirty members of Kokomo's Junior Klan, one hundred women from the auxiliary, and two floats, one a car decorated all in white, the other a miniature schoolhouse surrounded by an oversized American flag.[4]

With its conspicuous costumes, its bigoted rhetoric about the threats facing white Protestant America, and, of course, the customary cross burning, the Klan placed a distinctive stamp on the day's events. At the same time, it is apparent that the vast majority of Kokomo's citizens did not regard the order as a violent group of vigilantes who threatened danger and division. In fact, the Klan gave every indication of being the most unifying force in the community, a social and civic organization comprised of ministers, professional men, politicians, small businessmen, and, most important, an enormous percentage of the city's average citizens. At least a third of Kokomo's native-born white men paid their ten dollars to join up during the 1920s, making the Klan by far the largest organization of any type in the community.[5]

Not all chapters monopolized community functions as the Kokomo Klan did on the Fourth of July. The Klan's influence on local affairs varied from community to community, depending not only on the number of members but also on a variety of insular circumstances. Still, this event in one city where the Klan was particularly powerful was symbolic of the role played by the hooded order in communities throughout the state. Beyond the rhetoric of recruiting pamphlets and the antics of state and national leaders lay an organization that was driven to a large degree by grass-roots, community-oriented forces. Social activities—grand holiday celebrations, rallies, barbecues, weekly dances, family picnics, and other events—represented the most common means for the average member to be involved in the movement. Indeed, for many Klansmen, such activities, along with voting for a Klan-sponsored political candidate, may have been their only connection with the organization. The extensive involvement of the Klan in local civic and political affairs further indicates the extent to which the movement focused on community. Klan chapters throughout the state injected themselves into a wide range of local issues, including not only popular concerns about Prohibition enforcement but also such things as public education, taxes, moral and religious matters, and charity work.

A distinguishing feature of the Klan was its capacity to arouse a sense of solidarity among the citizens of cities and towns, to unite disparate social groups, to circumvent existing social and political institutions, and to assert a powerful populist influence in community life. Some of its appeal can be attributed to common attitudes about the perceived threat of immigrants, the growing dominance of the city, and other, primarily national issues. Perhaps the average Klansman threw himself into local activities in part because he wanted to construct a wall between himself and those places in America where urban sophisticates mocked traditional values and where Catholics, Jews, and blacks had made white Protestants a numerical minority. But most of the Klan's popularity stemmed from deeper, more immediate concerns about the nature of community institutions and the ability of the average citizen to have a voice in shaping them. Indiana Klansmen, whether they lived in industrial cities, smaller commercial and manufacturing centers, or rural villages, did not need to look to distant places to see the consequences of social change and the problems of modern society.

Prohibition, for example, had created a crisis in nearly every community in the state, demonstrating to many white Protestants that the will of the people could be easily, even arrogantly thwarted. Of all the issues affecting community life in Indiana during the 1920s, this one was the most divisive and raised the most difficult questions about popular control over community affairs. When the Klan appeared in individual communities, it could immediately become a champion of Prohibition, making instant allies of Protestant clergymen, local Anti-Saloon League and WCTU groups, and others working for the same goal.

As important as the Prohibition issue was in and of itself, it was at the same time a symbol for the wider process of changing social relationships and the frustrations of average people who were forced to deal with those changes. By 1920, decades of industrial growth and economic consolidation in Indiana had altered many of the structures of community life, created new institutions, and increased the power of economic elites to shape the course of public affairs. Ordinary men and women could see that communities all around them had become larger, more complex, more profoundly influenced by outside forces, and less subject to the will of their citizens. Through the Klan movement, a measure of popular control was temporarily restored.

Sources of Stress

In the late nineteenth and early twentieth centuries, as the United States struggled to reconcile its agrarian past with a now overwhelmingly industrial present and future, Indiana in some respects epitomized a changed American society. During this time, the state turned away from its nineteenth-century dependence on agriculture and instead became reliant on a variety of new industries. Its cities grew rapidly in just three decades, and by 1920, as was true for the nation as a whole, Indiana had become a predominately "urban" state.[6] After the state's centennial celebration in 1916, some Hoosiers even began to see their home as the "typical American state" and a "barometer of American temper." In the twenties, Robert and Helen Lynd gave this view even more credibility when they selected Muncie, Indiana, as "Middletown" for their pioneering study of the effects of industrialization on a "typical" American community.[7]

Although seemingly representative of the nation's transformation from an agrarian to an urban-industrial society, Indiana differed from other industrial states in two important ways. First, compared with other industrial states of the Midwest, industrial development in Indiana occurred slightly later and on a somewhat smaller scale. As recently as 1890, the U.S. Bureau of the Census had still classified as rural three-quarters of Indiana's residents. At the same time, the population of Indianapolis, the only large city in the state, had just reached 100,000, and among the other cities, only Evansville, Fort Wayne, and Terre Haute, had populations over 25,000. By contrast, during the same period Chicago had more than one million citizens, the population of St. Louis had reached nearly 500,000, and Cleveland and Cincinnati had almost three times as many residents as Indianapolis.[8] Much of Indiana's most heavily industrialized region, the northwestern corner of the state, had not even begun to develop in 1890. Gary, a U.S. Steel Corporation town of more than 55,000 in 1920, did not exist prior to 1906. East Chicago and Hammond, both of which had over 35,000 residents in 1920, had respective populations of 1,255 and 5,428 in 1890. In 1924 South Bend, which boasted one of the largest automobile factories in the nation, had more than 70,000 inhabitants; it had been only one-third as large in 1890. Also in 1890, the gas belt cities of central Indiana, such as Anderson, Kokomo, and Muncie, had just reached the height of their boom period. While each of these cities had become an established site of heavy industry by 1920, in 1890 they had been only slightly removed from their quiet, county seat/town traditions.[9]

By 1920, not only had industry been a dominant force in Indiana for a relatively short time, but also, and more important, it had brought about comparatively little change in the state's ethnic composition. While European immigrants poured into other midwestern states between 1880 and 1924, relatively few went to Indiana. In 1920, foreign immigrants represented nearly 20 percent of the populations of Illinois, Michigan, and Wisconsin and 12 percent of the population of Ohio. In Indiana, however, foreign-born residents made up only 3 percent of the population; of those, only half were "new" immigrants from southern and eastern Europe, and nearly a third lived in Lake County just across the border from Illinois and the city of Chicago. In all but a handful of Indiana's ninety-two counties, the foreign born represented only a small fraction of the population. Outside Lake County, only one major Indiana city, South Bend, contained a large number of immigrants; 19 percent of the population was foreign born in 1920. In other Indiana cities, foreign-born residents made up between 2 and 5 percent of the population; the figure for Fort Wayne was slightly higher at nearly 8 percent. At the same time, immigrants represented 30 percent of the populations of Chicago and Cleveland and 13 percent of the residents of St. Louis.[10]

The migration of southern blacks into the industrial Midwest also had a smaller effect on Indiana than on other states. According to the 1920 census, blacks represented just under 3 percent of the population of Indiana; by 1930, the figure had grown to only 3.5 percent. Among the major cities, only Indianapolis, Gary, and Evansville had large black communities (11, 10, and 8 percent of the population, respectively). In Muncie, Richmond, and Terre Haute, blacks represented less than 6 percent of the population, and in other cities the percentages were generally much smaller.[11]

Because its industrial development had been moderate compared with other areas, and because it attracted relatively few ethnic minorities, Indiana avoided some of the more disruptive manifestations of America's urban-industrial society, especially the sharp internal conflict between town and country that occurred in other states. Indiana's rural citizens, like those nationwide, could see numerous examples of the evils of cosmopolitan life throughout the Midwest: the overwhelming influence of alien cultures, Prohibition violations (considered particularly rampant among the immigrants), crime and political corruption, and the congestion, confusion, and filth of the urban landscape.[12] But in Indiana's industrial communities, with the exception of Gary and other Lake County communities, which were essentially satellites of Chicago, many of these problems were not nearly so troubling.

The largest and most diverse city in the state provided the best example. Indianapolis, James H. Madison has pointed out, "was not an urban alien set uncomfortably in rural and small town Indiana," even though its population had surpassed 300,000 by 1920.[13] Journalists and businessmen cited by Madison supported this conclusion. One author, writing in 1924, described Indianapolis as "a somewhat blurry, but nevertheless authentic mirror of Hoosierdom at large." Spokesmen for the Chamber of Commerce in the 1920s claimed that Indianapolis had been spared many of the undesirable characteristics of other large cities.[14] In the size of its native-born white population, Indianapolis was, in fact, more closely related to Indiana's smaller industrial cities and rural communities than to other large midwestern cities. In 1920, 70 percent of Indianapolis's residents were native-born whites. This ratio of foreign to native born compared favorably to the native white composition of the entire state (80 percent) as well as to the other industrial cities. Only Lake County cities and South Bend were similar, for example, to Cincinnati and St. Louis where only half the residents were native whites, or to Chicago and Cleveland where they represented only a quarter of the population. (See Table 4.1.)[15]

The continuity of white Protestant ethnic domination in Indiana, while it remained strong and lessened the sense of estrangement between town and country, could not stave off other consequences of industrial development that changed the structure of community life. The new role of community elites within the industrial setting, for example, provided a particular challenge to rural and small-town traditions—one that proved more fundamental than the growth of small neighborhoods of ethnic minorities.

The development of industry between 1890 and 1920 drastically altered the role of elites in most Indiana communities. The immense scale of industry gave business leaders obvious power to dictate the course of large sections of local economies and, in some instances, the affairs of entire cities. The most patent examples could be

Table 4.1

Native White Composition of Indiana Cities, 1920

City	Percent Native White*
Anderson	91.3
Evansville	70.1
Fort Wayne	66.6
Indianapolis	69.8
Kokomo	85.3
Muncie	84.6
Richmond	75.4
South Bend	47.8
Terre Haute	74.1
Lake County	
East Chicago	16.6
Gary	29.8
Hammond	41.5
Other Cities	
Chicago	23.8
Cleveland	26.6
Cincinnati	51.5
St. Louis	46.5

Sources: U.S. Bureau of the Census, *Fourteenth Census: Indiana Compendium*, p. 43, and *Fourteenth Census*, 2:47.

*Both parents native born.

found in Gary and in nearby Whiting, home to a massive oil refinery operated by Standard Oil of Indiana. Other cities typically became dependent on a small number of major industries. The production of automobiles governed much of the economy of Indianapolis and played an even more important role in smaller cities such as Anderson, Kokomo, Muncie, New Castle, and South Bend. The production of glass products, associated primarily with the Ball Brothers Company of Muncie, became a powerful force in many communities. Coal dominated Evansville, Terre Haute, Vincennes, and other smaller cities of southwestern Indiana. Food processing, much of it carried out by two of the nation's largest canning firms—the Van Camp Company of Indianapolis and the Morgan Packing Company of the small southern Indiana city of Austin—reached into many communities throughout the state.[16]

These industries, which became more concentrated during the 1920s (especially automobiles, which fell increasingly into the hands of Detroit's large manufacturers), embodied most of Indiana's industrial wealth. Owners and managers of these businesses, and many smaller firms that also operated on a previously unprecedented scale, controlled the fate of countless workers, few of whom were protected by labor unions. The business elite gained increasing control over local government as a result of its importance to the welfare of the community. Through social and philanthropic organizations they dominated civic matters such as the operation of charities and the building of hospitals, libraries, and other public facilities. Before the appearance of large-scale industry, community elites also had been disproportionately influential, of course, but as a group they had been more likely to include successful small businessmen, professionals, and clergymen who maintained contact and shared values with ordinary citizens. After industrialization, elites became further removed from the people who were their employees and neighbors. More than earlier generations of community leaders, the business elite spent its leisure hours at private clubs, sent its children to exclusive schools, and attended churches where other members were also of high social standing. Perhaps even more important, elites—through their social, political, and business organizations—had come to stand for a new definition of community, one that emphasized business success as a city's most fundamental unifying principle.[17]

One early example of how industrial elites had assumed more powerful roles and begun to alter community institutions and traditions could be seen in Terre Haute, one of Indiana's oldest industrial cities. Business leaders of the 1870s, whose wealth came from the local development of railroads and coal, espoused a point of view toward their community that was notably different from that of an earlier generation of businessmen. While the latter had attempted to keep personal success from interfering with long-standing community relationships and responsibilities, after 1870 the "best people" of Terre Haute, according to Nick Salvatore, "presented themselves as a separate group of singular importance."[18] In their social and business dealings, elites continuously grew apart from the rest of the community and asserted more and more control. They ministered to one another's businesses. Their children intermarried. Through politics, philanthropic works, and control of the newspapers they dominated civic affairs. In 1873, the new business leaders expressed the simple code with which they expected to oversee their community: "As a city we are altogether dependent upon the business tact and energy, or in other words, *life* and *vigor* of our business community."[19]

When Robert and Helen Lynd investigated Muncie in the 1920s, they found that five decades of industrial expansion had created a powerful "business class" that exercised stifling control over the citizenry.[20] This was perhaps too simple a means of depicting a complex set of social relationships, and there is evidence that on occasion Muncie's elite was successfully challenged, especially after the onset of the Great Depression.[21] Still, the expanded prerogatives of business leaders had clearly produced a new community identity based almost exclusively on business success. Local newspapers presented the idea of loyalty to hometown businesses as a test of citizenship. One editorial published during the Lynds' study advised that "the thing we must get into our heads about this out-of-town buying business is that it hurts the individual who does it and his friends who live here" and that "a dollar spent out of town never returns." Two other editorials, while they offered somewhat conflicting views, summed up the new community ethic: "The first duty of a citizen is to produce," and "The American citizen's first importance is no longer that of citizen but of consumer. Consumption is the new necessity."[22]

The creed of boosterism was certainly not new in the late nineteenth and early twentieth centuries, and the idea of business success had never been inherently inconsistent with rural and small-town values. The importance of the businessman's new vision of community as the Lynds viewed it and as it existed in other Indiana towns and cities was that it had become omnipresent. It came to symbolize the loss of individual involvement and control in community life. The heart of the Lynds' argument was that Muncie had become segmented and demoralized as the significance of face-to-face relationships faded in civic affairs; as more and more workers were employed by large corporations; as traditional institutions such as the church, the family, and representative government appeared to lose authority; and as new forms of community organization, less subject to popular influence and control, gained strength.[23]

The proliferation of formal business organizations in Indiana between 1890 and 1920 demonstrated the shifting focus of authority in communities. One of the first such groups, the Indianapolis Commercial Club, was founded in 1890 by a small group of reform-minded business leaders that included Colonel Eli Lilly, patriarch of the Indianapolis drug and pharmaceutical empire and perhaps the most well-known businessman in the state.[24] While the Indianapolis club—and others like it that soon appeared in other cities—expressed a genuine interest in civic improvements and governmental reforms, the long-term effect of these organizations was to give business leaders increased authority in the public domain. This process became more apparent in the early twentieth century as commercial clubs evolved into local chapters of the Chamber of Commerce, which, by the twenties, had become an active political force in most communities.[25]

At the same time that business organizations were asserting more political influence within communities, popular involvement in politics diminished. Voter turnout in Indiana between 1890 and 1920 followed the national trend downward. In national elections from 1888 to 1904, 90 percent of the state's eligible voters typically cast ballots. By the 1920s, however, the turnout had dwindled to 70 percent. In Muncie, the Lynds detected growing estrangement from the political process at all levels. Corruption in government caused part of the apathy. In addition, public interest in the electoral process had grown weaker as the relationship between voters and candidates became more impersonal and as the differences between party candidates grew more superficial. "In the city of today," the Lynds declared, "it is far less possible than in the eighties and earlier for a voter to know personally each of even the two or three dozen local candidates from whom he is expected at a given election to choose the 'best men.'" One man interviewed by the Lynds expressed a view they found to be common: political issues were not of great consequence. "I'm not going to hear ___speak tonight. It'll be in the papers tomorrow. And anyway, it doesn't make much difference."[26]

The decline of citizen involvement in civic affairs also affected areas outside the political arena. The Lynds found that much of the responsibility for assisting Muncie's poor had been shifted from individuals to business groups and social agencies. In the late nineteenth century, the poor of Muncie had been aided primarily on a neighborhood level through face-to-face giving, churches, and lodges. This type of direct contact with the homeless and the hungry continued into the twentieth century, but by the 1920s it was no longer the dominant means of charity. By that time, less than one-quarter of the money given to the poor came from churches, and lodges contributed even less. "Lodge charity," the Lynds noted, "plays a relatively smaller role today as other charitable agencies have developed, as the fraternal spirit declines, and as lodges are more preoccupied in using their resources to build competitive club houses." More and more, "Christian charity" had been reduced to a "secularized business proposition." Groups such as the Chamber of Commerce and Rotary assumed leading roles in the administration of charity, reorganizing it by 1925 into a centralized system more subject to "long range planning and control." Through the Community Chest, business leaders sponsored annual fund-raising campaigns and distributed the proceeds to Muncie's social agencies. Soon after its inception, the Community Chest became the primary means of distributing money to the poor; neither traditional face-to-face giving nor the modest programs supported by the county government compared in significance.[27]

The evolution toward segmentation, impersonalization, and the concentration of authority in civic affairs could be seen in industrial communities that were both larger and smaller than Muncie.[28] The effects of this process, however, were not confined to the city. Rural areas, too, had been disjoined by an expanding, increasingly centralized economy.

This was true first because of the relationship between farmers and the changing urban communities. Few farmers were so isolated that they did not have frequent contact with one of the cities or towns in Indiana's urban network. Because farmers were connected to towns by politics, economic necessity, and the need for schools, churches, information, and entertainment, there is little reason to conclude that changes in community life escaped their notice or concern. The link between town and country was even more significant because of the continuing flow of population from rural counties into the cities. This was by far the primary source of population growth in Indiana's cities, and by the 1920s few farm families had not lost a son or daughter to the city or moved there themselves.[29] Even for those who remained on the farm, hard times, such as those of the twenties, often meant that at least one family member had to take a job in a nearby city to make ends meet.

If the rural population was not entirely insulated from the changes in urban life, neither was it spared the social consequences of an increasingly modernized and centralized agricultural economy. Farm modernization significantly altered rural life between 1900 and 1920. In 1913, the state legislature established a system of county agricultural offices under the direction of scientists from Purdue University. The system disseminated information on advances in farm management and on new techniques in such areas as soil improvement, fertilization, and plant and animal disease control. These innovations greatly increased farm production, helping to create a prosperous agricultural economy between the turn of the century and the end of World War I.[30]

Modernization, however, had not affected all farmers evenly. Well-to-do farmers benefited most from scientific advances and the county agricultural system. With capital to invest in automobiles, trucks, farm machinery, and fertilizers, or to put toward a son's education at Purdue, affluent farmers increased production, expanded landholdings, and profited most as land values rose. Increasingly, those who worked small farms were placed at a competitive disadvantage. Without the ability to invest in new agricultural techniques and equipment, smaller farmers often fell far behind and were less able to turn a profit. More and more, unsuccessful small farms were consolidated, the tenancy rate increased, more farms came to be operated by managers, and farm families turned to the cities for employment.[31]

This process, of course, had begun long before the turn of the century, but between 1900 and 1920 it had a particularly strong impact. By 1920, agriculture in southern Indiana had fallen far behind that of more commercial areas in the northern and central part of the state. Low productivity and outdated practices had created a stagnant agricultural economy in which many farmers simply abandoned the land rather than become mired in a sinkhole of unprofitable tenancy. In northern and central Indiana, successful farmers consolidated more and more land. The average farm size had increased dramatically in that part of the state by 1920. The tenancy rate had also reached a new high. By that time, the proportion of all farms operated by renters had exceeded 40 percent in twenty-four counties—almost all of them in northern and central Indiana.[32]

The concentration of authority among the more well-to-do farmers was most apparent in the rise of the Indiana Farm Bureau movement. Established in 1919 generally for the more successful farmers in each county, the Farm Bureau became the dominant force in Indiana agriculture during the 1920s. Through its chapters in eighty-one counties and its close relationship with Purdue University and the county agricultural offices, the bureau was directly involved in the administration of local farm programs. It operated a strong cooperative network throughout the state and used its political influence to have a series of agricultural regulations enacted in Indiana.[33] While much of its activity appears to have benefited the successful more than the struggling farmer, the Farm Bureau was significant less for its specific accomplishments than for the new order it represented in agricultural communities. Just as organizations like the Chamber of Commerce had shifted more authority to businessmen in the cities, the Indiana Farm Bureau movement had given the most affluent farmers more control. The Grange and other more popular farm organizations had lost much of their influence by the twenties. In rural areas, as in the cities, the ability of the average citizen to influence public affairs had declined.

While industrialization was most responsible for fundamental changes in community institutions and traditions, the immediate circumstances of the early 1920s seemed to throw a particularly bright spotlight on the eroded concord of community life. Part of the additional pressure, even in Indiana, could be traced to the growing influence of minority ethnic cultures, the black migration, and the renewal of mass European immigration after the war. Radio, motion pictures, the automobile, and the rising youth culture all represented new, sometimes threatening intrusions into the state's established social and cultural patterns.[34] The greatest strain to community institutions, however, was provided by the Eighteenth Amendment, the Volstead Act, and the great underground economy in illegal alcohol.

Rampant violation of the Prohibition laws undermined the public's faith in government, frequently turning police and law enforcement officials into either helpless observers or corrupt facilitators of crime. Suspicions that city and county officials profited from the liquor trade surfaced in communities throughout the state, and in some cities the failure to enforce Prohibition seemed endemic. The Democratic leaders of the Lake County government, for example, gained a wide reputation for ignoring liquor and other vice laws.[35] Indiana's first federal Prohibition commissioner himself mocked enforcement of the ban in Indianapolis between 1921 and 1923, when a series of letters he had written to the chief of police found their way into a city newspaper. The letters to Jeremiah Kinney, which became known as "Dear Jerry" notes, asked him to provide confiscated alcohol to the notes' bearers—usually prominent Indianapolis businessmen. The next commissioner, Bert Morgan, also demonstrated a superficial interest in enforcing Prohibition. Appointed through Republican patronage, Morgan did little to stop the flow of illegal liquor and, in 1924, lost his position after siding with the wrong faction in a party dispute. Out of desperation, he personally led a series of highly publicized liquor raids, but they failed to save his job or alter the public perception that the enforcement of Prohibition in Indiana was mired in politics and corruption.[36]

Prohibition also undermined the credibility of the justice system throughout the state. First, as the number of arrests grew dramatically during the 1920s, judges in individual communities responded inconsistently to the crowd of violators who jammed the court dockets. One well-known supporter of Prohibition, Judge Albert B. Anderson of the Indiana Federal District Court, believed that prosecutors should spend their time going after the leaders of the alcohol rings and frequently expressed anger at county and city officials who tied up the court system with cases involving small offenders. Other judges were inclined to view most Prohibition violators only as marginal criminals; some even saw them as victims of public harassment. Still others, of course, were as corrupt as many local police and elected officials.[37] The lack of uniform treatment for those charged with breaking the liquor laws, however, was not nearly as detrimental to public faith in the justice system as the fact that only a tiny fraction of violators were ever caught. Persistent widespread consumption of illegal alcohol and the presence of drinking clubs and roadhouses in nearly every community provided the best evidence that local and state laws, and even the U.S. Constitution, could not stop the flow of alcohol.

Reforms in the state Prohibition laws in 1925 reflected the deep distrust with which antiliquor crusaders had come to view the police, the courts, and politicians. Besides creating harsher penalties, not only for selling alcohol but also for possessing it even in small amounts, the prohibitionists also took away the discretion of judges in imposing punishments and authorized railroad conductors, bus drivers, ticket agents, and others who worked with the public to arrest violators.[38]

State political leaders inspired no more confidence than city and county officials. Republican governor Warren T. McCray, elected in 1920, was serving a term in federal prison by 1924 for improperly obtaining loans from the state agricultural board and from banks where the state deposited funds. Governor Edward Jackson, who was elected in 1924 with the support of the Ku Klux Klan, barely avoided the same fate. Jackson was indicted for bribery in 1927 and escaped conviction only because of the statute of limitations. The careers of McCray and Jackson seemed particularly contemptible next to those of the preceding generation of governors. Democrats Samuel M. Ralston and Thomas R. Marshall and Republicans James P. Goodrich and J. Frank Hanley had each made moderate governmental reform the focus of their administration. Hanley was also an active social reformer, leading the temperance crusade in Indiana during his tenure as governor and becoming the presidential nominee of the National Prohibition party in 1916. The crisis of Prohibition had ushered in what may have been the most corrupt period in Indiana's political history, and many Hoosiers probably agreed with Meredith Nicholson, who in 1926 observed: "We are governed by swine."[39]

The Klan's Response

In Indianapolis, as well as in Atlanta, Klan leaders were doing little to address the problems that affected community life. Ensconced in a luxurious suite of offices in downtown Indianapolis, D. C. Stephenson was preoccupied with the cultivation of power and money, both of which he seemed to have in abundance, at least for a short time. As a result of his association with the Klan between 1922 and 1924, he probably accumulated more than $1 million, which he used to support a life-style that was grossly at odds with the traditional values for which the Klan claimed to stand. He drove a number of luxury automobiles and frequently entertained guests at loud late-night parties at his home in the Indianapolis suburb of Irvington. Stephenson was a mean, sometimes violent alcoholic and womanizer. He was especially fond of escorting women to his yacht, which he kept anchored in Toledo, Ohio, and on more than one occasion his drinking binges got him into trouble with the police. At his desk in the Klan headquarters, Stephenson kept a bank of telephones, one of which, he claimed, was connected directly to the Oval Office. Often, he sent pompous, generally irrelevant mass mailings to Klansmen and politicians throughout the state, and though only in his early thirties, he insisted on being called "The Old Man."[40]

As leader of the Indiana Klan, Stephenson did almost nothing to elevate the order's ideals above mere rhetoric. His scheme to purchase Valparaiso University failed; so did the "Trade with Klansmen" (TWK) campaign, which was briefly promoted by the *Fiery Cross*. Ostensibly a boycott of Catholic and Jewish businesses, the TWK drive had little effect and seemed to serve primarily as a sales promotion stunt for the more than one hundred small businesses that advertised in the Klan newspaper.[41] Stephenson also did little to advance Prohibition enforcement. His halfhearted interest in the issue was apparent in May 1923, when he attempted to organize "vice cleanup squads" in Indianapolis. Despite the enormous number of Klansmen who were devoted to the dry cause, the program dissolved without results after several weeks. Stephenson's main interest appeared to be his ongoing dispute with Hiram Evans and the national leadership. Soon after Evans refused to provide financial support for the purchase of Valparaiso University in August 1923, relations between the two Klan leaders soured. By late 1923, Stephenson began to denounce the Klan's national leadership with the same vehemence that he had previously reserved for the pope and the "immigrant menace." He even suggested that he might break away from Atlanta altogether and establish a new Klan organization for northern states. Evans responded in the spring of 1924 by appointing Walter Bossert, an ambitious Republican party politician, the new Grand Dragon of Indiana. In June, Evans ordered Joseph Huffington to banish Stephenson from his home chapter in Evansville.[42]

The deposed Klan leader would not go without a fight and continued to maintain a great deal of political influence even after being stripped of his official connection to the secret organization.[43] His struggle for power, however, had little to do with the influential role Klan chapters were able to play in individual communities. While historians have traditionally credited Stephenson and other Klan leaders with much of the responsibility for the order's popularity in Indiana, it would be more accurate to conclude that the Indiana Klan grew powerful in spite of, not because of, its mediocre leaders. Neither Stephenson nor his replacement displayed any real desire to act on the ideals of the Klan movement. Money and political power motivated Indiana's Grand Dragons. This was also true of Hiram Evans, who hovered jealously over the largest Klan organization in his domain, determined to extract every possible dollar and every bit of influence from the army of Hoosier Klansmen, even at the cost of dividing and weakening the state movement. Stephenson and the less enterprising Joe Huffington were themselves outsiders, salesmen who had gone to Indiana to seek their fortunes. It seemed to matter little to them what they sold; perhaps under only slightly different circumstances the product might have been bootlegged liquor instead of the Klan. In reality, the force behind the Klan movement did not come from the state headquarters in Indianapolis but from the communities themselves, where the average member appeared to view the Klan as an opportunity to express his dissatisfaction with local affairs.

The Klan succeeded on the local level first because of the role it played as a social organization. In some respects, the hooded order operated much the same as other community lodges. Many of the most active Klansmen were, in fact, members of, and had been recruited from, these groups. The Klan's weekly meetings easily could have been mistaken for those of any other popular fraternal or civic group. The number of Klansmen who attended these gatherings, for example, was not significantly greater than that of other community groups. This accounts for the fact that Klan chapters usually met in rented rooms and halls that could accommodate only a fraction of the large membership. In the city of Marion, where there were more than 2,300 members in 1925, weekly meetings were held in a room over the Woolworth's store. Some chapters used the buildings of the local Knights of Pythias or Odd Fellows, while others assembled in private homes. A few chapters made room for larger crowds by meeting outdoors when the weather permitted.[44]

The typical Klan meeting, far from resembling a secret gathering of conspiring vigilantes, followed the unremarkable pattern of other voluntary organizations. Chapter officials, usually the only members dressed in full regalia, began each session with designated ceremonies from the Klan's national handbook, *Kloran*.[45] Chapter business, future social events, and, during election campaigns, politics dominated discussions. One Richmond Klansman remembered that meetings moved at a rapid pace, usually lasting less than an hour, and were followed by a brief period of socializing. In Kokomo, the *Daily Tribune* conveyed the ordinary character of the weekly Klan gathering. Each week, information on upcoming Klan meetings appeared in the front-page column, "What's Doing in Kokomo," along with similar announcements about other community groups and activities.[46]

For the most zealous members, Klan chapters provided frequent social activities, particularly during the spring and summer when picnics, outdoor meetings, and travel to other towns were most convenient. Kokomo's Klansmen were especially active in this regard, making even their weekly meeting as entertaining as possible. Usually, they met outdoors in Malfalfa Park to the accompaniment of their brass band and drum corps. The chapter made numerous evening and weekend trips to Klan gatherings in central Indiana, or sometimes just to visit another chapter in a nearby town. On such occasions, which several hundred members might attend, Klan leaders would arrange for car pools or special rail transportation at reduced rates.[47]

Despite their resemblance to other fraternal organizations, however, Klan chapters did stand apart—both in their accessibility to the average citizen and in the degree to which they cut across the lines that separated other voluntary organizations. Unlike other groups, which often established narrow social qualifications for membership, or which defined their purpose in relation to a specific cause or activity, the Klan offered membership to all but a small fraction of the community and stood for a wide range of ideals with which most white Protestants could agree. Klan chapters, which enrolled hundreds or thousands of members, stood in marked contrast to influential business organizations such as the Rotary and Kiwanis clubs, which admitted only business leaders and managers. Conventional fraternal bodies also cultivated an exclusive image and sometimes took into consideration the social position of the prospective member. The appeal of these groups, such as the Odd Fellows, Knights of Pythias, and Masons, was also limited by the scope of their activities, which did not extend much beyond male fellowship and the practice of secret rituals. Other community organizations, from religious and veterans' groups to charities and the YMCA, reflected the narrow interests of a variety of social groups and causes.

The Klan chapter, then, occupied a unique position among other voluntary organizations. More than any other group, the Klan represented the community as a whole, not the special interests of individual groups of businessmen, the "lower middle class," blue-collar workers, or religious, social, or political reformers. If this was somewhat obscured by the ways in which Klan chapters followed the routines of other community groups in their weekly meetings, it could be seen clearly in the order's larger activities, which often involved a gigantic proportion of individual communities.

Large Klan demonstrations and holiday celebrations, which took place in communities throughout the state during the Klan era, represented perhaps the most important measure of the strong relationship between the Klan and the wider white Protestant community. Such events influenced rural towns and cities—large or small—in different ways, but in all areas the Klan generated mass support and acceptance and left local newspapers at a loss to explain the unprecedented crowds that were drawn to Klan festivities. In Indiana's smaller cities, from Vincennes in the south to Anderson, Elwood, Kokomo, Lafayette, Muncie, Richmond, and others farther north, the Klan's influence was so great that occasionally it turned traditional community celebrations into celebrations of the Klan itself. The Klan's dominance of Fourth of July festivities in Kokomo was by no means an isolated case. In 1924, Indiana newspapers and the *Fiery Cross* also reported large Klan-sponsored Fourth of July celebrations in Crawfordsville, Jeffersonville, Valparaiso, and other cities.[48] In Crawfordsville, the Klan prepared to entertain as many Independence Day celebrants as possible. Local leaders hired ten bands, ordered two thousand dollars worth of fireworks, and purchased thousands of pounds of food, including nearly a pound of frankfurters and hamburgers for every resident of Montgomery County.[49]

On Labor Day, 1924, Klan-sponsored parades, fireworks, and picnics again attracted huge sections of many communities. The *Fiery Cross* announced that the largest gatherings would be in Kendallville, Logansport, Seymour, North Vernon, Paoli, and Vincennes. The most extensive activities took place in Vincennes, the largest city within a region of several coal-mining counties in southwestern Indiana. By the fall of 1924, the influence of the Klan among Indiana mine workers had become obvious. The Klan's Labor Day picnic in Vincennes a year before had been a great success, and when the United Mine Workers of America held its national convention in Indianapolis in 1924, Indiana's delegates had offered the strongest resistance to an anti-Klan resolution.[50] The Vincennes Klan invited all members and their families and encouraged nonmembers to attend its Labor Day celebration of 1924, promising a "naturalization" ceremony for all new members at the end of the day. Despite threatening skies, more than a thousand people arrived at Klan Park to ride the merry-go-round, picnic, and listen to speeches by Klan leaders from Indiana and Illinois.[51]

Vincennes Klansmen also had taken over another annual ritual: the county fair. By the early 1920s the Knox County fair had fallen on hard times, and in 1923 the fairgrounds were sold to the Klan, which renamed them Klan Park and sponsored its own "Klan Karnival" as a substitute celebration. The *Vincennes Commercial* was enthusiastic about the change in management. In June 1924, as the festivities began their four-day run, it foresaw financial success and predicted that the crowds would "equal if not surpass [those] of the old Knox County fair days." The support of the *Commercial* was especially noteworthy because its editor, Thomas H. Adams, eventually became an outspoken critic of the Indiana Klan.[52] In the summer of 1924, however, Adams provided the Klan Karnival with abundant favorable publicity. The *Commercial* painted a glowing picture of the activities planned and stressed that all were welcome, not just Klansmen. "The Caterpillar [ride] will be a curiosity to most Knox County people," the newspaper reported, "and it is expected it will have its hands full, also will the spectacular Ferris Wheel and Merry-Go-Round." As if these were not inducements enough, the *Commercial* went on to describe the "large number of minor attractions" suitable for those in "every walk of life," the expected excitement of a speech by the Grand Dragon of Indiana, and a free tour of the interior of the Klan's new Imperial Palace. It concluded its pre-Karnival publicity with the following assessment:

> The Klan home, on the banks of the Wabash, is an ideal location for a gathering of this kind, as over a hundred large shade trees surround it and there is plenty of shade for the people these hot days. For the past several days the grounds have been lined with visitors viewing the many attractions as they arrive and watching the assembling of the same. Everyone is welcome at any time, day or night, when the grounds are open. Three cool and refreshing watering places have been placed on the grounds for the convenience of the visitors, in fact everything to make your visit enjoyable is being done as far as human hands are able.[53]

In Lafayette and Elwood, Klan chapters played a similarly dominant role in community celebrations. Lafayette Klansmen purchased the Tippecanoe County fairgrounds in 1923 and successfully operated the annual fair despite considerable opposition from Mayor George R. Durgan, one of the most determined anti-Klan politicians in the state.[54] Elwood, nicknamed the "Tinplate City," also witnessed the Klan's power to completely take over a yearly community event. In May 1924, Elwood's "Tinplate Day" became "Klan Day" as thousands of Klan members arrived from throughout central Indiana to participate in the daylong festivities and the nighttime parade. The *Kokomo Daily Tribune* estimated that as many as five thousand robed men and women marched in the parade.[55]

The Klan succeeded in monopolizing many community events, and in staging similar separate activities, primarily because it placed no important barrier between itself and the rest of the white Protestant population. Local chapters did not seek to establish isolated enclaves for true believers only but tried instead to represent and reach out to the average person. Like Billy Sunday revival meetings, Klan celebrations were structured for all whites who identified, even if only vaguely, with American Protestantism. And like the county fair, Klan celebrations provided entertainment that would appeal to the entire community.

Klan advertisements, which appeared in the *Fiery Cross* and community newspapers statewide, demonstrated the desire of Klan chapters to attract as many people as possible to their celebrations, regardless of whether they were official members. One *Fiery Cross* ad for a large gathering in Evansville announced that "the White Gentile Protestant People of Indiana and the Tri-State Territory Are Cordially Invited." Two months later the Logansport Klan made a similar appeal, inviting "all Klansmen, families and friends" to attend its "first all-day celebration." An advertisement placed in the *Fiery Cross* by the Valparaiso Klan (see Figure 4.1) gives an indication of the carnival atmosphere Klan chapters attempted to create in their celebrations. Entertainment such as that provided by circus performers and "Imported Texas Cowboys" represented a powerful inducement to community members.[56]

One of the most significant aspects of large Klan demonstrations and celebrations was the similar effect they had on different types

> # KU KLUX KLAN
> ### and The Women's Organization
> ## Home Coming and May Festival
> # Saturday, May 19th
> #### VALPARAISO, INDIANA
>
> ONE DAZZLING DAY OF DIVERSIFIED DELIGHT
> 100,000 KLANSMEN THE WOMEN'S ORGANIZATION
>
> ### Gigantic—20 Brass Bands—Free Acts—Colossal
> # A Big Barbecue
>
> High, Tight Wire Walking, 100 Feet in the Air—Wild Broncho-Busting—Outlaw Horses—Imported Texas Cowboys—National Speakers—200 Horsemen—Evening Fire Works—Illustrated Parades—Visit Valparaiso University—The Sand Dunes—See the Calumet Region
>
> **ALL DAY** **ALL NIGHT**
>
> *All Klansmen Are Cordially Invited—Come One—Come All*
>
> On the Lincoln Highway, Yellowstone Trail and Liberty Way
> ### ALL ROADS LEAD TO VALPARAISO, MAY 19th
> *You Are Welcome to Our City*

Figure 4.1
Valparaiso Klan Barbecue Advertisement
Source: *Fiery Cross*, May 17, 1923.

of communities. Events that occurred in small cities and medium-sized towns such as Kokomo or Vincennes stood out because they overwhelmed important population centers. But the order's social events in small, rural towns also generated extremely large crowds even if they attracted less attention than those occurring in urban areas. Indiana newspapers reported crowds of several hundred—and, in some instances, several thousand—at Klan parades, initiation ceremonies, and picnics in rural villages throughout the state.[57]

Even a city as large as Indianapolis could be temporarily engulfed by massive Klan celebrations and rallies. Support for the Klan was so strong that public officials, including those who opposed the hooded order, were forced to accommodate the Klan's requests for parade permits, police protection, and the use of public grounds. When Indianapolis Klansmen planned a massive parade to celebrate the Klan's victory in the primary election of 1924, Mayor Lew Shank, who had just been defeated as an anti-Klan candidate for governor, promised full cooperation from the city. He announced that the Klan could parade at any time and would receive police protection. The parade, which snaked through northern Indianapolis from the fairgrounds to the center of the city, took nearly one and a half hours to pass a given point. Local newspapers estimated that between 75,000 and 100,000 spectators viewed the columns of marching Klan members. Several months later, the Indianapolis Klan received a similar reception when it announced plans for "Klan Day" at the state fair. The State Board of Agriculture, which directed the fair, quickly acquiesced, recognizing the Klan's ability to inundate public events. A representative told the *Indianapolis Times*: "There is no special program for the Klansmen, but we shall be glad to welcome them as citizens."[58]

Another important part of the Klan's role as a social organization involved the incorporation of women into its activities. Every major Klan demonstration and rally included an appearance by the Klanswomen; often, local women's orders would be identified as cosponsors of Klan celebrations (see Figure 4.1). It seems certain that the women's chapters had smaller memberships.[59] At the same time, there were many indications that enthusiasm for the Klan among Indiana women was significant even if it did not match that of men. When the women's organization held its first state convention in Mooresville in July 1923, thousands of members attended.[60] Membership fees that flowed into the women's office in Indianapolis were at least large enough to cause arguments and financial scandals similar to those that characterized the men's order.[61]

The involvement of women and, to a lesser extent, children added even more weight to the Klan's populist character. Because most of its celebrations were occasions for family outings, women and children—whether or not they were official members of Klan organizations—swelled the attendance at these events and clouded even further the separation between the Klan and the wider white Protestant community. Social activities planned specifically for the women's and junior organizations provided additional opportunities for the Klan to present itself as a respectable community group. Klanswomen often generated their own excitement with weekly meetings and rallies. The women's organization, like other women's groups, also assumed particular responsibility for charity work, the schools, and the "values of home life."[62] Through the junior orders, the Klan conducted various traditional youth activities. In 1924, for example, Klan chapters from twelve Indiana cities sponsored a Junior Klan basketball tournament.[63]

What stood out most about the Klan as a social organization was its remarkable ability to create a sense of congruity within Indiana's predominantly white Protestant communities. Catholics, Jews, and blacks were excluded from the Klan's definition of community, of course, and continued, along with many white Protestants, to resist the Klan movement. The fact remained, however, that no other religious group, political organization, or fraternal or civic association possessed a similar capacity to place itself at the center of a community's social life and generate such massive support for its activities. The Klan's social activities were more than entertaining. They were expressions of the pent-up desire of the white Protestant majority to assert the primacy of its traditional beliefs and its presumed rightful place as the dominant force in community life. In effect, the Klan's social activities represented acts of resistance to the forces that were transforming community life. While communities had become more impersonal, their citizens more isolated from one another and from increasingly concentrated centers of economic and political power, and while traditional institutions such as the church, the family, and respect for the law seemed to be losing ground, Indiana's Klan demonstrations expressed continued faith in traditional institutions and proclaimed the authority of the average person within the community.

To further promote a greater measure of popular control in community life, the Klan took direct action as a civic organization. Statewide, the Klan's involvement in local issues centered most often on Prohibition enforcement.

While the Klan's state organization made almost no attempt to aid the enforcement of Prohibition laws, individual chapters often took aggressive steps to assist local law enforcement officials—and to exert pressure on them if they failed to show proper enthusiasm for the task. Fort Wayne Klansmen were among the most diligent antivice crusaders in the state. In March 1923, they launched a campaign against liquor sales, prostitution, and gambling, declaring that "next to Gary," Fort Wayne was the "Sodom of Indiana." An article in the *Fiery Cross* spelled out the details:

> Whiskey is sold over the bars, in restaurants, candy kitchens and hotels. Pearl Street is "open" and houses of ill repute are permitted to operate without interference. . . . Dope is distributed freely. But of the evils that are sapping the life of the community . . . the greatest harm is seen in the increase of gambling. The city houses roulette, chuck-a-luck, no limit poker, and crap shooting in more than a dozen places, and to the knowledge of the police, and without intervention. Booze, bonded and "moonshine" liquor, is flowing as freely as the Miami River. . . . The town is, saying it liberally, on a drunk.

Predictably, the Klan newspaper promised that the town's growing chapter would put a stop to the corruption.[64]

The primary tactic of the Fort Wayne Klan was to collect detailed information on illegal activities—with the use of private detectives, it claimed—and then to present sworn affidavits to the police with a pledge to publicize the information if action was not taken. In July, their labors resulted in a major raid on local liquor outlets. City officials downplayed the Klan's role in bringing about the raid, but Klansmen countered by printing copies of affidavits and their correspondence with the state Prohibition enforcement office. During the next year, Fort Wayne Klansmen continued their watch on vice and turned in other bootleggers.[65]

In many communities, Klan chapters followed the same pattern, gathering information about illegal activities and working with established dry advocates to apply public pressure on law enforcement agencies. An organization known as the Committee of Ten demonstrated how this process worked in Vincennes. Established in the early twenties, the committee was made up of Protestant ministers and other longtime supporters of Prohibition and was publicly identified as an affiliate of the local Klan organization. In fact, the head of the committee was a leading Vincennes Klansman. The Committee of Ten held regular meetings to evaluate the state of Prohibition enforcement in the area and report their findings to the press.[66]

In Logansport, the Klan and other dry forces applied more direct pressure on the local government. In March 1924, a large group of Klan members attended a meeting of the city council to demand that the mayor "clean up flagrant law violations in Logansport." The Klansmen claimed that police "tip offs" to bootleggers had diminished the success of recent liquor raids. According to the *Fiery Cross*, the Logansport Klan presented the council with "enough information to keep the police busy" and insisted that future raids net more lawbreakers. Similar protests by Muncie Klansmen led to a federal investigation of liquor law violations. In February 1924, Muncie Klansmen testified before a grand jury in Indianapolis that the police were lax in enforcing dry laws.[67]

The focus of Klan outrage and activism, and the real obstacle to enforcement of the dry laws, was the apathy of community leaders, the police, the business elite, and much of the public. Klansmen sensed that those who had gained the most influence over the administration of government did not necessarily display a strong interest in traditional morality. The "Dear Jerry" episode in Indianapolis showed the ease with which well-to-do businessmen could circumvent the law, corrupting public agencies in the process. The Indianapolis Chamber of Commerce, in one instance, demonstrated that the business leaders of that city were more concerned with saving tax dollars than in apprehending Prohibition violators. In a report that drew criticism from Indiana's dry forces, the Chamber advocated that the Indianapolis police department disband its special Prohibition enforcement units. These units, the Chamber claimed, were a waste of time and had been done away with in other large cities.[68] Dissatisfaction with the many examples of Prohibition-related corruption in government, and the apparent willingness of some community leaders to tolerate higher levels of crime, lay at the root of the Klan's Prohibition enforcement activities.

In 1924, when political slates of the Klan swept established leaders out of office in communities throughout the state, both political parties were dumbfounded.[69] Perhaps they would have been less shocked if they had been better able to gauge public displeasure with the state of Prohibition enforcement.

The desire of Klan chapters to inject more citizen involvement into community life could be seen not only in their efforts to uphold Prohibition laws, but also in their frequent charitable activities. While the Indiana Klan was at its height, newspapers throughout the state routinely made note of the order's donations to schools, churches, and other organizations.[70] Often these gifts reflected the order's ethnocentric and nationalistic concerns; Bibles and American flags or small amounts of money were usually given. To the Klan's critics, such acts were nothing more than publicity stunts, and to some degree they were. Like other civic and business groups, the Klan did seek to extract all the public relations value it could from its charitable works. When robed, silent Klansmen suddenly appeared during church services, as they often did when local chapters were in the early stages of organization, it could be safely assumed that the dramatic visitation had been carefully arranged with the minister and even a newspaper reporter. The amounts of Klan church donations almost always found their way into print.[71]

On another level, however, it was clear that the philanthropy of Klan chapters attempted to revive the type of direct involvement in community affairs that the Lynds had observed to be rapidly disappearing from community life. Without directly attacking business organizations such as the Chamber of Commerce or the Rotary club, which had come to dominate the administration of funds for charity in many communities, the Klan undertook independent projects calling for spontaneous, direct public involvement and bypassed elite-dominated community institutions. On Christmas 1922, Indianapolis Klansmen distributed twelve truckloads of food and clothing to the poor, including, they claimed, blacks and Catholics. The notion of helping neighbors in need—more appropriate, in reality, for a small town of the nineteenth century than a modern industrial city—lay behind such an endeavor. While a Christmas basket did little to alter the plight of the destitute, it was a symbol of community that appealed to Klansmen. The next year, they intensified their efforts. On Christmas Eve 1923, proud Klansmen posed for a photograph in a large warehouse where they had assembled hundreds of bushel baskets of food that they were about to distribute in Indianapolis neighborhoods.[72]

In Kokomo, the Klansmen and Klanswomen of Howard County undertook the most significant philanthropic project of Indiana's Klan movement to help build a county hospital. For two years, the Kokomo chapter sponsored a variety of events to raise money for the cause. Before the massive Fourth of July Klan convention in 1923, the local organization pledged to give all the money it raised to the hospital fund. It did the same on Independence Day the following year, as well as collecting donations at other events. At the time, the only hospital in Howard County was operated by the Catholic church. This situation served as a catalyst for the Klan's efforts, but beneath the anti-Catholic sentiment lay a genuine interest in civic improvement. Because no other group showed similar enthusiasm for such an undertaking, it is doubtful that the new hospital would have been built without the groundswell of community support stimulated by the Klan. In fact, the hospital did not survive long after the Klan movement declined. Ironically, the Sisters of St. Joseph purchased the empty building and moved their facilities there in the early 1930s.[73]

One important aspect of the building of the "Klan hospital" in Kokomo was that it was only part of a broader Klan-inspired populist insurgency in community affairs. Rather than deposit the Klan's funds and the all-important hospital fund in one of the city's banks, for example, local Klan leaders founded their own institution, the American Trust Company. The "Klan bank," as it was known, did not last long, and its president, an officer in the Kokomo klavern, was eventually indicted for embezzlement and grand larceny. Still, the fact that the bank even came into being indicates a measure of popular dissatisfaction with the power of Kokomo's business establishment. One of the more contentious political issues in Kokomo during the 1920s, the decision to use public money to dredge a section of Wildcat Creek, further exemplified the intensity of this disapproval. The project, which was supported by the Chamber of Commerce and the local Republican establishment, elicited a storm of protest. Critics charged that the dredging was unnecessary and was being undertaken only for the benefit of a plate glass company located on the creek. In 1925, an officer in the Kokomo Klan, Silcott Spurgeon, ran for mayor, attacking the Chamber of Commerce in general for its domination of political and economic affairs and the Wildcat Creek dredging in particular as an example of corruption in city government. Much to the dismay of Kokomo business leaders, Spurgeon and a number of other Klan-endorsed candidates were victorious in the city election.[74]

Local Klans would launch assaults against elite-dominated political organizations in communities throughout the state, charging that their leaders had failed to enforce Prohibition and other vice laws and demanding that local political decisions be made more subject to popular control. Before examining the political consequences of Klan populism, however, it is important to take a closer look at the social conditions that made the Klan such a significant force in community affairs.

5. City, Town, and Village

Within the Indiana Klan, it would be difficult if not impossible to identify a typical Klan chapter. The movement incorporated too many distinctly different geographic regions and communities. One might as well attempt to choose a typical Klansman among farm owners, farm tenants, coal miners, automobile workers, doctors, lawyers, the owners of small businesses, department store clerks, hill country Democrats, Yankee Republicans, Methodists, Lutherans, and nonchurchgoers—all of whom joined the organization in substantial numbers. Even if one could select an average klavern and Klansman, their examination would doubtless be limited by the scarcity of Klan records.

If the idea of a "typical" Klan chapter is not valid, however, the records that do exist make it possible to look closely at three different types of communities that, together, are at least representative of many other communities in the state. The complete list of members for the Wayne County Klan provides an opportunity to examine two types of communities: (1) the medium-sized manufacturing and commercial town of central Indiana, and (2) the outlying rural community that primarily served the needs of farmers. Both types showed particularly strong support for the Klan movement and played vital roles in Indiana's social, economic, and political life during the 1920s. The partial but extensive membership list for Indianapolis opens the door to some analysis of the Klan in a third type of community: the large industrial city.

Richmond

Richmond had much in common with other cities its size, but certainly it was not a microcosm of Indiana in the 1920s. As one of the state's oldest industrial centers, Richmond had maintained a more diversified economy and had been changed less by industrial expansion in the late nineteenth and early twentieth centuries than other cities of the same size. Moreover, its heritage had been touched to an uncommon degree by the Society of Friends. Quakers originally settled Richmond and had always been disproportionately represented in its population. Earlham College, just across the Whitewater River from the central business district, gained a reputation as a leading Quaker intellectual center. Compared with Muncie, thirty-five miles to the northwest, as well as numerous other cities in Indiana, Richmond also enjoyed a rather pacific political era during the twenties. Its politicians generally remained untainted by political scandal, and its political climate was remarkably uninfluenced even by the Ku Klux Klan. Richmond's Klan, for the most part, seems to have been a subdued group compared with chapters in other cities.

At the same time, however, Richmond was not exempt from the forces that had undermined traditional community institutions and values. And the Richmond Klan was far from insignificant. As in Muncie, industrial growth had gradually eroded the cohesiveness of Richmond's community life. The population had grown larger and more diverse in the thirty years preceding 1920. The city's average citizens, still overwhelmingly white Protestant, had become more segmented by social and economic differences and more removed from a position of influence in civic affairs. The power of business leaders to control community events had increased continuously since 1890, and business success had become the dominant force in community life. As it did in other Indiana cities and towns, the Klan movement in Richmond tapped into a great reservoir of dissatisfaction with this new structure and, through social and civic activities, offered the means of expressing a more traditional sense of community. In fact, the Richmond Klan came to include a huge proportion of the population, enrolling 3,183 members—or 41 percent of the city's native-born white men—between 1922 and 1926.[1]

Because Richmond had been an established manufacturing center prior to 1890, its growth after that time was not as dramatic as that of other Indiana cities. Still, with more than 26,000 residents in 1920, the population had increased by nearly 40 percent since 1890, and it continued to grow during the next decade.[2] Following a pattern particularly common for Indiana, most of Richmond's population growth was fueled by white Protestant migrants from surrounding rural areas. Small neighborhoods of blacks, Italians, and immigrants from eastern Europe also appeared, adding to the complexity of the city's development. Most of these ethnic minorities lived literally on the "wrong" side of the railroad tracks, north of the business district; many found employment at the Pennsylvania Railroad switching yard nearby. South of the city's center lay a relatively large community of German-Americans. Residents of the area were divided almost equally between Lutherans and Catholics, and the neighborhood contained some of Richmond's most successful merchants.[3]

Richmond's expansion resulted from a growing local economy. In addition to the Pennsylvania Railroad, the city's other major corporate employer was International Harvester. By the 1920s, the manufacturing giant had taken over much of Richmond's business in agricultural equipment. Other companies continued to make farm machines, and in 1924 Richmond still boasted that it manufactured more lawn mowers than any other city in the world.[4] Among other important employers, the Star Piano Company and several firms that manufactured coffins and church pews played a vital role in the local economy. All had extensive national markets in the twenties. Other Richmond factories produced gloves, underwear, work clothes, automobiles, cabinets, and tools. In all, approximately five thousand workers were employed by Richmond businesses in 1920. This represented an increase of nearly 34 percent since 1910. The five largest enterprises employed half of the city's factory workers.[5]

As the local economy grew, Richmond's business elite, like that of other cities, gradually became more conscious of itself as a distinct and powerful group. During the first two decades of the twentieth century, it formed new organizations that underlined the growing authority of business leaders in community affairs. These associations also separated in a more formal way the wealthy from the rest of the city's inhabitants and ultimately promulgated the idea that business success and "community" were synonymous.

Around the turn of the century, business leaders displayed enthusiasm for two organizations that had received little support up to that time. In 1899 the Richmond Commercial Club took on new life, bringing together several of the city's industrial families and many of its more successful merchants. Within a few years the club had a membership of over two hundred and, through the beginning of World War I, acted in various ways to represent Richmond's business interests. "It is the aim and special attention of the club," one newspaper article explained, "to foster and encourage and develop the industries already established here and it will systematically and continually endeavor to bring other worthy industries to the city." To a significant degree, the group also perceived itself as a guardian of the people's welfare—to be the "most efficient" civic organization in the community and to "advance and promote the best interest for all the people of the city of Richmond." To this end, the Commercial Club promised to "cooperate with city, county and state officials" to obtain better roads, rail transportation, schools, and other public improvements, and "to arouse a universal spirit of civic loyalty" by encouraging citizens to "buy at home."[6]

A similar organization, more heavily influenced by the successful German merchants of southern Richmond, also gained new popularity at about the same time. The South Side Improvement Association (SSIA), like the Commercial Club, had existed since the late nineteenth century, but it was not until 1903 that businessmen began joining in significant numbers.[7] Many of the organization's members also belonged to the Commercial Club, and over the next two decades the South Side Improvement Association took a similarly active role in promoting the growth of industry in the city. The group's booster activities ranged from simple promotional stunts to direct involvement in politics. In 1904, the SSIA sold "I'm for Richmond" buttons. In 1917, it began to pressure the city government to establish a planning commission to help direct Richmond's expansion.[8]

In addition to the Commercial Club and the SSIA, there were other signs of the growing separation of the city's business elite from the rest of the community. In 1908, business leaders published a book that pointed out the degree to which they had come to consider themselves a group of exceptional significance. Entitled *Men of Affairs in Richmond, Indiana*, this publication featured caricatures of the leading industrialists, professionals, corporate managers, and retail merchants drawn by a newspaper cartoonist. Those who financed the private printing depicted it as a "Hall of Fame" to the city's most prominent citizens. Many of the men whose likenesses appeared also had by this time become involved in the foremost social organization, the Richmond Country Club. The club was launched in November 1900 and for two decades moved to a variety of locations in the city, each time expanding its facilities. By 1927, it had constructed a golf course and a clubhouse in the southeastern section of Richmond, where "Men of Affairs" and their families could socialize.[9]

By the beginning of the 1920s, two new organizations had come to symbolize the special position of Richmond's business elite and the predominance of boosterism in civic affairs. Soon after its formation in 1917, the Richmond Rotary Club established itself as the most powerful and exclusive voluntary organization in the city. Membership in the Rotary was restricted to industrialists, the top executives of the largest businesses, and the most successful retail merchants and professionals. In 1924 this included just ninety-two men, almost all of whom regularly attended weekly luncheon meetings.[10] A second organization, the Richmond Kiwanis Club, was founded soon after the Rotary and generally included the city's managers and smaller merchants. More than one hundred men had joined the Kiwanis by November 1920, and hundreds more were admitted in the next few years.[11]

The Rotary and Kiwanis clubs represented a new refinement in the organization of Richmond's business leaders. Whereas the old Commercial Club—which dissolved in 1920—had introduced the notion that businessmen should exert a guiding hand in community matters, the Rotary and Kiwanis no longer needed to promote this idea; they only had to put it into action. Instead of defining themselves primarily as boosters of the city's economic interest, as the Commercial Club had done, the Rotary and Kiwanis regarded themselves as "service organizations" in the traditions of their national orders. Much of their activity focused on the Community Chest, which their members controlled and which represented the main source of support for social services in the city.¹² Yet the old Commercial Club and the newer businessmen's organizations played essentially the same role. Through these groups, Richmond's most powerful men exerted their influence in local business and governmental matters. The prominence of the Rotary and Kiwanis, their central role in the city's social, economic, and political affairs, demonstrated the degree to which the businessman's concept of community had become an accepted standard.

While the Rotary and Kiwanis together illustrated the ascendancy of a business culture in Richmond, taken separately they provided one example of how the community had actually become more segmented by the process of industrial growth. When the Commercial Club first gathered the business leaders of Richmond into a formal organization, its membership included those in both the first and the second levels of the commercial hierarchy—the owners of factories as well as their managers and those who operated shops in the business district. By 1920, those two groups had been divided. The Rotary accepted only the city's most successful businessmen and professionals. Less prominent men were confined to the Kiwanis, and later, as the Kiwanians set their own membership limits, a Lions Club formed and drew together yet another class of middle-class men. As anyone seeking admission to one of Richmond's service organizations would quickly discover, the Rotary, Kiwanis, and Lions were reserved respectively for the city's owners, managers, and, as one man remembered, "those who did all the work."¹³

The stratification of Richmond's businessmen into separate voluntary organizations was symptomatic of the social and economic divisions that had magnified as a result of several decades of industrial expansion. The manufacturing economy had created a large and distinct class of factory workers, and their lives moved in patterns fundamentally different from those of more affluent citizens. While the city's businessmen, with their optimistic boosterism, may have symbolized the "prosperity of the 1920's," its blue-collar workers endured less cheerful realities.¹⁴ More than 60 percent of Richmond's workers held blue-collar jobs, and approximately one-quarter of the work force was employed in semiskilled and unskilled occupations. Like the automobile and glass workers of nearby Muncie, whom the Lynds found to be only marginally secure even in the best of times, Richmond's factory workers existed on subsistence wages, without job security or protection from the consequences of layoffs, injury, disease, or old age. A lifetime of steady work, for example, did not guarantee home ownership. In 1910, 57 percent of the homes in Richmond were rented. That percentage remained the same in 1920 and declined only slightly by 1930. Business success meant that people had jobs, not necessarily that they prospered.[15]

In addition to the increased distance between businessmen, merchants, and professionals on the one hand and workers on the other, there were other indications of a less cohesive community. For example, in the first twenty-five years of the twentieth century Richmond's religious institutions had become noticeably more fragmented. Black migrants to the city built their own churches, and immigrants greatly expanded the Roman Catholic population. Protestant fundamentalists began to separate themselves from more traditional denominations. Between 1903 and 1923, four new Protestant denominations and nine new churches appeared. The total number of churches increased by 26 percent.[16] Most of the growth could be attributed to the establishment of new fundamentalist churches. Churches were also divided by the economic status of their members. The wealthiest families in Richmond attended primarily three churches: the First Presbyterian, the First Lutheran, and St. Paul's Episcopal Church. The Disciples of Christ, Methodist, Quaker, Catholic, and other Lutheran churches, which represented the great majority of church members, generally attracted a broad range of middle- and working-class families. The small Baptist and fundamentalist churches tended to attract those at the lower end of the economic spectrum.[17]

Another indication of decline in the cohesiveness of community life could be seen in the decreasing involvement of citizens in the political process. In the late nineteenth century and continuing into the first years of the twentieth century, Richmond's eligible voters usually went to the polls in very high numbers. By the 1920s, however, voter turnout had decreased markedly. Table 5.1 clearly demonstrates this trend. In the general elections of 1896 and 1904, approximately 90 percent of all eligible voters in Wayne County cast ballots for the offices of president, governor, and U.S. representative. In 1916, voter turnout shrank to less than 75 percent, and in

Table 5.1

Percentage of Voter Turnout, Wayne County and Richmond, 1896–1925

Wayne County

Year	President	Governor	U.S. Representative
1896	92.3	90.9	91.0
1904	92.7	89.3	89.4
1916	74.5	72.5	73.6
1924*	61.1	59.2	60.1

Richmond

Year	Mayor
1902	68.5
1905	68.8
1909	70.0
1913	79.6
1917	51.0
1921	50.8
1925	61.6

Sources: U.S. Bureau of the Census, *Eleventh Census*, 1:777, *Twelfth Census*, 2:182, *Thirteenth Census*, 1:565, and *Fourteenth Census: Indiana Compendium*, p. 43; State of Indiana, *Biennial Report*, 1896 (pp. 228, 237, 252), 1904 (pp. 333, 335, 361), and 1916 (pp. 175, 191, 207); State of Indiana, *Yearbook, 1924*, p. 51; *Richmond Evening Item*, May 7, 1902; *Richmond Palladium*, November 8, 1905, November 3, 1909, November 5, 1913, November 7, 1913, November 9, 1921, November 4, 1925.

*Women voting.

1924, when newly enfranchised women could be counted among the eligible voters, the turnout declined to approximately 60 percent. The same trend occurred in local elections. During the first years of the twentieth century, voter turnout for the city's mayoral elections showed a gradual increase, reaching a peak of approximately 80 percent in the election of 1913, when a candidate representing

Theodore Roosevelt's Progressive party unseated a longtime Republican incumbent. Just four years later, however, when a Republican candidate was again returned to office, the turnout had declined to 51 percent. It remained low in the next two local elections as well.

The estrangement of growing numbers of citizens from the political process demonstrates the degree to which Richmond had become a more segmented, less cohesive community. Perhaps those who did not vote were preoccupied with earning a living or simply symbolized the decline of politics as a form of popular entertainment. The erosion of the progressive spirit in politics probably also contributed to the lower voter turnout. Whatever motivated individual nonvoters, together they transmitted a message of doubt that their vote had any particular importance, that they as individuals could have a significant impact on politics either in their own city or beyond.

By the early 1920s, growing social divisions and a more complex urban environment had done much to erode the traditional idea of community—that of a generally homogeneous, like-minded people who shared common concerns and values and acted in concert in civic matters. At the same time, a newer definition of community, asserted primarily by an economic elite and centered on the idea of business success, was on the rise. The rapid growth and widespread popularity of the Ku Klux Klan in Richmond resulted to a large extent from a continued belief in the older definition of community and a reluctance to accept fully the newer one.

The most significant characteristic of the Richmond Klan—Whitewater Klan No. 60, as it was officially known—was that except for the wealthiest citizens and, of course, Catholics and blacks, virtually any man was a likely candidate for membership. In almost all parts of the city, among various religious and occupational groups and within popular social organizations and clubs, men joined the Klan in representative numbers. Those from the working and middle classes, shopkeepers and professionals, and Methodists, Baptists, Episcopalians, Quakers, and Lutherans all paid the ten-dollar fee to enter the Invisible Empire. Of all the men in Richmond who were eligible for membership, probably 40 to 50 percent joined the Klan between 1922 and 1926.[18]

Robert Lyons, the son of a local minister, introduced the Klan in

Richmond in 1922. Lyons had grown up in that city during the years his father pastored the Reid United Presbyterian Church. By the early 1920s, he had moved to Indianapolis, where he became one of D. C. Stephenson's lieutenants in the early phase of the state Klan movement. In the late summer of 1922, when Lyons and Stephenson traveled together to Richmond, Lyons evidently began his recruitment drive among his acquaintances at the Reid church. One member of the church at the time recalled that it quickly became a hotbed of Klan activity, and several of its members became officers in the new klavern. More concerned with Klan affairs at the state level than with those of his hometown, however, Lyons did not play a dominant role in the Richmond Klan once it got off the ground.[19]

Leadership of the Richmond chapter fell into the hands of Albert Anderson, the owner of a coal and ice delivery company. It is not clear whether Anderson was appointed to this position or whether he was elected by the klavern's early members. In either case, he generally kept a low profile. He did not become seriously involved in local politics, nor was his name frequently linked with the Klan in the newspapers. Apparently Anderson's business was successful, though he was clearly not part of the city's business elite. He probably retained the recruiter's commission for new members. One Richmond Klansman remembered that Anderson collected all the money.[20]

If Anderson was not a dynamic leader, he was at least representative of the men in Richmond who were first attracted to the Klan. Compared with all those who eventually joined the chapter between 1922 and 1926, the early members were a decidedly more affluent group.[21] To a significant degree, they were more likely to have held white-collar jobs (see Table 5.2). Many of the klavern's first members were small businessmen, clerks, and managers, and a large number held influential positions in the community. Among the early joiners were the pastors of several of the largest Protestant churches, almost all of the important department heads and many elected officials in city and county government, the county judge and the prosecuting attorney, and the president of the Richmond Electric Company.[22]

The disproportionately high middle-class composition of the Richmond Klan in its earliest phase resulted from a variety of factors,

Table 5.2

Occupational Differences among Early Klansmen, All Klansmen, and Non-Klansmen in Richmond, 1922–1926

	Early Klan		All Klan		Non-Klan	
	Number	Percent	Number	Percent	Number	Percent
High white collar	71	14.2	46	9.2	56	11.2
Low white collar	207	41.4	151	30.2	103	20.6
Skilled	136	27.2	176	35.2	162	32.4
Lower manual	83	16.6	116	23.2	156	31.2
No occupation	3	0.6	11	2.2	23	4.6
Total	500		500		500	

Chi-square (Early and Non-Klan, 4 dof) = 76.6 $P \leq .01$

Source: See Appendix.

the first being that many of its members were recruited from other local voluntary organizations with strong middle-class orientations. To those who were traditional joiners, the Klan doubtless had a particularly strong appeal. Also, the image of the Klan as an organization that stood for traditional values and law enforcement probably generated special enthusiasm among those in white-collar occupations; early membership by the county's law enforcement officials underscored the importance of the crime issue. Still another significant factor was the high cost of becoming a Klansmen. The ten-dollar initiation fee could easily represent several days' pay to men at the lower end of the occupational spectrum. Those who could afford the initiation fee naturally joined the Klan more readily.[23]

The middle-class orientation of the Richmond Klan soon shifted, however, as—despite the ten-dollar barrier—the chapter gained solid support among white Protestants throughout the city regardless of their occupational status or religious affiliation. The Richmond Klan came to represent a near–cross section of the city's occupational groups: businessmen and professionals joined in representative numbers, lower white-collar workers were slightly overrepresented, roughly the same percentage of Klansmen and non-Klansmen were skilled workers, and nearly a quarter of all Klansmen worked in semiskilled and unskilled occupations—a figure that corresponds closely with the percentage of the white Protestants in general who worked in such jobs. The religious affiliations of the Klansmen also closely approximated the city's Protestant spectrum (see Table 3.12 in Chapter 3). The large, traditionally evangelical denominations (Methodist, Baptist, Disciples of Christ, and Presbyterian) were strongly represented, but so too were the equally consequential German (Lutheran and United Brethren) and Quaker churches. In addition, Richmond Klansmen were not significantly more or less likely than non-Klansmen to be unaffiliated with a church.[24]

Among distinctly white Protestant social groups in Richmond, only the economic elite seemed uniquely immune to the Klan's appeal. While many high white-collar workers could be found in the ranks of the Richmond chapter, their positions were clearly a step below those of the most affluent and powerful. As mentioned earlier, 30 percent of the city's doctors and 27 percent of its lawyers were Klansmen, but none of its bank executives or most powerful business leaders were members. The rejection of the Klan by Richmond's economic elite could be seen with particular clarity within the ranks of the Kiwanis and Rotary clubs. Among the members of the Kiwanis club in 1920, 40 percent later joined the Klan. In contrast, the Klan attracted only 4 percent of the Rotarians.[25]

In its activities, the Richmond Klan worked primarily to assert the conventional idea of community and the validity of traditional white Protestant cultural hegemony. These aims did not lead to instances of vigilante violence by the membership. As it did in other Indiana communities, the Klan in Richmond functioned chiefly as a social and civic organization for white Protestants, leaving the city's black, Catholic, and immigrant neighborhoods generally undisturbed.

Richmond's newspapers, which followed closely the activities of the local klavern, did not report a known case of Klan-inspired violence between 1922 and 1925. One of them, the *Richmond Palladium*, surely would have done so if violence had erupted. From the inception of the Klan movement in Indiana, the *Palladium* maintained a staunchly anti-Klan stand. Eventually, its editor joined other Indiana journalists in an effort to unearth the Klan's corrupt involvement in state politics. Throughout the Klan era, the editorial policy of the *Palladium* was to give the hooded order no favorable publicity. In the process, it often ignored major community events that involved the Klan. The *Palladium* presented the Klan only in a negative light—when, for example, in other parts of the country, it could be linked with violent activities or corruption.[26]

Of course, the absence of violence did not mean that Richmond's ethnic minorities viewed the hooded order as a benign organization. Some Catholic citizens remembered the fear they had experienced when cross burnings illuminated the night sky after the Klan's outdoor meetings. The granddaughter of a prominent attorney, Henry U. Johnson, recalled a period when Klansmen threatened her family and burned a cross on her grandfather's lawn after Johnson had used his influence to help admit a black attorney to the Wayne County bar.[27] Blacks in Richmond, like those in other communities, could not help but feel trepidation and anger at the sight of the Klansmen and the indications of their vast numbers.

Still, it would be incorrect to assume that the growth of the Richmond Klan resulted primarily from mounting hostilities between ethnic groups. Whatever sense of conflict existed between the white Protestant majority and Catholics, blacks, and recent immigrants, it burned at a low temperature in the background. One black citizen remembered that he cast his first vote for a Democrat after hearing rumors that a Republican candidate had been associated with the Klan, but when asked if he or any of his friends had ever been bothered by the Klan, he replied in the negative. The only person he could recall who had had trouble with the Klan was a white friend: "They [the Klan] was marching in the street in Richmond and this white friend, he knew one of them and hit one of them. The law came and got him." Another black man who lived through the Klan era in Richmond recalled a certain amount of hostility but downplayed its significance. He could remember the Klansmen's masks and cross burnings, and their warnings to blacks to stay away from

Klan ceremonies. At the same time, however, he spoke of the period with great fondness: "if you were hungry and were sick, people would bring food and would send teams to pick your crops, free as a neighbor.... We had nothing, except togetherness. We discussed neighborhood problems, settled them then, and everyone trusted one another. I wish and long for those times to return."[28]

During the 1920s, blacks and immigrants in Richmond did not encroach on white Protestant neighborhoods nor did Klansmen concentrate in areas surrounding minority neighborhoods. Blacks, as well as Italian and Slavic immigrants, generally resided in well-defined neighborhoods at the northern end of the city, bounded on the north and west by the Whitewater River and on the east by undeveloped parkland. To the south, railroad tracks marked an unofficial border between the minority neighborhoods and the rest of the city. Large numbers of Klansmen lived in virtually all other areas of the city. Therefore, it is doubtful that many joined the order out of a sense of residential competition with blacks and immigrants.[29] In fact, the white Protestant neighborhood that was nearest to those of ethnic minorities was the most affluent in the city and the least likely to be populated by Klansmen. The wealthiest citizens lived in locales with large houses and great green lawns north of Main Street, between the central business district and the railroad tracks. Blacks did not move toward the central part of the city until later, when the most affluent citizens began to migrate to outlying areas. Unity among white Protestants, not the suppression of already well-contained ethnic minorities, guided the actions of the Richmond Klan.

Like other chapters in Indiana, the Richmond klavern achieved its greatest impact on the community as a social organization. Each week the most enthusiastic members gathered at the Knights of Pythius meeting hall (later known as the Medical Arts Building). Only a tiny fraction of the membership attended these fraternal assemblies—usually between one hundred and two hundred men. Surviving records of the klavern contain few indications of the issues that dominated the discussions. Two Klansmen who attended these meetings sporadically remembered them to be generally unexciting and focused on the recitation of ceremonies from the *Kloran*. The details of occasional political deliberations did not stand out in their recollections. Both men recalled frequent reminders that the Klan stood for Prohibition enforcement and law and order—and that terrorism played no part in the Klan's activities.[30]

Those who attended the chapter's weekly meetings probably were most likely to participate in its frequent social events for Klansmen and their families. Fliers and unsold tickets appearing in klavern records evidence the numerous dances, fish fries, barbecues, and picnics. One Richmond Klansmen recalled that these had been the most satisfying and well attended of the regular Klan events. He remembered in particular a barbecue outside Richmond, near the town of Centerville, that attracted Klansmen and their families from all parts of the county.[31]

The Richmond Klan reached beyond its fraternal core to unite the wider white Protestant community during its larger demonstrations, its summer-night rallies, its "naturalization" (initiation) ceremonies, and, with a particular force, its huge parade in October 1923. Like no other organization in the city, the Klan was capable of bringing together great numbers of citizens. During the summers of 1923 and 1924, klavern officials often conducted weekly meetings in fields on the outskirts of Richmond. The excitement of these occasions, much of it generated by the expectation of a cross burning at the meeting's culmination, usually swelled attendance. One of the largest such events occurred on May 25, 1923, when the chapter conducted a huge naturalization ceremony in Glen Miller Park. According to the *Richmond Evening Item*, which had supported the Klan from the time of its first appearance in the city, more than three thousand Klansmen and spectators attended. The festivities included speeches by Klan leaders, an initiation ceremony for new members, fireworks, and the customary cross burning. A large advertisement in the previous day's *Item* undoubtedly contributed to the success of the event.[32]

The chapter generated its highest level of excitement among white Protestants later that year, when it sponsored a massive parade through the downtown streets. As it had in May, the Klan announced its plans for the celebration in a full-page advertisement in the *Item* on the previous day. Proclaiming "EVERYBODY WELCOME" in large letters, the October 4 ad promised speeches, band music, and a parade down Main Street to Glen Miller Park, followed by a naturalization ceremony for new Klansmen, fireworks, and an appearance by an airplane that would swing a huge fiery cross in the dark sky. After the giant parade, the *Item* noted: "The largest Ku Klux Klan demonstration ever given in Wayne county was viewed last night by approximately 30,000 people, including beside Richmond residents, visitors from this vicinity and outlying towns. Fully 6,000 members of the Klan participated in the monster parade at 8:15 o'clock, which in magnitude and impressiveness has had few equals in this city."[33]

It is doubtful that Richmond had ever experienced a greater spectacle. Early in the day, traffic began to congest the city; by evening, policemen—some of them adorned in their Klan robes—were forced to stop all traffic in the downtown area. At five o'clock, Klansmen began to assemble in Glen Miller Park, where they were entertained by a band concert and a speech by a national Klan speaker. At eight, the parade formed and began its march down Main Street to the courthouse. There it turned south to "A" Street, then looped back to Main Street and returned to the park. Richmond Klansmen constituted the majority of the marchers, but others came from klaverns in Muncie, Marion, Anderson, and Dayton, Ohio. Several hundred members of the women's order in Richmond also appeared in the parade, along with at least ten marching bands; the Muncie Girls Band, the *Item* commented, "attracted more than usual interest." Floats added to the festivities. According to the *Item*, they were "many, varied and interesting" and "depicted either in symbolic form or told by banners the aims and feelings of the Klan on different questions." When the celebrants returned to the park, uniformed Klansmen holding red flares formed a cordon around the naturalization ceremony; nonmembers watched from a large grandstand. After the candidates were initiated, the fireworks show began, featuring three set pieces that outlined the American flag, "K.K.K.," and "100 Percent." As promised, an airplane circled overhead carrying a large cross lighted by electric bulbs.[34]

As a civic organization, the Richmond Klan failed to generate such excitement. Compared with other chapters, the Richmond Klan devoted far less energy toward specific social or political improvements in its city. The public school issue, for example, sparked little concern within the Richmond order, even though its ranks included the president and several other members of the school board. When

Richmond Klansmen did act, their efforts, like those of other klaverns, focused on the defense of the traditional idea of community.

Like other chapters, the Richmond Klan paid particular attention to the enforcement of Prohibition. The issue of whether or not to outlaw alcohol had been extremely divisive for more than a decade before the onset of state Prohibition in 1917 and later national Prohibition. In 1908 and again in 1914, local option elections had deeply divided the city's electorate and in both cases the narrow defeat of the dry forces had produced controversy and charges of election fraud. When the Klan appeared, it quickly enrolled prominent ministers who had been longtime supporters of Prohibition and, in combination with other citizens, exerted pressure on the city and county governments to make sure that drinking and other vice laws were enforced.[35]

Some of the Klansmen operated under the auspices of the Horse Thief Detective Association, the nineteenth-century vigilante organization that Indiana lawmakers once had empowered to perform police duties. In some communities, Klansmen had resurrected it to lend authority to their law enforcement activities. There is no evidence that members of the Horse Thief Detective Association in Richmond broke the law or attacked suspected criminals. Richmond Klansmen had no need to take the law into their own hands. The president of the police commission and the district attorney were themselves Klan members, and when Klansmen uncovered evidence of gambling and bootlegging in their city, they turned it over to the authorities. On one occasion, the *Richmond Evening Item*, long a supporter of the dry cause, credited the Klan for the conviction of "notorious" bootleggers; on another, it specifically defended the Horse Thief Detective Association. The Richmond police, an *Item* editorial stated, "are powerless to deal with gangs of criminals these days and need the help of citizens in such an organization. . . . It's the American Way for citizens to take care of their communities in such a fashion."[36]

The Richmond chapter became involved in a number of other civic, charity, and church causes, aiming primarily to rekindle a sense of popular involvement in civic activism, which had once been a hallmark of community life. The Klan's most ambitious goal was to build a 6,500-seat public auditorium for Wayne County, which, conveniently, could be used for Klan meetings. The effort failed. The community facilities that had been constructed in preceding years, such as the Morrisson-Reeves Library, Reed Hospital, and Reed Church, owed their existence to wealthy benefactors. Without similar support, the Klan's grass-roots attempt to finance a public building languished, then disappeared. Richmond Klansmen met with more success in their activities for charity. On several occasions, members of the men's and women's orders made the customary appearance in Richmond churches, leaving donations with the respective pastors. A particularly strong relationship existed between the Richmond Klan and the local chapter of the Salvation Army. The captain of the latter organization was a Klansman himself and arranged for the chapter to make large donations, especially during the Christmas season. In 1922, the *Item* reported that money and food contributed by the Klan allowed the Salvation Army nearly to double the number of Christmas baskets it would distribute to Richmond's poor.[37]

In local politics, as in other civic matters, the Richmond Klan generally played a subdued role. Many elected officials of the city and county belonged to the Klan, but apparently the secret order had no organized agenda of reforms and members who held public office did not appear to look to Klan leaders for direction. Occasionally the chapter made its presence felt in local politics, especially in defense of traditional community institutions. One incident in the winter of 1924 demonstrated this tendency and, at the same time, symbolized the inherent conflict between the Klan's vision of community and that of Richmond's powerful business elite.

Late in 1923, executives of the Terre Haute, Indianapolis, and Eastern Traction Company went before the Richmond Public Service Commission to ask for permission to install in the city a high-power electric line to operate its traction cars. The commission denied the request on the grounds that the company's intention to sell surplus current from the line to Richmond power users would threaten the city's municipally owned power plant. The traction company's officials reacted angrily to the decision, one of them informing the commission members that they would be "damn sorry some time that you did not agree to this contract."[38] The company then made plans to construct the power line around the city, close enough to the municipal boundaries to sell electricity to Richmond residents. This, the commission admitted, it could not stop. In response, the Richmond City Council proposed to annex large areas of unincorporated land, creating a buffer zone that would block the traction company's incursion into the city.

The decision of whether or not to expand Richmond's boundaries touched off a heated political battle, pitting the city's business elite against a coalition composed of Mayor Lawrence A. Handley, who was not a Klansman, and his supporters on the city council, the majority of whom were members of the Klan. Richmond's elite objected to annexation on the simple grounds that it would hinder business expansion. The rejection of the traction company's proposed expansion by itself violated the spirit of boosterism so deeply ingrained in the minds of business leaders. Perhaps they envisioned that competition between the traction company and the Municipal Light Plant would lower power rates, decreasing business expenses. The main concern of corporate executives, however, was that by drawing wider boundaries, the city would absorb existing and future industrial sites that lay just outside the city limits and thus were not subject to municipal taxes. Without this advantage, business leaders argued, established companies would be hurt and new firms would look elsewhere for more hospitable treatment.

The argument against annexation, not surprisingly, was taken up by the *Richmond Palladium*. Its publisher, Rudolph Garr Leeds, was a member of one of Richmond's wealthiest families. The editor, Edward H. Harris, was active in the Richmond Rotary and a leading booster of business interests. Under the control of these two men, the *Palladium* had long articulated the views of Richmond's business elite. The newspaper's campaign against annexation began after it became clear in January 1924 that there were enough votes on the city council to pass the proposed ordinance. In an attempt to sway public opinion and the votes of councilmen, the *Palladium* ran a series of stories predicting a host of dire consequences that would result from annexation. These included an increase in fire insurance rates and city taxes, since municipal services would have to be extended to a variety of sparsely populated outlying areas. One editorial provided a price list of new city expenditures if annexation passed: $600,000 to expand the city sewer system, $20,000 to

$40,000 to increase fire insurance coverage, thousands of dollars more to construct new fire stations and hydrants, and increased utility rates for water and gas.[39]

As evidence that annexation would injure the local economy, the *Palladium* claimed that a factory under construction on the outskirts of Richmond was planning to reduce its operations if the city extended the municipal boundary. Under the front-page headline, "Factory Not to Expand If Line Extended," an article disclosed that officials of the Fibre Conduit Company would cut their proposed plant size in half if annexation passed. According to the *Palladium*, "practically all prospective industrial sites will be taken into the city if the ordinance goes through in the present form, it is said. Those favorable to amendment of the measure believe this fact to provide an important argument for such action, as cities seeking to attract factories usually make it a point to emphasize that the land available for industrial sites is not within the city and consequently free from many hampering restrictions." If the ordinance could not be amended to maintain a favorable climate for business investment, the *Palladium* argued in an editorial, annexation should be defeated and the city should simply enter into an agreement with the traction company that the company would not sell its surplus current if allowed to lay the power line.[40]

Despite the considerable ability of Richmond's economic elite to make its voice heard, it was far from clear at the outset that it would be able to persuade the city council to abandon its plans for annexation. Mayor Handley represented one formidable obstacle. Elected in 1921, he had been the only candidate in recent memory to deliver a major defeat to the local Republican establishment. He was the first Democratic mayor in more than thirty years. A majority in the city council also favored annexation when it was first proposed. Of twelve councilmen, nine initially supported the measure. Party loyalty did not account for this alignment; only one Democrat held office on the city council. The largest block of supporters were Klansmen. Seven members served on the city council and five originally endorsed annexation.[41]

A natural alliance existed between proannexation politicians and the city's other daily newspaper, the *Item*. Its editor, Guild A. Copeland, had supported Handley's election. He had also supported the Richmond Klan, even though he was not a member himself. In his newspaper, Copeland had long lamented changes in community life, the decline of traditional values, and the failure of government to enforce Prohibition laws. The city's business leaders, in Copeland's view, were responsible for much of this instability, and their campaign against annexation demonstrated their tendency to place personal gain above community interests.

Copeland characterized the annexation issue as a struggle between the common good and the will of the economic elite. The *Item*'s articles and editorials stressed the importance of defending the city power plant from corporate competition and the basic fairness of asking industrial plants and other residents of unincorporated areas using city services to pay their share of municipal taxes. "Annexation," one editorial stated, "is the only way in which we can protect our great Municipal Light plant from the outside interests that have already begun to try to coax away its business.... And who is there who is public spirited and who knows what the plant means to Richmond who wants to stand by and see it wrecked?"[42] In response to the *Palladium*'s claim that annexation would create a bad business environment, the *Item* downplayed the idea that municipal taxes would hurt local businesses. These taxes, another editorial pointed out, could be deducted from earnings when companies paid state taxes and thus did not represent a significant hardship. A third editorial emphasized the danger of granting too many favors to business:

> The idea that a city should be run chiefly to favor its factories has never been tremendously popular in Richmond, although this city is always glad to welcome a new industry and always aims to treat every industry fairly. In our neighboring city of Hamilton, Ohio, however, we can see a pretty good example of the policy of building up a "factory city" rather than a city of homes. Hamilton is not very much larger than our city, but it is far more typically an industrial city and because of its industrial type it has grown faster than Richmond. It now has something like 10,000 more population than our new city; but its growth

has been chiefly in the way of bringing workers to its factories almost wholly. It has not the diversified business that Richmond has.[43]

As the *Palladium* continued to campaign against annexation, the *Item* took every opportunity to counter its rival's charges and defend the city councilmen who supported the measure. The claim that annexation would increase city taxes, fire insurance rates, and utility fees, the *Item* protested, was propaganda. "Anybody who argues that adding two millions [sic] to our property is going to increase our taxes must be a congenital idiot!" one editorial asserted. The campaign against annexation served only the interests of Richmond's wealthy businessmen, the *Item* repeatedly argued, and the power of this small circle of individuals to persuade the public and manipulate the political process constituted a grave threat to the community. "Those who oppose the ordinance," Copeland declared, "admit very frankly that they are doing so just as a favor to one or two industrial plants, here, that don't want to pay city taxes for the city benefits they get. . . . On one side are the people's interests. On the other side are the interests of a few factories which want about everything—but don't want to pay a cent for what they get." Copeland and his newspaper urged the public to stand firmly behind the city council: "On the plain face of it, who are the men who are working for what they know to be the interests of all the people of Richmond? If the people of Richmond can't trust the men who have brought the finances and the public service of our city to the very highest rank among Indiana cities, whom can they trust then? The advocates of special privilege for the few, at the cost of all the rest of the people of Richmond?"[44]

In the end, the city council succumbed to the public campaign, and doubtless the private lobbying, of Richmond's business leaders. Despite furious last-minute debating by representatives of the Handley administration and proannexation supporters, the measure was defeated by a vote of seven to five—only two weeks after a preliminary vote had favored the bill by a nine-to-three margin. Two of the four defecting councilmen were Klan members, one of whom made a rather long speech on the night of the final vote explaining that in the last two weeks he had been persuaded that the majority of Richmond's citizens had turned against the idea of annexation. Guild Copeland expressed another view of the sudden shift in the council. In an *Item* editorial two days after the final vote, he asked Richmond voters to remember the antiannexation councilmen in the next election:

> Every one of them should be replaced with a man who has the character and sand enough to stand up for the interests of the people of Richmond. This idea that the city affairs should be run chiefly to oblige a group of men who employ labor and that those men owe the labor thus employed no duty, is a bad basis on which to run the affairs of any city. . . . It is not at all fair to the 25,000 [people of Richmond] to say that the 25 shall not pay taxes for the city benefits which their industries enjoy. And we need, on our city council, men who have the nerve and the backbone to stand up for the interests of the 25,000 in spite of the pressure brought by the 25.[45]

On the surface, the role of the Richmond Klan in the annexation debate appears to have been relatively insignificant. While Klan members represented a majority on the city council, ultimately they were divided almost in half by the decision not to expand the city boundaries. A year later, Klansmen who had both supported and opposed annexation were returned to office; others representing both sides of the issue decided not to seek reelection.[46] As we shall see in the next chapter, Klans in other cities were more successful in challenging local political establishments; nevertheless, the Richmond chapter was not alone in failing to make use of its considerable potential for political power. The significance of the annexation debate in Richmond was not that it demonstrated the lack of unity among Klan officeholders, but that it revealed so clearly the contending views of community that existed in the city. There is no doubt that the Klan movement in Richmond represented the interests of the traditional vision of community, that it owed its existence, in fact, to the deep-seated desire of most of the citizenry to defend and revitalize traditional community institutions and values. If they and like-minded non-Klansmen failed in this instance to defend their vision of community, it only indicated the formidable power of the boosters and their belief that a community should attend to its businesses before turning to less weighty concerns.

Rural Wayne County

With its factories, shops, churches, newspapers, college, and more than 26,000 inhabitants, Richmond easily dominated affairs in Wayne County. In 1920, more than 65 percent of the county's population lived in Richmond. That percentage had grown constantly for thirty years and would continue to do so. The vast majority of Wayne County's Klansmen also lived in Richmond, or at least close enough to belong to the Richmond klavern. Of the 4,037 men who joined the Wayne County Klan in the twenties, 3,183 appeared on the Richmond roster; the rest were named on much smaller lists for seven other communities. As of 1920, however, half of Indiana's population still lived in communities with less than 2,500 residents, and the Klansmen of rural Wayne County probably represented to some degree the thousands of men from rural communities across the state who generally joined the Klan at the same rate as men in more populous areas. The 854 Wayne County Klansmen who belonged to the village klaverns, then, are important not only for the part they played in local Klan affairs, but also for the insights they offer about rural Klansmen as a whole.[47]

Just as Richmond had been one of the first commercial and industrial centers in the state, rural Wayne County had prospered from an early date. Many of its towns were established not long after Richmond in 1804 and before most other communities in central or northern Indiana. The National Road, which traveled straight west to Indianapolis after leaving Richmond on the eastern side of the county, formed a transportation backbone for the rest of the region as early as 1829 and ran almost directly through the center of the county from the Ohio border into Henry County. Corn and oats were the largest crops in Wayne County in the nineteenth and early twentieth centuries, when farmers enjoyed relatively easy access to commercial towns along the National Road—if not Richmond, then Centerville or, in the western part of the county, Cambridge City.

Quakers were strongly represented in the rural townships, just as they were in Richmond. German and, to a lesser extent, Irish immigrants also left a noticeable imprint on the character of the rural population, and each group built its own small enclaves in the towns of Dublin and Germantown, located respectively just to the west and east of Cambridge City.

Most of Wayne County's other rural communities had been established north of the National Road. Hagerstown, Dalton, and Economy lay in the northwestern corner of the twenty-by-twenty-mile-square county. Greensfork and Williamsburg were located toward the center of the northern section, while Webster, Fountain City, Chester, Middleboro, and Whitewater were farther to the east, directly north of Richmond. Only three communities existed south of the National Road: Milton, just south of Cambridge City, and Abington and Boston, both in the southeastern corner of the county. Of all the Wayne County communities outside of Richmond, only Cambridge City, with 1,963 residents in 1920, came close to being classified as an urban place. The next largest towns, Centerville and Hagerstown, each had populations of approximately 900. The other communities generally contained between 300 and 600 residents. In 1920, there were 2,410 farms in Wayne County. Most of them were owned and operated by families, and more than half were between 50 and 175 acres. Outside of Richmond, approximately half of the population lived on farms, while half resided in towns. Ethnic minorities represented only a tiny fraction of the farm population. Immigrants operated only 38 farms in the county; blacks owned or rented a total of 16 farms.[48]

While thirty years of economic expansion and growth in population naturally had made Richmond the center of social change in the county, less powerful but significant changes had also affected life in the rural communities. In the two decades before 1920, farms had become more modern and productivity had generally increased. The appearance of automobiles and tractors had contributed to this process; so, too, had the expanding telephone network. By 1919, seventy-nine tractors were in use in Wayne County, 62 percent of all farmers owned automobiles, and 73 percent of all farms had telephones.[49] After the disastrous decade of the 1890s (when farm ownership shrank from 72 percent to less than 54 percent of all farms), the county's farm economy generally experienced two decades of growth and prosperity. The rate of farm ownership grew again to approximately 65 percent and remained at that level throughout the period. The number of acres in farmland also remained stable—at a level of just under one-quarter million acres. At the same time, however, modernization appeared to lead to growing consolidation. Between 1910 and 1920, the number of farms in the county decreased by 217, or 8 percent. During the same period, the average farm size increased by 7 percent, from 94 acres to 101 acres. The rural population declined both in real terms and as a percentage of the overall population. Ten of the county's fourteen rural townships showed a general trend toward population decline from 1900 to 1920. At the turn of the century, residents of the rural townships had represented 45 percent of the county's population, but by 1910 it had declined to 39 percent and by 1920 to 35 percent.[50]

These gradual changes in the county's rural communities were compounded by the depressed farm economy of the early 1920s. Continued low prices for corn and oats put more farmers out of business and took more farmland out of production. Between 1920 and 1925, the amount of farmland in the county decreased by more than 16 percent, the total number of farms dropped by another 9 percent, and the number of farms operated by tenants increased by 20 percent.[51]

It is difficult to judge with certainty the affect of these shifts on the popularity of the Ku Klux Klan in rural Wayne County. Newspapers, township directories, and other records for these small communities generally have not been preserved, and interviews with longtime members of several towns have revealed only limited information. Nevertheless, it seems fair to conclude that long-term changes in rural communities coupled with the farm crisis of the early 1920s contributed to some degree to the broad support that the Klan gained in these areas. If community life in Richmond was being altered by persistent growth, Wayne County's rural townships faced their own set of pressures which related to stagnation and decline. In any event, the evidence that does exist strongly suggests that the county's rural Klansmen were not profoundly different from their counterparts in Richmond. They seem to have represented a wide cross section of the population in their communities and did not engage in violence or the persecution of ethnic minorities. Social activities and community cohesiveness played a central part in the affairs of the village Klans, and support for Prohibition enforcement represented a powerful common interest.

Like the Klansmen of Richmond, those in the rural areas of the county were strongly oriented toward their own communities. The klavern headquarters in Richmond kept separate lists for groups of Klansmen in six other Wayne County towns. Klan members for one additional town, Cambridge City, seemingly remained completely separate from the main county organization. There is no information about Cambridge City in the Wayne County Klan records, but in the statewide Klan report for 1925, Cambridge City is listed as a separate chapter with 315 members. Without detailed membership lists for other counties, it is impossible to determine whether this pattern was common among rural Klansmen. The 1925 report generally gives only one Klan organization in each county; Cambridge City was a rare exception in this regard. At the same time, the general lack of hierarchical control that characterized the relationship between the state headquarters and the county organizations may have extended in many instances to the relationship between county headquarters and township. This may have been particularly true in counties such as Wayne, where one relatively large population center was so dominant. Perhaps in counties with purely rural populations, Klansmen gravitated less to individual townships and more to one central location. In any event, slightly more than 21 percent of Wayne County Klansmen became members of chapters located in towns outside of Richmond (see Table 5.3).[52]

For the most part, the Klan appeared to be almost as popular in the countryside as it was in Richmond. In addition to the 854 known members of the rural klaverns, approximately 450 more farmers belonged to the Richmond chapter. Most of the farmers who were registered in Richmond resided in or near Wayne (Richmond) township. Some, however, lived in other parts of the county and probably would have found it easier to associate with one of the rural chapters. No doubt, many of these men became members during one of the large social events in Richmond that attracted people from throughout the county and beyond. As a group, they were probably not as active in Klan affairs as other members. Taken together,

Table 5.3

Klan Membership in Incorporated Towns, Wayne County, 1922–1926

Town	Population	Number Klan Members
Boston	190	66
Cambridge City	1,963	315*
Centerville	917	224
Dublin	630	Unknown
Fountain City	375	67
Greenfork	380	79
Hagerstown	1,238	86
Milton	580	17
Mount Auburn	142	Unknown
Richmond	26,765	3,183
Spring Grove	76	Unknown
Whitewater	96	Unknown

Source: Membership List, Wayne County Ku Klux Klan Collection, Indiana

*Membership for Cambridge City taken from Local Officers of the Ku Klux Klan, Indiana Historical Society.

Klansmen from all parts of the county outside Richmond represented more than 32 percent of the total Richmond membership. This compares favorably with the 35 percent of the general population that resided beyond Richmond's city limits in 1920. In the rural townships, Klan membership was divided fairly evenly between townspeople and farmers. Of the 439 men whose names appear on the Klan lists for townships, 232, or 43 percent, were farmers.[53]

The Klan attracted all classes of Wayne County farmers. A sample of one thousand farmers in the county indicates that the Klan gained a significant following among both owners and tenants; among those who worked large, medium, and small farms; and among farmhands and skilled workers who made their living in rural areas. But the sample also shows that Klan members tended to come slightly more often from certain categories of farmers. Klansmen were more likely than non-Klansmen to be owners of medium-sized farms (see Table 5.4). More than 41 percent of the Klan farm owners worked between forty and two hundred acres. Among non-Klan farm owners, less than 38 percent fell into this category. At the same time, owners of both large and small farms were less likely to be Klan members. In the case of small farm owners, the ten-dollar Klan initiation fee may have represented a luxury that many could not afford. Many of the farmers in this category worked such small plots of land that they had to have had outside income of some sort just to survive. The county's most successful farmers could pay the initiation fee, of course, but generally seemed less inclined to join the Klan. Owners of over two hundred acres were more than twice as likely to be non-

Table 5.4

Occupations of Klan and Non-Klan Rural Residents, Wayne County

	Klan		Non-Klan	
	Number	Percent	Number	Percent
Farm owners				
200 acres or more	4	1.3	24	3.4
100–199 acres	51	16.8	98	14.1
40–99 acres	76	25.0	165	23.7
Less than 40 acres	24	7.9	85	12.2
Farm tenant				
100 acres or more	83	27.3	158	22.7
Less than 100 acres	33	10.9	118	17.0
Owner/Tenant	6	2.0	7	1.0
Farmhand/skilled worker	27	8.9	41	5.9
Total	304		696	

Chi-square (7 dof) = 19.6 $P \leq .01$

Source: See Appendix.

Klansmen. A separate examination of the county's twenty largest farm owners (holding over three hundred acres) shows that only three became Klan members.[54]

There were also important differences among farm tenants and farm workers. Tenants who worked larger farms had a stronger tendency to join the Klan, while those working smaller farms were less likely to be Klansmen. Again, the economic barrier to Klan membership almost certainly played a role in shaping this pattern. The importance of the issue can be seen in the tendency toward Klan membership by farm workers. While men in this category generally had the same occupational status as small farm owners and tenants, they showed a higher rate of Klan membership. In all likelihood, this was because they worked for wages and were not as dependent on income produced by the sale of crops.[55]

The Klan's wide popularity among county farmers appears to have been matched by its appeal to residents of the rural towns. Without directories for individual townships, it is impossible to estimate the social characteristics of these Klansmen with the same precision as farmers and residents of Richmond. The membership totals listed in Table 5.3, however, give some indication of the Klan's ability to attract members from these areas. Fifty-six percent of the Klansmen who were registered on rural membership lists appear to have been townspeople. These men represented not only a majority of the rural Klan membership, but also a substantial portion of the adult male population for each town. Taken together, Klansmen made up 25 percent of the estimated adult male population in these communities. In four of the six towns with separate Klan lists (Boston, Centerville, Fountain City, and Greenfork), they probably accounted for more than one-third of the adult male population. The percentage of Klan membership was noticeably low in only two of the communities for which separate Klan lists were available (Hagerstown and Milton).[56]

Interviews with long-standing residents and former Klansmen in two rural towns (Hagerstown and Centerville) suggest that membership in the village Klans was open to almost everyone and was not confined to any narrow segment of the population. In both communities, the Klan seems to have been extremely popular among Main Street merchants. Each of the four people interviewed believed that nearly all of the most successful men in each town were members. In Hagerstown, this included shop owners as well as several members of a family of businessmen who operated a small but successful piston ring manufacturing company on the eastern side of town. In Centerville, it included the owner of a bank, several lawyers, and, again, virtually all of the town's leading merchants. Also among the Klansmen were shop hands, foremen, and clerks from the piston ring company in Hagerstown and factory workers who lived in Centerville and commuted to jobs in Richmond. Teachers, postal workers, store clerks, and other low-level white-collar workers could also be found on the Klan rosters for both communities. Members of each of the Protestant churches appeared on the membership lists. Hagerstown's two churches (Methodist and Christian) were both well represented, although slightly more Methodists may have been members of the Klan and their church may have been a focus of local Klan activity. In addition to other Protestant churches, Centerville contained a large congregation of Quakers, a substantial number of whom joined the Klan.[57]

Former Klansmen from Hagerstown and Centerville did not remember violence playing a part in the Klan's affairs. Other longtime residents recalled that the men on the Klan lists were good citizens and neighbors and not prone to unlawful activities. There were almost no ethnic minorities to persecute in either of these communities, even if the memberships had been so inclined. Few if any blacks ever lived in Centerville and only one black man resided in Hagerstown. This was due primarily to the fact that blacks were not welcome in these communities before, during, or after the Klan years. Hagerstown had what residents generally recognized as an unwritten law against black families taking up residence. Apparently there was no such policy against Catholics, and some Catholic families did live in both communities. Neither town, however, contained a Catholic church.[58]

Social activities were common and seem to have been a primary reason for the existence of the township klaverns. For several years, Hagerstown Klansmen met once a week in the same home used for Grange meetings. One Hagerstown Klansman remembered that these were purely social affairs—a chance for townspeople and farmers to meet and discuss community issues. The Centerville

Klan, in particular, was a hub of social activities. In fact, one of the town's Klansmen recalled little about the local klavern other than its many dinners, picnics, fish fries, and dances. A Richmond Klansmen remembered that he had had several friends in the Centerville klavern and enjoyed attending its functions more than Richmond's because of the emphasis on social activities.[59]

Probably the single greatest concern of Wayne County's rural Klansmen, like their counterparts throughout the state, was the enforcement of Prohibition laws. Both of the rural Klansmen who were interviewed remembered that this was the main issue stressed by the Klans in their own communities as well as Klan leaders in Richmond. But neither could cite any instances when Centerville or Hagerstown Klansmen took action against violators, nor is there evidence that other rural klaverns in Wayne County took steps to crack down on bootleggers. Still, the county's rural townships had demonstrated a tradition of solid support for laws against alcohol. By 1908, saloons had been banned through local option elections in every township in the county outside of Richmond—and attempts to make Richmond dry in 1908 and 1914 were only narrowly defeated. In Hagerstown, alcohol appears to have been the only local political issue of consequence for most of the early twentieth century. The town had been the last rural community in the county to go dry, in large part because workers at the piston ring factory (which, at an earlier time, had produced other machine products) had always resisted the idea. During the 1920s, many of the men who joined the Hagerstown klavern were longtime supporters of the dry cause, and several had been active in the local option campaigns of 1908 and 1914. Perhaps one reason that Klan membership in Hagerstown was low compared with other rural communities in Wayne County was that its factory workers, who represented an unusually large segment of the population, had a history of being at odds with local supporters of Prohibition.[60]

Regardless of Hagerstown's smaller membership, the Klan's identification with the cause of Prohibition enforcement undoubtedly accounted for a large part of its popularity in rural Wayne County. Control of the sale of alcohol had long stood as a symbol of order, cohesiveness, and traditional values in these communities. The Ku Klux Klan offered citizens a chance to demonstrate their support for

Prohibition in their own towns as well as in the rest of the state and nationwide. In this sense, the rural Klansmen of Wayne County shared a powerful bond with their compatriots in Richmond.

If the rural klans differed in any important way from the Richmond chapter, it was in their ability to attract leading citizens into the local klavern's ranks. In both Hagerstown and Centerville, prominent businessmen joined the order and probably took part in directing its operation. The reasons for this were twofold. First, these communities had remained smaller and more closely knit than Richmond or other larger towns. Community organizations of all kinds had not become as stratified as they had in Richmond. Town merchants, whose economic existence depended on the business of a relatively small number of townspeople and farmers, had every reason to be closely involved with community organizations such as the Klan. Second, these small-town elites had not become part of the group of boosters and businessmen who played such a dominant role in Richmond's public affairs. The Rotary club did not open its membership to leading businessmen from surrounding towns until sometime after the 1920s. Thus, the line that separated Richmond's boosters from the rest of the community also apparently separated them from business leaders in other parts of the county.[61]

Indianapolis

In some respects, the Indianapolis Klan had little in common with the chapters that operated in Richmond and rural Wayne County. The idea of community, which played such a significant part in the Klan movement in towns with 300, 3,000, or even 30,000 residents, could not convey the same meaning in an industrial city of 300,000. Klansmen in Indianapolis could not assemble in one place for weekly meetings and could not hope to know personally more than a small number of their fellow members. Klansmen in comfortable tree-lined suburban neighborhoods in the northern and eastern sections of the city probably had little contact with Klansmen in distant working-class neighborhoods in central, western, and southern sections. Ministers from one or two leading churches could not play the same influential role in Indianapolis that they could in Richmond or Centerville. Massive social events and demonstrations could have a powerful impact, even in a large city, but they could not overwhelm and energize an entire population in the same manner as those that inundated town squares and Main Street shopping districts.

Unlike Klan movements in Richmond, rural Wayne County, or most other communities in the state, the Indianapolis movement took place in an environment where ethnic minorities were present in significant numbers and were the focus of considerable concern. Of course, the overall size of the foreign-born population did not compare with that of cities like Chicago, St. Louis, or Detroit, and the largest immigrant group was German rather than of southern or eastern European origin. Still, at more than 5 percent of the total population, Indianapolis's foreign-born groups were large enough to form their own ethnic neighborhoods and leave a noticeable imprint on the city's social, economic, and political affairs. After Germans, who comprised 30 percent of the immigrant population, the next largest group of foreign-born residents came from eastern and southern European countries—primarily Greece, Italy, Poland, Romania, Russia, and Yugoslavia. Together, these groups made up more than 27 percent of the city's foreign-born population. The Irish were another important immigrant group, representing more than 14 percent of all foreign-born residents. The great majority of the city's immigrants lived in working-class neighborhoods south of the downtown district. These neighborhoods did not expand during the 1920s, but there is evidence that more prosperous families, particularly from the Jewish community, were beginning to move to suburban districts in the northern part of the city.[62]

During the twenties, blacks were by far the largest and, to many whites, the most disturbing ethnic minority group in Indianapolis. The black population had grown from 21,816 in 1910 to 34,678 in 1920 and had come to comprise 11 percent of the total population. Historically confined to a section along Indiana Avenue northwest of the downtown area, the black community had been gradually expanding, generally in a northern direction toward more affluent suburban neighborhoods. Blacks had also begun to move into previously all-white neighborhoods northeast of downtown. The expansion of the black community ignited a great deal of controversy and resulted in the appearance of white neighborhood "protective" associations, a new system of racially segregated public schools, and an attempt to segregate residential neighborhoods by city ordinance. Indianapolis Klansmen naturally supported these measures and used their political influence to help bring them into effect. Thus, conflict between white Protestants and blacks—as well as Catholics and Jews—played a more direct role in the Indianapolis Klan movement than it did in Wayne County.[63]

While recognizing the differences between the Indianapolis Klan and chapters in smaller, less diverse communities, it is important not to exaggerate the significance of these differences or to conclude that Indianapolis Klansmen joined the order for fundamentally different reasons than other Klansmen in the state. While the Klan movement took a distinct form in a large urban setting, the main forces driving it were essentially the same as those in other communities. The order still attracted a wide cross section of the white Protestant population rather than being confined to any narrow social group or set of groups. Ethnic conflict, though an issue in Indianapolis, still was not the main focus of the Klan's activities and not the primary reason for its popularity. And even if the Klan could not bring the same sort of cohesiveness to community life in Indianapolis that it did in Wayne County towns, it still had its greatest impact as a force for popular control at the local level. In fact, in a large city like Indianapolis, the Klan could not rely simply on sensational public demonstrations or social activities to make its presence felt. Instead, it was forced to turn directly to politics. As a result, the Indianapolis Klan achieved more influence in local government and a greater voice in civic affairs than any of the Wayne County chapters.

As noted earlier, in the early stages of its growth the Indianapolis Klan attracted white Protestant men from all walks of life. These individuals joined the order in representative numbers from each of the city's major occupational and religious groups. The important exceptions were that leading businessmen and other economic elites did not join, lower middle-class individuals were somewhat more likely to be members, and those who belonged to the city's relatively new, overtly fundamentalist Protestant churches rejected the Klan. It is likely that as the Klan movement reached its zenith, the membership in Indianapolis was even more widespread. This cannot be proven, of course, since the surviving list of the city's Klansmen does not extend past early 1923. But if the pattern of membership growth in Indianapolis paralleled those in both Richmond and Denver, Colorado, in any meaningful way, as time went on new members were more likely to come from the working class, making the city's Klansmen even more representative of the general population.[64]

Residential patterns in Klan membership—even in the early period—further demonstrate the order's broad appeal. An analysis of the residential distribution of five hundred Klansmen and five hundred men from the general population in 1923 shows that while Klan membership was more concentrated in some areas, it had a significant following throughout the city (see Table 5.5). In four of the six areas investigated (north central, south central, east, and north), the percentage of Klansmen was higher or nearly equal to the percentage of all men sampled. The two areas where Klansmen were less concentrated (west and south) were overwhelmingly working-class neighborhoods. But at the same time, the percentage of Klansmen in these areas was far from inconsequential and, by the summer of 1924, probably became more representative of the total male population.[65]

Given the heightened significance of ethnic minorities in the population, it is important to note that the Klan does appear to have been particularly popular in the north-central section of Indianapolis, where racial tensions ran especially high. While the figures in Table 5.5 make it appear that the percentage of Klansmen was roughly equal to the percentage of males in the general population, in reality, at least one-third, and perhaps one-half, of the men residing in the north-central area can be assumed to have been black. Compared with the percentage of *white* men, then, the percentage of Klansmen in this area was quite high and can be attributed, at least in part, to white concerns over the consequences of continued growth in the black population. Even in neighborhoods not adjacent to the black community, racist fears about the growing number of blacks in the city probably helped stimulate support for the Klan. Heightened ethnic tensions also may have played a role in the Klan's popularity in the south-central region, which contained most of the city's Jewish population. Klan membership was relatively high in other neighborhoods of southern and eastern European immigrants as well.[66]

Table 5.5
Residential Distribution of Klan Members and All Males, Indianapolis, 1923

| | Klan | | All Males | |
Area	Number	Percent	Number	Percent
North Central*	88	17.6	94	18.8
South Central	109	21.8	92	18.4
West	43	8.6	71	14.2
East	142	28.4	103	20.6
North	69	13.8	73	14.6
South	41	8.2	67	13.4
Other	8	1.6	—	—
Total	500		500	

Chi-square (6 dof) = 29.01 $P \leq .01$

Source: See Appendix.
*Contained a large black community.

If ethnic conflict in several neighborhoods contributed to the Klan's appeal, however, it was only part of a wider pattern of social and political concerns that enticed men into the secret order. As shown in Table 5.5, the Klan was popular in suburban areas in the north and especially in the east, where ethnic minorities represented no threat to generally homogeneous white Protestant neighborhoods. Even in south-central Indianapolis, the Klan's attraction appears to have involved more than a turf battle between native-born whites and ethnic minorities. In her recent history of Indianapolis's Jewish community, for example, Judith E. Endelman observes that while Jewish citizens were naturally outraged by the Klan's ideology and disturbed by its popularity, Jewish neighborhoods were not torn by conflict with surrounding white Protestant populations during the 1920s. By that time, Endelman argues, the Jewish community generally had "earned the respect of the larger community" and sporadic episodes of anti-Semitism were of relatively little consequence. Ultimately, the Klan had "little direct effect on the Jewish community."[67]

The Klan's appeal to south-side Protestant German immigrants and assimilated Germans further complicates the picture. Anti-Catholic and anti-Jewish sentiment in the German community may have contributed to the Klan's popularity. On the other hand, working-class German immigrants had always lived in close proximity to other immigrant groups in that part of the city and there is no evidence that tensions increased significantly during the Klan years. Given the powerful trend toward assimilation by German-Americans in the twentieth century and then particularly after World War I, it is likely that many ethnic Germans perceived the Klan as a patriotic citizens' organization and joined primarily for that reason.[68]

The Klan can be tied more directly to the racial conflict in north-central neighborhoods. In 1925, the Indianapolis Klan gained control of the Republican political machine and made a clean sweep in the municipal election. Under the at-large scheme for electing city councilmen, six new members of the council were chosen in November, all Klansmen and all garnering approximately the same number of votes. Although only two of the new councilmen lived in the north-central section, all appeared sympathetic to the white neighborhood protective associations that were pressing the city to restrict the movement of blacks into white neighborhoods. Shortly after taking office early in 1926, the new Klan councilmen passed a residential segregation ordinance that gave white citizens the right to exclude black families from their neighborhoods. The ordinance was overturned by the courts and never put into effect, but its passage represented a clear example of the racist sympathies of the Klan councilmen.[69]

One of the more significant, and perhaps ironic, aspects of the residential segregation ordinance episode was the relatively small role it played in the larger context of the Klan's involvement in Indianapolis politics. The segregation campaign predated the Klan's emergence as a force in the city. First directed at the public schools, it resulted in a decision by school officials in 1922 to reorganize elementary schools along racial lines and build a new high school that all black students would be required to attend. The attempt to extend a legally sanctioned system of segregation of residences in 1926 was the next step in the ongoing campaign, rather than something new, and actually generated relatively little controversy among the white citizens of Indianapolis. While Klan politicians supported the measure, it had not been an important campaign issue or the subject of weighty debate between Klan and (white) anti-Klan forces.[70] Two other issues, in fact, engendered a good deal more political strife. One involved the Klan's assault on the city's Republican machine and the battle over patronage that ensued once the Klan slate had been swept into office. The other issue—by far the biggest of the election—involved the public schools but had nothing to do with racial segregation. Instead, it centered on the Klan's support for a widely supported school building and modernization program and the refusal of school officials to get it under way.

Although the state Klan movement had begun to lose momentum by November 1925, the hooded order was still strong enough in Indianapolis to propel two of its members into top leadership positions in the local Republican organization. One of these men was John L. Duvall, an attorney who since 1909 had made a living operating a series of small suburban banks and whose previous experience in politics was limited to one term as Marion County treasurer. Duvall joined the Klan sometime in 1922 or early 1923 and became its candidate to replace the anti-Klan Republican mayor, Lew Shank, in 1925. Klansman George V. Coffin became even more powerful than Duvall. The former Indianapolis chief of police and Marion County sheriff became a high official in the city's Republican machine beginning in 1924 and surpassed all other leaders of the organization once Duvall and the other Klan candidates were elected in 1925.[71]

The issue of patronage surfaced immediately after Duvall won the mayoral contest and revealed the Klan's powerful new role within Indianapolis's Republican organization. Duvall quickly established that the Klan would be repaid for its support. The day after the election, he left Indianapolis for a secret location in Illinois where he could meet with Klan leaders away from the glare of the press and the pressures that were sure to emanate from the Republican establishment. During the next several weeks he issued a series of announcements about expected appointments in the upcoming administration, almost all of which met with the Klan's approval. A number of Klan insiders were put on the city payroll. One job in the park administration went to the leader of the Indianapolis Klan, George Elliot. An editorial appearing in the anti-Klan *Indianapolis Times* within a week of the election concluded with obvious dejection that the Klan's takeover of city politics had been nearly complete: "The city hall will be turned over to the Ku Klux Klan on January 1. Mayor-elect John L. Duvall has rewarded his friends."[72]

The Klan had indeed won control of both city politics and the local Republican organization, but the Old Guard did not give up power without a fight and Klan politicians themselves were far from unified as they took command. As the new chairman of the Marion County Republican party, George Coffin attempted to mediate between the Klan faction that had brought him to power and the Republican establishment, represented by attorney William H. Armitage, the Republican boss during the Shank administration. As the election drew near, Coffin apparently came to believe that the new administration should contain a mixture of Klan and Old Guard loyalists. Coffin's willingness to work with Armitage infuriated Elliot, Duvall, and the rest of the Klan's political leadership. On the eve of the election, at a massive rally for the Klan slate, Elliot denounced Coffin as a traitor and a "politician" and declared that the Klan would not be connected in any way with the Republican political machine. Over the next few weeks and into the first few months of the Duvall administration, factional struggles between Duvall and the regular Klan leadership on the one hand, and Coffin, other Klansmen, and a few remaining Old Guard Republicans on the other, were at the center of city politics.[73]

Coffin's show of independence was not surprising. Unlike Duvall, whose political support was derived almost entirely from the Klan, Coffin had deep roots in Indianapolis politics and maintained a network of allies and supporters that extended well beyond Duvall and Elliot. Coffin had been a popular figure in the city ever since 1913 when, as a police captain, he personally rescued several hundred people and led relief efforts in flood-ravaged West Indianapolis. Later, when he became chief of police and county sheriff, Coffin made inroads into the Republican establishment and became particularly useful to the party in maintaining relations with leaders in the city's black community. Even though Coffin used the Klan to further his career, he refused to be controlled by its leaders once he became county chairman, because doing so would have cut him off from traditional Republican supporters. Coffin's attempt to hold the middle ground eventually paid off. In the short run, however, he was able to wrestle away only a few patronage positions as the new administration took office.[74]

While the election thrust Klan factions into a struggle for power at city hall, it had also achieved something more substantive. Along with Duvall and the new city council, the Klan had elected a slate of candidates for the Indianapolis Board of School Commissioners. Their election had been the central issue of the campaign and the focus of a bitter struggle between a powerful group of business leaders and the Klan—much like the battles that took place in Richmond and other communities—over who would control public affairs.

Since the end of World War I, the city of Indianapolis had been engaged in a protracted debate over conditions in its public schools. Newspapers and civic groups had criticized the overcrowded classrooms as well as poor heating, ventilation, and plumbing, outdoor toilets, broken windows, and other indications of disrepair. In 1921 and again in 1923, the voters passed bond measures intended to finance a building program. The program was to include the repair and modernization of existing buildings and the construction of two or perhaps three new high schools, six new elementary schools, and a number of other new classroom buildings. In 1921, in the midst of enthusiasm for the building program, a number of business leaders organized the Citizen's School Committee and offered a slate of candidates for the Board of School Commissioners who would "establish sound management and efficiency" in a school administration that was perceived by the public as poorly run. While the citizen's board won election by giving the impression that it supported the building program, over the next four years it demonstrated instead a determined commitment to hold down expenditures for the schools and generally block the building program.[75]

The campaign against the building program was carried out by the Indianapolis Chamber of Commerce, the Indiana Taxpayers Association, their allies on the school board and other supporters in state and local government, and the *Indianapolis News*. The first blow came when the state tax board refused to approve the 1921 school bond after the voters had passed it. Then in 1922 and 1923, the board members of the Citizen's School Committee worked to block other attempts to raise revenues and to postpone decisions about plans for the new school buildings. Further delays grew out of a rupture within the citizen's committee's ranks early in 1923. Two of the school commissioners who had been elected with the committee's support defected and upset the balance of power on the board.[76] In response, the Chamber of Commerce Education Committee issued a report attacking several of the new building designs for their "extravagance" and pointing to various other examples of waste and inefficiency in the schools. One of its recommendations called for the resignation or impeachment of the two "traitorous" commissioners and another who had joined with them in opposing the Citizen's School Committee. The besieged commissioners refused to resign and vigorously defended the building plans in the press. One commissioner, Dr. Marie Halsep, revealed that from the beginning of her term she had been under pressure to oppose the building program and support the position of the citizen's committee and the *Indianapolis News*. "I was warned that I must obey the *News*," she told a reporter. "One person told me 'if you do as the *Indianapolis News* says, your time on the board will be pleasant. If you do not, then watch out.'"[77]

The city's two other major newspapers rushed to defend the school board from the criticisms leveled by the chamber of commerce. The *Times* and the *Star* both concluded that the problems in the city schools could not be blamed on school board mismanagement. They criticized the report as unfairly biased against the building program, since two of the committee members had also sat on the state tax board, which had undercut the 1921 school bond, and two other members were employees of the *Indianapolis News*. Faced with growing opposition—and with another school bond election just one month away—the chamber of commerce softened its position, stating that it would no longer oppose the building program so long as board members agreed to consult "civic bodies" before making major decisions.[78]

The Klan's involvement in the school controversy began with the 1923 school bond referendum. As the March election date approached, the *Fiery Cross* printed a series of stories on conditions in the city schools and the opposition to the building program. The Klan newspaper pointed to the "outside toilets, old stoves, stench and filth and revolting conditions" and reminded its readers that previous attempts to finance the building program had been undermined. The main culprit, in the view of the *Fiery Cross*, was the president of the Board of School Commissioners, Charles W. Barry. Much of the criticism of Barry, a Roman Catholic, came in the form of traditional Klan anti-Catholicism. The *Fiery Cross* concocted a number of schemes whereby Catholic bishops were directing Barry to undermine Indianapolis's public schools. At the same time, however, it made more valid criticisms of the opposition to the building program that came from the Indianapolis Chamber of Commerce, the Indiana Tax Board, and the *Indianapolis News*. When voters passed the school bond, the Klan newspaper declared in a front-page headline: "Sure They Want More Schools."[79]

When the Board of School Commissioners came up for reelection in 1925, the Klan led the fight against the Citizen's School Committee. Five candidates, all backed by the Klan and all pledged to endorse the building program, organized as the Protestant School Ticket. By the time of the election, the citizen's committee and its supporters realized that public support for the building program was too strong to be completely thwarted. Some of the new elementary school buildings had been constructed in 1924, and as the election drew near in 1925, the school board broke ground for two of the new high schools and announced that it had agreed on the plans for constructing the Shortridge High School (the land for which had been purchased more than five years earlier). But the citizen committee's change in policy came too late to satisfy the voters. All of the Klan's school board candidates were elected, and despite continued resistance from business interests, they presided over the completion of three new high schools and several new elementary schools.[80]

One of the high schools finished by the Klan school board was racially segregated Crispus Attucks, located in northwestern Indianapolis. The completion of the school during the Klan's reign, along with the attempt by the Klan city council to enact the residential segregation ordinance, led to a pervasive belief in later years that the segregation campaign of the 1920s grew out of the Klan movement and was implemented primarily by Klan politicians. While the Klan made an excellent scapegoat for later generations of politicians attempting to justify decades of legally sanctioned discrimination, this simply was not the case—despite the fact that the hooded order was a natural home for activists in the segregation campaign and Klan leaders did their part to promote it. The key to understanding segregation and the Klan in Indianapolis is to recognize, first, that Klan politicians were far more interested in patronage and power than they were in ideology and, second, that the Klan and segregation movements were, for the most part, independent of each other. The decision to segregate the public schools was made in 1922 by the board of the Citizen's School Committee at the urging of not only the white neighborhood protection associations but also the chamber of commerce and other business groups that backed the citizen's board.[81] The segregation program did not depend on the Klan's support and would have been carried out had the Klan never existed. The real source of controversy was the building program, not segregation. During the twenties, there were many vehicles for racial prejudice in Indianapolis; the Klan, however, represented one of the few vehicles to challenge the power of commercial business elites in city politics.

6. Political Power

Early in 1924, as they looked toward the primary election in the spring and the general election in November, Indiana Republicans had reason to worry that their control of state politics might be in jeopardy. In a contest for the U.S. Senate just a little more than a year earlier, a Democrat had defeated the hoary dean of Indiana Republicanism, Albert J. Beveridge. Worse, the first-term Republican governor, Warren T. McCray, had been indicted for embezzlement and mail fraud; shortly, he would be convicted and resign his office. Under normal circumstances, such political setbacks might not have caused great concern. Calvin Coolidge was on his way to easy reelection, and in staunchly Republican Indiana almost any respectable GOP gubernatorial candidate could have expected to ride the president's coattails into office. But 1924 was not a normal year in Indiana politics. By that time, the Indiana Ku Klux Klan had reached its zenith and showed signs of becoming a powerful and, perhaps, destabilizing political force. It was generally believed that Beveridge had been defeated in 1922 in part because, unlike his opponent, he had fallen into disfavor with the Klan.[1] Added to this was the fact that Klan leaders already had become embroiled in election-year politics by announcing their intention to support Klansman Ed Jackson, then secretary of state, in the Republican gubernatorial primary. Whether individual Republican politicians applauded or objected to the Klan's presence in politics, none could ignore its importance, and in an uncertain political climate, many would be forced to seek its support.

The takeover of the state GOP by the Indiana Klan produced a shocking political victory. Jackson was elected governor along with almost an entire slate of Klan-endorsed candidates for other state offices. In local elections, the order's candidates won numerous contests and in some communities completely overturned entrenched political establishments. Like Beveridge earlier, politicians who alienated the Klan suffered near-complete failure. Only one openly anti-Klan candidate won a congressional seat in 1924. The other twelve successful contenders had either allied themselves with the Klan or modified their views to avoid the wrath of the Invisible Empire. Furthermore, the Klan's political influence was not confined to the Republican establishment. By this time the secret order had also made deep inroads into the Democratic party, forcing Democratic leaders to deal with an insurgency within their own ranks as they attempted to develop a strategy for defeating the Klan-dominated Republicans.

The ability of the Indiana Klan to influence the workings of both parties and elect pro-Klan candidates at all levels of government represented its greatest political achievement. In 1924, the Klan had been the central issue in Indiana politics and the Klansmen had emerged victorious. The populist energies that had ignited support for the Klan in individual communities also transformed state politics and in the process affirmed that the average white Protestant could exert a powerful influence in public life. At the same time, however, the Klan's victories at the polls did not produce any great changes in the government of Indiana. Klan-dominated officials at the state level enacted little significant legislation, since Klan leaders remained divided and were far more interested in personal gain than in passing any new laws. Klansmen elected to local office found that they could not easily make disappear the social conditions that had stimulated public ire. As candidates, Indiana's Klan politicians were amazingly successful, but as officeholders, they were failures.

The State Election of 1924

More than a year before he was elected governor, Ed Jackson already had positioned himself as the man to beat in the race for control of the statehouse. With the incumbent under criminal investigation and his eventual short-term successor, Lieutenant Governor Emmett F. Branch, showing no signs of launching his own campaign, Secretary of State Jackson appeared to have a clear field between himself and the nomination. Perhaps even more important, as far as many political observers were concerned, Jackson had established a close association with D. C. Stephenson, the person who presumably controlled the massive voting block represented by the Indiana Ku Klux Klan. As early as mid-1923, some journalists predicted that these combined circumstances would ensure Jackson's election.[2]

Jackson's path to high office was also made easier by the boundless ambition of the dominant figure in the Indiana GOP, Senator James E. Watson. Elected to the U.S. Senate in 1916, Watson wrestled control of the Republican state committee from former governor James P. Goodrich and former U.S. senator Harry S. New in 1922 and envisioned running on the national ticket as a candidate for vice-president of the United States in 1924.[3] Toward this end, he quickly accepted the front-runner Jackson and his Klan supporters into his political camp. Watson placed the party organization at their disposal, apparently requiring only two things in return: first, that Jackson and Stephenson keep the persistent Goodrich-New faction at bay; and second, that they put together an Indiana delegation to the Republican National Convention that would stand committed to Watson's vice-presidential nomination.[4]

With the firm support of the party organization and the Indiana Klan, Jackson ran a confident, low-key primary campaign. In his speeches around the state he recited an uncontroversial political gospel of government efficiency, better public schools, and lower taxes. While newspapers identified him as the candidate of the Klan, Jackson steered clear of the issue as much as possible, denying any connection with the secret order. Meanwhile, Stephenson worked to deliver the Klan vote. From his Indianapolis headquarters, he sent more than 200,000 letters in support of Jackson and ordered individual Klan chapters to distribute bulletins providing information and official Klan voting slates. Stephenson called his operation a "military machine" and claimed absolute control over Klan voters organized on township, ward, precinct, and block levels statewide. It is doubtful that Stephenson actually enjoyed such extensive political power or that many chapters bothered to form such elaborate political structures; indeed, neither were necessary to ensure a pro-Jackson consensus among Indiana Klansmen. On election day, Jackson won an easy victory, accumulating more than twice as many votes as his closest rival, Indianapolis mayor and anti-Klan candidate, Lew Shank.[5]

After the election, Indiana newspapers rushed to assess the Klan's political influence. The *Fiery Cross* and other publications that supported the movement attempted to minimize its importance, hoping to deflect potential charges that the Klan was about to begin a reign of terror or corruption in Indiana state government. The pro-Klan *Kokomo Daily Tribune* attributed Jackson's victory in Howard County to the fact that he possessed the "high personal regard" and the trust and respect of the citizens. Jackson himself piously reported that he owed no allegiance to any "voting bloc" and that he opposed "radicalism." Most newspapers, however, interpreted Jackson's victory as proof that the Klan was the dominant political force in the state. In one postelection editorial, the anti-Klan *Indianapolis Times* wrote: "The only answer to the results of the primary is the power of the Ku Klux Klan. While some may not like the idea, there is no longer a particle of doubt that at the present time the Klan is the most powerful influence in Indiana politics. Its influence extends not only to the point of persuading voters to cast their ballots for candidates approved by the Klan, but also to the point of influencing thousands to vote for candidates who are opposed by the Klan. . . . In other words, the Klan was the only big issue in the primary."[6]

In addition to clearly demonstrating the Klan's broad political base, Jackson's victory brought to a head the heated conflict between D. C. Stephenson and the Klan's national leadership. While Stephenson technically had been removed as Grand Dragon of the Indiana Klan before the spring primary, neither he nor Walter Bossert and Hiram Evans had been interested in a showdown over who really controlled the state movement. The week after Jackson's victory, however, Stephenson was ready to make his move to separate the Indiana Klan from the national organization. At a press conference on May 10, he called for an immediate meeting of representatives from every chapter in the state: "I command you in the name of mutual love of our country to assemble in the city of Indianapolis in Cable Tabernacle at one p.m. on the twelfth day of May, 1924, for the purpose of overcoming and driving from our ranks the treacherous and despotic individuals who threaten, if not checked, to excite the indignation of the whole country."[7]

The hastily called convention was a failure, and Stephenson's attempt to rid the Indiana Klan of its "Southern influence" quickly ended. Newspaper accounts of the meeting varied. The *Indianapolis Star* gave it the most credence, reporting that Klansmen from all but a few Indiana counties had attended to denounce Bossert and elect Stephenson as their Grand Dragon. Indianapolis's *Times* and *News* were more skeptical. The *News* related Stephenson's election but commented that "politicians" seemed doubtful that the rank-and-file membership had gone along with the "insurgent Klan." Articles in the *Times* showed that Stephenson himself did not regard the convention as conclusive. Three days after his supposed election, Stephenson again declared that "Bossert rule must go" and called for another meeting of Indiana Klansmen (which never took place) to establish their right to self-determination. The regular Klan leadership naturally discounted Stephenson's revolt. "Nobody can keep a jackass from braying," declared Joe Huffington, the former Stephenson ally, who still headed the Evansville klavern. One week after Stephenson's convention, Bossert and Evans called a Klan meeting of their own, The *News* reported that 1,500 Klansmen from both factions attended and that the insurgent movement had been "crushed." As a last resort, Stephenson attempted to exert control of the all-important Marion County (Indianapolis) klavern, but this, too, failed. Marion County Klan leaders demonstrated their continued loyalty to the national organization by sponsoring a Klan victory celebration later in May. Bossert, not Stephenson, was asked to preside. Only a month after he began his revolt, Stephenson announced that he was no longer associated with any Klan organization.[8]

Stephenson's inability to assume control of the state organization represented an important turn in the course of the Indiana Klan, but it did not significantly affect the former Grand Dragon's standing as a political boss. This can be explained, in part, by the Klan's secret nature, the wildly conflicting reports and the general confusion as to who actually controlled the state movement, and the reluctance of politicians to attack anyone who might be regarded as a leader by members of the massive organization. But the main reason for Stephenson's continued power was that he had already embedded his hooks deeply into Ed Jackson. In 1923, when Stephenson was still the unquestioned leader of the Indiana Klan, he had given thousands of dollars in secret, illegal contributions to Jackson. Also, in the fall of that year, the two men attempted to bribe the embattled governor, Warren McCray, offering him $10,000 and immunity from prosecution if he would appoint a Klansman as Marion County prosecutor.[9] These and, in all likelihood, other indiscretions had welded Stephenson's political career to Jackson's, and his nomination, therefore, ensured Stephenson an influential position.

Empowered by his hold over the popular gubernatorial nominee, and perhaps determined to show that he had not been undone by his break with the Klan, Stephenson played an extremely active role at the Republican state convention two weeks after the primary. Journalists covering the convention paid special attention to the large number of Klansmen among the delegates and to the former Grand Dragon who circulated on the convention floor, lobbying for what became known as the "Klan slate" of nominees for state offices. When all but one name on Stephenson's slate were chosen to accompany that of Jackson on the November ballot, most observers concluded that Stephenson was the dominant figure in state Republican politics, that he had nearly become, as he liked to boast, "the law" in Indiana.[10]

This assessment, however, greatly exaggerated Stephenson's strength and distorted the role of the Klan in Indiana's Republican party. It is not clear, for example, that Stephenson's power could be attributed to his control of Klan delegates; after all, his attempt to take over the state movement had failed just one week earlier. Further clouding the situation was the fact that Walter Bossert and his lieutenants also supported Jackson. They attended the convention and circulated their own slate, which differed from Stephenson's by only a few names.[11]

Stephenson's slate prevailed primarily because he was better connected than Bossert to the party establishment. Bossert had allied himself with the anti-Watson wing headed by James Goodrich and

Harry New. The alliance was a natural one, not only because the Goodrich-New group needed a link with the obviously popular Klan, but also because Bossert himself, even more than his allies, had been a long-standing political opponent of Watson. Before the convention began, however, it became obvious that the Goodrich-New-Bossert faction could not overturn Watson's control of the party organization; the group had tested its strength immediately after the election but failed to unseat the chairman of the Republican state committee, Clyde Walb. On the other hand, Stephenson, through his close association with Ed Jackson, operated safely beneath Jim Watson's political umbrella. Stephenson had worked in district meetings to protect Walb from the Goodrich-New-Bossert assault. As a party leader at the state convention, Stephenson had helped give Watson what he wanted—a delegation to the Republican National Convention that was resolved to support Watson's quest to become Calvin Coolidge's running mate.[12] Therefore, Watson allowed Stephenson to act as a power broker for minor state offices, and delegates to the state convention, aware of Stephenson's link with the party establishment, adopted his slate.

Neither Stephenson nor Bossert took over the Indiana GOP in 1924, and to whatever degree Klan leaders succeeded in injecting themselves into the party's upper echelon, regular Republican leaders remained dominant. The real influence of the Klan within the Republican organization on the state level could be traced not to the power of Klan leaders, but to the enormous Klan vote and the eagerness of Republican leaders and candidates to exploit it. Ed Jackson proved to be the most successful in this regard, and his easy victory over an openly anti-Klan candidate in the primary election demonstrated to the rest of the party the political power inherent in the massive Klan movement. To ensure that the Klan's identification with their party continued, GOP leaders were more than ready to accept Klan leaders into their ranks—even if it was unclear that any of them actually controlled the rank-and-file membership. The dominant figure in the party, James Watson, demonstrated how Klan leaders could be manipulated for political gain. Watson not only controlled Stephenson but he also made agreements with Bossert and Evans.[13] As Indiana Republicans began to anticipate the contest with Democrats in November, one of Watson's more candid statements seemed to epitomize how the party had come to view the Klan. "All I want to do," declared Indiana's senior senator, "is elect Ed Jackson for governor, not because he belongs to anything, but because he belongs to the Republican party. . . . The fact that Mr. Jackson is a Klansman, or is charged with being a Klansman will not in the slightest deter me from using every ounce of power I possess in his support."[14]

Indiana Democrats, too, wanted their candidates elected, and elements within that party entered the primary season determined to garner their share of Klan votes. One gubernatorial candidate, Olin R. Holt of Kokomo, campaigned openly for Klan support. A known pro-Klan candidate had no chance of winning the Democratic nomination, but Holt showed surprising popularity in some districts.[15] The party leadership decided on a neutral strategy for the primary: Klan votes were necessary, but so were those of the traditionally Democratic Catholic constituency. As a result, the party's leading candidate, Carleton B. McCulloch, refused to comment on the Klan during the campaign.[16]

The state Democratic machine, headed for more than twenty years by former Indianapolis mayor Thomas Taggart, hoped to gain several advantages through this neutral strategy in 1924. First, and most important, it would keep McCulloch out of the cross fire between the party's pro- and anti-Klan elements. Second, it would deemphasize the Klan as an issue, allowing the eventual Democratic nominee to attack the Republicans at their weakest point—corruption in both Indianapolis and Washington, D.C., during the McCray and Harding administrations. Refusal to antagonize the Klan would also aid the dark-horse presidential aspirations of Indiana senator Samuel M. Ralston. As both Ralston and Taggart recognized, the Klan would be a central issue at the Democratic National Convention in June, one that had the potential to divide the party. Since Ralston, through his defeat of Albert Beveridge in 1922, had demonstrated that he could satisfy both pro- and anti-Klan voters in a state where the Klan was particularly strong, he and Taggart reasoned that the Indiana senator might be an acceptable compromise candidate in a deadlocked convention. Throughout the spring political season, Ralston urged Indiana Democrats to avoid the Klan issue as much as possible.[17]

The results of the primary election, however, made such a position difficult to maintain. McCulloch had come in first in the Democratic race for governor, but he had not gained a majority of the votes. The second-place finisher was Lafayette mayor George R. Durgan, who had run on the single issue of opposing the Klan. To secure the nomination at the Democratic state convention in early June, McCulloch was forced to concede to the demonstrated strength of the party's anti-Klan wing. In mid-May, much to the delight of the *Indiana Catholic and Record*, McCulloch formally announced his opposition to the Klan. Fortified by McCulloch's conversion, anti-Klan Democrats prevailed at the state convention. Over the objections of the party's vocal Klan supporters, and despite the wishes of some Democrats who thought it wise to remain neutral, the convention delegates approved an anti-Klan plank in the party platform. In the debate over how the article would be worded, anti-Klan Democrats conceded that the Klan need not be mentioned by name; but there was no doubt about the plank's intent. Observing that "the Republican party of our state has, for the time being, retired from the political arena, having been delivered into the hands of an organization which has no place in politics," the platform resolved, "We condemn the efforts of our opponents to make religion, race, color or accidental place of birth a political issue."[18]

The reluctant but eventually firm rejection of the Klan by Indiana's Democratic party established an unambiguous theme for the November election. The Republicans had become deeply entwined with the Klan movement and would count on the electoral support of its membership. The Democrats would place their hopes with those who opposed the Klan. The parties' gubernatorial nominees, Ed Jackson and Carleton McCulloch, both dodged the central issue of the campaign as much as possible. Jackson continued to deny his association with the Klan, often claiming that the Democrats, not he, had introduced the issues of race and religion. He insisted that he intended to protect the rights of all citizens including blacks, Catholics, and Jews. Other Republican leaders urged black voters to stand behind the "party of Lincoln."[19] For most of the campaign, McCulloch resorted to his original neutral strategy, making, in the words of one newspaper, "only passing reference" to his party's opposition to the Klan.[20]

While the candidates pandered to each other's constituencies, Indiana newspapers made it clear that the election was essentially a referendum on the Klan. Many papers, particularly those that opposed the hooded order, gave limited attention to the Klan's role in the campaign. Other publications created enough commotion over the issue to ensure that only the most isolated, out-of-touch voter could fail to know by election time that Jackson was closely associated with the Klan. The state's leading anti-Klan newspaper, the *Indianapolis Times*, ran the boldest campaign against Jackson. As the election approached, the *Times* printed a copy of stolen Klan records that showed Jackson's name among Indianapolis members. It depicted the election as a choice between secrecy, suspicion, and hate on the one hand and democracy and peace on the other, and it compared the "Ku-kluxism of Ed Jackson" to Russian bolshevism. One unusually large *Times* headline, appearing a week before the election, implored Indiana voters simply to "STOP THE KLAN."[21]

On election day, the majority of those voters decided instead that the hooded order deserved their support. Jackson won 53.4 percent of the vote to McCulloch's 46.6 percent.[22]

An Analysis of the Vote

Journalists and political observers who witnessed Jackson's victory generally believed that the Klan had made a shambles of traditional party loyalties. The editors of the *Indiana Catholic and Record*, the *Indiana Jewish Chronicle*, and the *Indianapolis Freeman* naturally were among the most disturbed by an apparently new political alignment that was based almost exclusively on race and religion. After the spring primary, the *Freeman* had declared that "the Republican party in Indiana exists today only in name," that it had been turned into "an agency for the promotion of religious and racial hate." By all accounts, blacks abandoned the Republican party in November, throwing their support to McCulloch.[23] Jewish and Catholic leaders eagerly welcomed the new Democrats. The *Catholic and Record* commended Indianapolis blacks on their "splendid courage and intelligence to rise above party and vote against the enemies of their race." It seemed obvious that the Democrats could use these new supporters, and more, to make up for the many white Protestants who had defected to the Republicans. "When you go into the factories and mills," a Republican party loyalist reported in 1924, "they are all for him [Jackson]. I was out in West Indianapolis recently, the Democratic stronghold, and it looked as though there was a Jackson picture in every window."[24]

Regression analysis shows that the Klan indeed played a powerful role in the election of Ed Jackson and that many Klansmen who had voted Democratic in the previous gubernatorial election switched to the Republicans in 1924. As indicated in Table 6.1, Klansmen preferred Jackson to McCulloch by a wide margin. More specifically, an increase of 1 percent in Klan voters from a given county could be expected to increase the Jackson vote by 0.48 percent, while it would have, at best, no affect on the McCulloch vote. Expressed another way, the percentage of Klansmen who voted for Jackson was 48 points greater than that of non-Klansmen who voted for Jackson. A comparison of the Klan vote for governor in 1924 with that in 1920

Table 6.1

Influence of Klansmen on Votes for Governor and President, 1920–1924*

		b	SE	R^2
Gov. 1924	Rep. (Jackson)	.48	.17	.23
	Dem. (McCulloch)	−.07	.06	.17
Gov. 1920	Rep. (McCray)	.10	.16	.38
	Dem. (McCulloch)	.08	.18	.26
Pres. 1924	Rep. (Coolidge)	.35	.15	.41
	Dem. (Davis)	.05	.18	.44
	Prog. (La Follette)	.10	.05	.19
Coolidge minus Jackson		−.12	.05	.28
McCray minus Jackson		−.45	.11	.36

*Controlling for southern residence and percentage urban, Protestant, Catholic, and renters.

reveals that Jackson's candidacy enticed many Klansmen to cross party lines. In 1920, Klansmen had not yet gravitated significantly toward either the Democratic or the Republican candidate.

Klan membership also seems to have had a positive impact on the vote for two of the three presidential candidates in 1924. Not surprisingly, Indiana Klansmen strongly supported Calvin Coolidge over John Davis. Throughout the campaign the president had refused to make a formal condemnation of the Klan, whereas Davis eventually went on record against the order. The Klan also gave noticeable support to Robert La Follette, the Progressive candidate, a fact that is surprising in light of the candidate's vigorous anti-Klan position, established early in the campaign. La Follette captured only 7 percent of the vote in Indiana. Nevertheless, the percentage of Klansmen who voted for La Follette was 10 percent higher than that of non-Klansmen. To some members of the Klan, it seemed that La Follette's support for working-class political interests outweighed the importance of his stand against the Klan.[25]

Table 6.1 also shows the relationship between Klan membership and two "anti-Klan" variables. Both Coolidge in 1924 and McCray (the Republican gubernatorial candidate) in 1920 gathered more votes than Jackson in 1924. Assuming that those who voted for Coolidge or McCray, but not for Jackson, were put off, at least to some extent, by Jackson's association with the Klan, the difference between the totals for Coolidge and McCray and that for Jackson can be viewed as a measure of "anti-Klan" sentiment. Not surprisingly, regression analysis indicates a strongly negative relationship between Klan membership and this anti-Klan political position.

While Jackson obviously derived some of his strength from Klansmen who had not supported his party in the previous election, it does not follow, as many suspected, that the entire party system in Indiana had been thrown into disarray. Apparently, one of the important aspects of Jackson's election was that while the Klan caused some disturbance and shifting loyalties in the political system, it did not fundamentally alter or realign party allegiances. The great majority of Hoosier voters supported the same party in 1924 that they had in 1920 when the Klan was not an issue. Table 6.2, which gives the results of a regression of voting totals for governor in 1924 with

Table 6.2
Party Alignment in Vote for Governor, 1920–1924

	Republicans 1924	Democrats 1924	Not Voting 1924	Total
Republicans 1920	.81	.06	.11	.42
Democrats 1920	.07	.79	.14	.33
Not Voting 1920	.15	.09	.76	.25
Total	.40	.31	.29	

those for governor in 1920, demonstrates the general continuity in party loyalty.

Technically a "contingency table," Table 6.2 is not difficult to interpret. The "Total" figures represent the percentage of voting-age adults who cast ballots for the Republican and Democratic candidates or who did not vote. The figures in the cells of the table represent percentages of those totals. We can see, therefore, that 81 percent of those who voted for the Republican gubernatorial candidate in 1924 had also voted Republican in 1920, 79 percent of the Democratic voters in 1924 had also supported that party in 1920, and 76 percent of the nonvoters in 1924 had also been nonvoters in 1920. Both parties appeared to lose a similar percentage of its 1920 voters to the other party in 1924 (the Republicans losing 6 percent of its 1920 supporters to the Democrats and the Democrats losing 7 percent to the Republicans). Blacks surely accounted for a great deal of the Republican defection, while Klansmen would have been the most likely to shift from the Democratic to the Republican camp.[26] The Republicans appeared to gain the greatest advantage in 1924 by attracting more support from those who had not voted in 1920. Overall, the percentage of nonvoters increased by 4 percent. Fifteen percent of the Republicans' support in 1924, however, came from those who had not voted in 1920, while 1920 nonvoters accounted for only 9 percent of the Democratic vote in 1924. When these figures are compared with the losses each party experienced in the nonvoting category in 1924 (11 percent for the Republicans and 14 percent for the Democrats), the Republicans emerged with a net gain of 4 percent, while the Democrats suffered a net loss of 5 percent.

The ability of the Klan-dominated Republican party to retain the vast majority of its supporters and at the same time attract more votes from the Democratic and nonvoter ranks than it lost to those categories is a second powerful reason for its victory in 1924. Klansmen rushed to endorse Jackson, but, perhaps even more important, only a relatively small number of Republicans were dissatisfied enough with Jackson to abandon the party. The general picture of stability in the election of 1924 implies that support for Jackson outside the ranks of the Klan was widely dispersed among Indiana voters, not concentrated within specific social groups. Another indication of this trend can be seen in the markedly smaller R^2 figures that accompany regressions of the 1924 governor's race (see Table 6.1 and subsequent tables in this chapter). The smaller R^2 figures mean that the social groups under consideration generally had a less powerful influence in this race than they did in the other elections. In other words, support for the candidates in the election involving the Klan was less concentrated in these groups and more widely dispersed throughout the electorate. In this sense, those who voted for Jackson were much like those who made up the Klan movement—representative of a wide cross section of society.

Religious affiliation, for example, appeared to have only a minor impact on Jackson's victory. Given the traditional association between the Klan and the emotional Protestantism of the 1920s, one might assume that Protestant church members gravitated strongly toward the candidate of the Ku Klux Klan. Regression analysis demonstrates that this was not the case; in fact, it shows a notable trend in the opposite direction. As indicated in Table 6.3, evangelical Protestants (Methodists, Baptists, Disciples of Christ, Presbyterians, and United Brethren) voted for both parties in the gubernatorial election of 1920 and the presidential election of 1924 but supported the Democrats at a somewhat higher level. But in the 1924 gover-

Table 6.3

Influence of Evangelical and Nonevangelical Protestants on Votes for Governor and President, 1920–1924*

		Evangelical			Nonevangelical		
		b	SE	R^2	b	SE	R^2
Gov. 1924	Rep.	.08	.12	.17	−.14	.14	.16
	Dem.	.16	.08	.14	−.05	.13	.11
Gov. 1920	Rep.	.16	.06	.40	.18	.09	.36
	Dem.	.22	.05	.35	−.03	.04	.32
Pres. 1924	Rep.	.15	.06	.42	.05	.03	.33
	Dem.	.22	.05	.46	−.14	.06	.35
	Prog.	−.09	.03	.19	−.08	.05	.11
Coolidge minus Jackson		.10	.03	.32	.23	.06	.30
McCray minus Jackson		.08	.04	.29	.42	.12	.26

*Controlling for southern residence and percentage urban, owners, foreign born, and Klan.

nor's race, many evangelical Protestants reacted negatively to Jackson's candidacy. Members of evangelical churches showed less support for Jackson than the other Republicans studied; they also exerted a significant positive influence on the anti-Klan vote. Nonevangelical Protestants (Episcopalians, Lutherans, and Quakers) gravitated toward the Republicans in the 1920 gubernatorial and 1924 presidential races. That trend was broken in the contest involving Jackson; and even more strongly than evangelical church members, nonevangelicals supported the two measures of anti-Klan sentiment. Nonevangelicals, it should be noted, represented only a small percentage of the state's voters; still, they appear to have been well represented in the group of regular Republicans who refused to support the election of a Klan governor.

If the difference between evangelicals and nonevangelicals was not that great, neither was the difference between all Protestant

Table 6.4

*Influence of Protestant Church Members and Nonchurch Members on Votes for Governor and President, 1920–1924**

		Protestant Church Member			Nonchurch Member		
		b	SE	R^2	b	SE	R^2
Gov. 1924	Rep.	.09	.12	.14	.07	.08	.14
	Dem.	.15	.10	.10	.11	.13	.11
Gov. 1920	Rep.	.15	.07	.38	.11	.04	.31
	Dem.	.22	.05	.26	.09	.03	.24
Pres. 1924	Rep.	.14	.06	.40	.11	.03	.38
	Dem.	.21	.06	.29	.10	.04	.29
	Prog.	−.08	.04	.17	.09	.04	.11
Coolidge minus Jackson		.10	.03	.31	.06	.04	.26
McCray minus Jackson		.09	.03	.25	.10	.06	.24

*Controlling for southern residence and percentage urban, renters, foreign born, and Klan.

Table 6.5

*Influence of Southern Residence on Votes for Governor and President, 1920–1924**

		b	SE	R^2
Gov. 1924	Rep.	−.02	−.02	.18
	Dem.	.05	.02	.14
Gov. 1920	Rep.	−.04	.02	.34
	Dem.	.03	.01	.46
Pres. 1924	Rep	.02	.02	.41
	Dem.	.07	.02	.44
	Prog.	.00	.01	.17
Coolidge minus Jackson		−.03	.01	.21
McCray minus Jackson		−.02	.01	.12

*Controlling for percentage urban, owners, foreign born, and Protestant.

church members and Indiana voters who did not belong to any church (see Table 6.4). Like Protestant church members, nonchurch members showed support for both parties in the 1920 gubernatorial and 1924 presidential contests (although the nonchurch vote appears to have been more equally divided than the Protestant vote). In the 1924 governor's race, there seemed to be some change in the nonchurch vote, with some evidence of anti-Klan sentiment but, still, no overwhelming movement away from the Republicans. Thus, both Protestant church members and nonchurch members were put off—at least to some extent—by Jackson's candidacy, but not enough to cost the Klan candidate the election or dramatically change the party system. Support for Jackson remained broadly distributed across the religious spectrum, and any notion that his victory can be attributed primarily to a coalition of Klansmen and Protestant church members must be rejected.[27]

While religious affiliation mattered little in the decision to support Ed Jackson, geographic differences mattered even less. Voters from southern counties generally favored the Democrats by a small margin in each of the elections considered (see Table 6.5). However, the negative influence on the Jackson vote was slight and insignificant, whereas the two measures of anti-Klan sentiment in this case suggest that southern Republicans remained loyal when it came to supporting the Klan candidate. Regression analysis also shows that the Klan's political triumph did not hinge on either the urban or the rural vote. As Table 6.6 demonstrates, urban and rural status actually exerted little influence on any of the elections in question. There is no consistent pattern of positive or negative influence on the parties, and, more important, the standard errors are too large to make any of the b coefficients significant.

Economic status, measured by owner and renter demarcations as well as by the percentage of wage earners in each county, also seems to have had little effect on Jackson's victory (see Table 6.7). Both owners and renters generally supported candidates in both parties, but, again, the standard errors are large, suggesting that the coefficients are not reliable. For the most part, the same can be said of wage earners. The percentage of wage earners in a given county had no significant effect on the votes for governor and president in 1924

Table 6.6

*Influence of Urban and Rural Residence on Votes for Governor and President, 1920–1924**

		Urban			Rural		
		b	SE	R^2	b	SE	R^2
Gov. 1924	Rep.	.01	.04	.14	.02	.05	.12
	Dem.	.00	.04	.13	.01	.06	.13
Gov. 1920	Rep.	−.05	.02	.32	.00	.03	.29
	Dem.	−.02	.03	.40	.05	.03	.41
Pres. 1924	Rep.	.01	.03	.37	−.04	.03	.32
	Dem.	−.03	.03	.42	.02	.05	.40
	Prog.	.02	.01	.17	−.03	.01	.19
Coolidge minus Jackson		−.09	.05	.14	.07	.07	.12
McCray minus Jackson		.04	.05	.10	−.02	.05	.06

*Controlling for southern residence and percentage owners, Protestant, and foreign born.

(see Table 6.8). In 1920, wage earners did exert a strong negative influence on the Democratic candidate yet had no positive influence on the vote for the Republican candidate. The generally negative coefficients attached to wage earners in each of the elections considered suggest that, as a group, wage earners were less likely to vote. Analysis of nonvoters supports this conclusion. In both gubernatorial races, wage earners had a significant positive influence on the percentage of nonvoters.

It is unlikely that either women or immigrants had a significant impact on the outcome of the 1924 governor's race. Statistical problems make the influence of females difficult to evaluate in this case, but an analysis of the voting behavior of women in all states outside the South shows that female voting patterns differed little from those of males in the elections of 1924 and 1928.[28] Indiana women probably did not deviate from this pattern in voting for governor in

Table 6.7

Influence of Home Owners and Renters on Votes for Governor and President, 1920–1924*

		Renters			Owners		
		b	SE	R^2	b	SE	R^2
Gov. 1924	Rep.	.16	.12	.16	.30	.22	.18
	Dem.	.17	.28	.10	.29	.19	.14
Gov. 1920	Rep.	.07	.11	.38	.21	.28	.34
	Dem.	.06	.26	.26	.28	.17	.46
Pres. 1924	Rep.	.11	.20	.34	.35	.31	.37
	Dem.	.07	.21	.36	.26	.16	.48
	Prog.	.04	.05	.19	−.06	.05	.31
Coolidge minus Jackson		.04	.16	.12	−.03	.14	.12
McCray minus Jackson		.02	.14	.06	.10	.14	.06

*Controlling for southern residence and percentage urban, foreign born, and Protestant.

1924, especially since there is no evidence that women in particular opposed the Klan movement. In the case of immigrants, regression analysis indicates that, as a group, they generally had a negative influence on candidates in both parties. Like wage earners, immigrants showed a tendency to be nonvoters.[29]

The election of Ed Jackson, then, appeared to result primarily from two factors. First, he enjoyed the support of the massive Klan membership, which previously had not voted as a group for a Republican gubernatorial candidate. The Klan bloc was large and instrumental to Jackson's victory. Of equal—perhaps greater—importance, however, was the fact that the Klan issue failed to polarize the electorate in any other significant way. While the evidence presented above suggests that the idea of Indiana's governor being closely tied to the Klan obviously distressed some voters who fit into a variety of social categories, together they had only a slight impact

Table 6.8
*Influence of Wage Earners on Votes for Governor and President, 1920–1924**

		b	SE	R^2
Gov. 1924	Rep.	−.28	.33	.14
	Dem.	−.34	.25	.16
	NV	.08	.03	.17
Gov. 1920	Rep.	−.12	.11	.33
	Dem.	−.30	.12	.45
	NV	.06	.03	.30
Pres. 1924	Rep.	.13	.11	.38
	Dem.	−.06	.11	.50
	Prog.	−.14	.10	.21
	NV	.05	.36	.09
Coolidge minus Jackson		.16	.36	.13
McCray minus Jackson		.41	.36	.09

*Controlling for southern residence and percentage urban, foreign born, owners, and Protestant.

on the outcome of the election. For many more voters, the Klan seemed to be a worthwhile addition, or at least an acceptable one, to party politics and state government.

Local Contests

While the state Republican party managed to abet its continued dominance of state government by accommodating the Ku Klux Klan, local politicians in both parties found the Klan to be a thorny problem. The populist energies inherent in the Klan movement, which had benefited Ed Jackson's statewide campaign, compelled incumbent congressmen and county party organizations to flow with the strong Klan current or risk defeat. By and large, incumbents chose not to oppose the hooded order and were reelected. Yet, in a number of local contests throughout the state, established politicians and party organizations were turned out of office by the Klan vote. Some political leaders simply refused to bend to Klan pressure even if an anti-Klan label jeopardized their careers. In other cases, entrenched political organizations, dominated by economic elites and generally not connected with the movement, were overwhelmed by the groundswell of support for Klan candidates, many of whom were political newcomers, outsiders, or previously unsuccessful contenders. In still other contests, the primary issue was not the Klan itself, but the related issue of enforcing Prohibition and other laws against vice. While the Klan appeared to be the champion of popular concerns about crime and the breakdown of moral standards in society, local politicians often stood as symbols of corruption and failure in city and county government. As such, they represented targets for political assault by the Klan.

In 1924, the candidates for Indiana's thirteen congressional seats, like the candidates for statewide office, generally attempted to gain politically from the Klan movement; those who did not by and large suffered defeat. Five new congressmen were elected, all Republicans and, according to the *Indiana Catholic and Record*, all "subservient or friendly to the Klan." They included, from the First District, Harry E. Rowbottom (Evansville); from the Fifth District, Noble J. Johnson (Terre Haute); from the Seventh District, Ralph E. Updike (Indianapolis); from the Eleventh District, Albert R. Hall (Marion); and from the Twelfth District, David Hogg (Fort Wayne). All but one of the new representatives defeated incumbents in either the general election or the primary. Among the congressmen who won re-election, almost all had placed themselves in a favorable position with the Klan. In the view of the *Catholic and Record*, two incumbents, Albert H. Vestal (Anderson) and Fred S. Purnell (Attica), Republicans from the Eighth and Ninth districts, respectively, had joined the five new congressmen in a pro-Klan position. Four other successful incumbents had assumed neutral positions in their campaigns against openly anti-Klan candidates. They included Democrat Harry C. Canfield (Batesville) from the Fourth District and three Republicans: Richard N. Elliott (Connersville) from the Sixth District, William R. Wood (Lafayette) from the Tenth District, and Andrew J. Hickey (La Porte) from the Thirteenth District. Only two incumbents who risked Klan disfavor were returned to office. Frank Gardner (Scottsburg), a Democrat from the Third District, campaigned as a neutral against a pro-Klan candidate. Democrat Arthur H. Greenwood (Washington) from the Second District ran an openly anti-Klan campaign.[30]

The defeat of incumbent congressmen by Klan candidates provided the most glaring example of Klan populism overwhelming Old Guard political leaders and their organizations. Perhaps the most significant defeat was that of Merrill Moores, the U.S. representative for Indianapolis and the rest of Marion County. After five terms in Congress, Moores epitomized Indianapolis's Republican establishment and under normal circumstances would have been invulnerable. In the 1924 primary, however, Klan leaders, determined to assume control of the party, sponsored their own candidate, Ralph Updike, an Indianapolis attorney. Although a political neophyte and outspent four to one, Updike deposed Moores in a close race.[31] In November, Updike easily defeated anti-Klan candidate, Joseph P. Turk. The Klan slate noted that Updike "bears a splendid reputation," while Turk had an "antagonistic and bitter attitude toward the Knights of the Ku Klux Klan."[32]

In Evansville, Klan populism undid the political leadership of both parties. In the primary, state assemblyman Harry Rowbottom, supported by the Klan and local labor unions, easily won the Republican nomination over Roscoe Kiper, a Dubois County judge who, according to the *Evansville Evening Journal*, was endorsed by the city's "bigger businessmen, especially those identified with the Chamber of Commerce." In the general election, Rowbottom faced incumbent congressman William Wilson, who had refused Klan overtures while running unopposed in the Democratic primary. By not yielding to the Klan, Wilson ensured his own defeat. According to his son, who recounted the events of the campaign in an article published years later, his father realized this fact long before the November election. Wilson's son also recalled that the family had endured the alienation of old friends and a summer of harassment from anonymous telephone callers and midnight pranksters. When the Klan issued its slate in late October, it identified Rowbottom as "a thorough gentleman, capable and reliable" and Wilson as "unfavorable" toward the Klan and "running on an anti-Klan platform." Rowbottom easily defeated the incumbent Democrat.[33]

Congressmen Samuel Cook and Lewis Fairfield were removed

from office in similar fashion. Cook, a Democrat whose district included six counties in the Klan stronghold of north-central Indiana, lost to Albert R. Hall, a Republican school superintendent from Grant County. The Klan slate characterized Cook as a candidate who "tries to assume a neutral attitude" but is "considered to be in sympathy with the anti-Klan element." Hall, in contrast, "bears a splendid reputation" and "is capable and reliable." Fairfield, a Republican, was defeated in the primary by Klan-backed Fort Wayne attorney, David Hogg. Hogg trounced an avidly anti-Klan opponent in November, carrying every county in the Twelfth District.[34]

These and other Klan victories, as significant as they were, represented only the tip of the political iceberg. In all of the congressional contests mentioned above, the election of Klan candidates was accompanied by a general upheaval in local party organizations. Updike's win in Marion County was joined by a Klan sweep of all county offices except that of county prosecutor.[35] In Cass County, where Hall defeated Cook, the Klan assumed strong roles in both parties, the county chairmen, according to the *Logansport Morning Press*, having been "reduced to figureheads." In the primary, Klan candidates captured every county GOP nomination, and each Republican candidate was elected in November. In Evansville, Rowbottom's triumph over the Republican establishment in the primary placed the Klan in a dominant position within the Vanderburgh County GOP. In November, the Klan's Republican ticket won every precinct but three in the usually Democratic county.[36]

The Klan also challenged established political organizations in numerous counties where congressional seats were not seriously contested. Postelection articles in the *Anderson Daily Bulletin* reported that the Klan had taken over the Republican party in Madison County. The newspaper's editor, Dale J. Crittenburg, who himself had been a candidate for the Democratic gubernatorial nomination in May, and who generally omitted any mention of the Klan in the *Bulletin*'s pages, in one editorial reluctantly admitted the political strength of the hooded order. Noting the influence of the Klan in state politics, Crittenburg observed: "In this county they also licked the political platter clean—and balloted all their candidates into office.... There is no controverting this fact." In other counties, party establishments—though not overturned—were at least seriously challenged. By winning a sheriff's race and a county commissioner's seat in Johnson County, Klan-backed Republicans broke a Democratic monopoly of county offices that had lasted nearly three decades. In La Porte, Klan leaders challenged the local Republican establishment in court after the party organization had kept the names of Klan-backed candidates off the primary ballot.[37]

Perhaps the best instance of the Klan's considerable political influence, even in a county where it did not succeed in taking over local government, could be seen in Allen County. Ed Jackson failed to carry the county in the November election—the only major urban county in the state he did not win—probably due to the high proportion of Catholics living in Fort Wayne. (In 1925 Fort Wayne's residents elected a Catholic mayor, suggesting that by 1924 the county may have had a particularly low Klan membership.) Nevertheless, the Klan movement showed considerable signs of political vitality, especially within the Republican party. As mentioned above, the Klan candidate in the Sixth District, David Hogg, unseated the incumbent congressman in the Republican primary and defeated an anti-Klan opponent in November, winning every county in the district and sweeping into office with him a slate of Klan-endorsed county officials. Jackson also won the county in the primary without having established an official local organization.[38]

Regular Allen County Republican leaders could not have been more stunned by the Klan's sweep in the spring primary:

> Local leaders of the Republican party rubbed their eyes and then gasped for breath when they awoke yesterday morning to find that the Ku Klux Klan had dictated every nomination made on their ticket in the county primary Tuesday. The G.O.P. klansmen clucked over the victory, the G.O.P. eagle screamed with disapproval. It is not to say that every man on the ticket is a klansman, although several of them know themselves to be trusted members of the "invisible empire." But Republicans freely admitted that every man who was nominated won his place on the ticket with heavy Klan support. They could not deny that every nominee, with a single exception, had been endorsed on a pink ticket passed out by the Klan on the night before the election.[39]

Popular support for the Klan candidates in Allen County placed an unlikely trio in the forefront of local Republican politics. One member of this group was James G. Jackson, brother of Ed Jackson, Great Titan of Indiana Klan Province No. 12 (the Twelfth Congressional District), and superintendent of the Fort Wayne Home for the Feeble Minded. Fred J. Wehrmeyer, a Fort Wayne jeweler and leader of the Allen County Klan, was also transformed into a Republican party leader as a result of the election. The third and most controversial new Republican power broker was Robert A. Buhler. A previously unsuccessful office seeker and a disbarred attorney who had been convicted of accepting bribes while serving as a judge on the police court, Buhler won the nomination for county prosecutor in the Republican primary. Buhler, according to the *Journal Gazette*, had worked closely with the politically inexperienced Wehrmeyer in selecting the Klan slate in the primary. Some Allen County Republican leaders had been willing to accept Ed Jackson as the nominee for governor, the *Journal Gazette* reported, but Buhler's political rehabilitation through the Klan "stuck in their craw."[40]

Along with Ed Jackson, Buhler lost Allen County in November. His candidacy, like Jackson's, gained such notoriety that it became a focus of the anti-Klan vote; Buhler's nefarious background surely discouraged many Klan voters as well. Still, other Klan-endorsed candidates were elected in Allen County—Hogg for Congress and the rest of the county Republican slate. That, and the fact that Buhler had been nominated in the first place, demonstrated the vulnerability of local political leaders to Klan populism. In Fort Wayne and in communities throughout Indiana, the Klan was such an accepted symbol of popular will and traditional values that the endorsement of a candidate by the hooded order could propel almost anyone, regardless of their background, into elected office and, in the process, displace candidates supported by community business leaders. The issue of the Klan by itself was enough to undermine the Old Guard.

The Klan also threatened established politicians as a result of its close association with the Prohibition and crime issues. Its reputation as a champion of law enforcement and traditional morality contributed to Klan political victories even where these issues did not appear to play a direct role in campaigns. In Fort Wayne, for example, rampant violation of drinking, gambling, and prostitution laws had stimulated public controversy for a year before the 1924 election and surely strengthened the appeal of Klan candidates in Allen County, even though the law enforcement issue did not dominate either the primary or the general election.[41]

In other areas, such as Lake County, Prohibition enforcement and public corruption had a more preponderant influence on the Klan's political victories. By the early twenties, Gary, Hammond, East Chicago, and Lake County's other industrial communities had become Indiana's leading symbols of big-city crime and corruption. Gary, according to one historian, was "an open city, where prostitutes paraded their charms in a manner that no immigrant worker could fail to comprehend, and where criminal entrepreneurs violated the Volstead Act with impunity." The government of Gary, led by Mayor Roswell O. Johnson, had gained a reputation for cooperating with the vice trade and sharing in its rewards. When the Klan appeared in Lake County, crime and governmental corruption became the focus of its energies. The Johnson administration, responding to both its own self-interest and its large immigrant Catholic constituency, naturally opposed the Klan's presence, banning its meetings within the city limits.[42]

The Klan's enmity for Mayor Johnson and the Lake County Democratic organization came to a head in the 1924 election. Disbelieving that regular Republican leaders in the county would fight vigorously to clean up local government, the Klan offered its own slate in the Republican primary. In what the *Gary Post-Tribune* called "the most hotly contested primary election in Gary's history," the voters elected almost all of the Klan's candidates, including those running for the key offices of sheriff and prosecutor. Although it had supported an anti-Klan congressional candidate, the *Post-Tribune* viewed the prospect of Klan-dominated city and county government in a favorable light. In a postelection editorial assessing the new Klan ticket, the newspaper concluded:

> As far as the character of the ticket is concerned there can be little fair criticism. For the most part the candidates are good citizens who ought to serve their country well. Indeed we might go further and say the ticket as a whole is one of the best that has been named in many years in Lake county. And we have no

question that if this ticket is elected Lake county will enjoy an era of law enforcement which will be the beginning of a new day. It is high time, and if the klan [sic] can be held responsible for such an accomplishment it will have much to its credit.[43]

The Klan swept the Republican slate, the editor reasoned, because "people have become dissatisfied with the failure of law enforcement since the country went dry and are now going to break away from the politicians and put into office some men who have no political debts to pay." Noting the Klan's inclination toward religious intolerance, the editorial expressed the hope that the involvement of Klansmen in local government would not exacerbate conflicts between Protestants, Catholics, and Jews: "An intensification of religious differences is to be deeply deplored." The editor believed, however, that "good Americans" would not allow any serious threat to religious liberty and that the Klan deserved a chance to clean up Lake County: "In an orderly attempt to enforce the law either the klan [sic] or any other organization will get much public support as the people are heartily sick of this era of bootleggers and criminals."[44]

Championing reform, and regarding the primary results as evidence of public support for their cause, Lake County Klan leaders entered into a struggle with local Republican leaders for control of the county organization. For a week after the primary, each faction lobbied precinct representatives in an attempt to secure enough votes to have its candidate elected county chairman. Neither side, however, could obtain the required support, and eventually both groups agreed on a compromise candidate, Gary attorney Oliver Starr. In accepting the post, Starr observed: "I take it I was elected county chairman as a neutral." And he promised: "I shall not swerve from my determination to keep the middle of the road." For both factions, the decision to appoint Starr had not been difficult. The large Republican vote in the primary suggested an easy victory over the Democratic machine in November, and neither side wanted to weaken the party's position with a protracted internal struggle. The Lake County Klan did not remove the Republican establishment; it did, however, place itself on an equal footing with the party's Old Guard and make law enforcement the central issue in Republican and Lake County politics. In November, every candidate on the Klan slate was elected.[45]

Prohibition enforcement also dominated local politics in Vincennes in 1924. Unlike the situation in most other Indiana counties, where the Klan worked primarily within the Republican party, in Knox County the Klan was particularly strong within the Democratic ranks. As discussed earlier, local coal miners were extremely active in the Klan, demonstrating their link with the hooded order during Labor Day celebrations and in United Mine Workers politics.[46] The county's leading Democratic newspaper, the *Vincennes Sun*, had also adopted a favorable editorial policy toward the Klan.[47] The Vincennes Republican establishment, led by *Vincennes Commercial* editor Thomas H. Adams and the mayor, real estate broker John M. Grayson, showed much less enthusiasm for the Klan but appeared to be resigned to its importance in politics. For example, the *Commercial* had given favorable publicity to local Klan activities and to Ed Jackson's candidacy, even though Adams was not an avid supporter of the gubernatorial candidate. In later years, the paper would spearhead the anti-Klan campaign within the state Republican party.[48]

During the fall campaign for county offices, Vincennes Republicans showed their willingness to make political use of the Klan movement while demonstrating the importance of the law enforcement issue. A series of articles appearing in the *Commercial* the week before the election charged that the Democratic incumbent prosecutor, Floyd Young, and the Democratic challenger for judge, Joseph Kimmell, had both worked to keep local bootleggers out of jail. The Republican newspaper asserted that Young had refused to file cases against the "liquor pets"; he also had allowed banditry and murder to become "prominent" in the county. Kimmell's law practice had defended more bootleggers than any other local firm.[49]

The *Sun* quickly came to the defense of the Democratic candidates, refuting the charges against Young in particular and maintaining that Mayor Grayson, not Young, was responsible for the "poorly enforced liquor situation." On behalf of Young and Kimmell, the *Sun* requested the help of Edward S. Shumaker, superintendent of the Indiana Anti-Saloon League, and Vincennes's Committee of Ten, the citizen's organization dominated by the Knox County Klan. Shumaker, who had defended Young in an article in the Anti-Saloon League's *American Issue*, arrived in Vincennes a week before the election to investigate charges that Young and Kimmell were "anti-dry." His inquiry, he reported to a meeting of the local ministers' association, showed that the Democratic candidates had clean records. The Committee of Ten did not need to be convinced that the Grayson administration was primarily responsible for continued violation of the liquor laws in Vincennes. For most of 1924 it had been attempting to gather evidence against Grayson and the Vincennes police force, and when the attacks against Young and Kimmell began, it sided with the Democrats. As the campaign came to an end, candidate Young took his case directly to the Klan's meeting hall, the Knights of Pythias building in northern Vincennes. Young spoke there on the Monday before election day—a time that happened to coincide with the date of a regular Klan meeting.[50]

Young's personal appeal to the Klan may have made the difference in the campaign; he won reelection by less than 140 votes. Kimmell was not as lucky. He lost by 70 votes, the narrowness of his defeat, as well as that of Young's victory, demonstrating the reason leaders of both parties had labored to bring in the "law enforcement" vote.

Failure at the Top

By the end of 1924, the Indiana Klan had more than proven its ability to shape the outcome of both local and state elections. Steering the course of state government was another matter, however, for in this area the Klan would have to depend on the ability of its leaders. When the legislature convened in Indianapolis in January 1925, it soon became apparent that those leaders were not up to the task.

While the majority of state senators and representatives had been elected with the support of the Klan, it was clear almost immediately that they would not act in concert to adopt legislation.[51] The lack of unity among Klan legislators became evident when the senate killed a number of anti-Catholic bills that had been passed by the assembly. The first had been a proposal to require daily Bible readings (without comment from the reader) in the public schools. Other measures would have required that no person wearing religious garb be allowed to teach in the public schools (nuns had been teaching in public schools in some counties), all public school teachers themselves be graduates of public schools, and parochial schools use the same textbooks as public schools. Klan representatives in the lower house also attempted to restructure the State Board of Education and to adopt a plan that would permit public school students to be released from classes for the purpose of religious education. None of these bills reached the governor's desk. Only one Klan proposal, requiring that students in all Indiana schools study the U.S. Constitution, was enacted into law.[52]

The Klan's "Americanization" program failed primarily because the men who stood at the center of Indiana's Klan-dominated political arena were not sufficiently committed to its passage. Had Ed Jackson received the anti-Catholic bills, he would have been forced either to undermine a central concern of his Klan constituents or, by signing the bills, to invite a storm of controversy over an obvious attack on religious liberty. A politician, not a Klan ideologue at heart, Jackson probably used his influence to block the potentially controversial legislation.[53]

D. C. Stephenson, who had riveted himself to Ed Jackson, also had sufficient reason not to favor the anti-Catholic bills and to help arrange their legislative death.[54] One reason he opposed the bills was that their passage would have represented a victory for Walter Bossert and the Klan legislators who had proposed them. Even though Stephenson's revolt against the regular Klan organization had failed, he still attempted to present himself as the true leader of the Indiana Klan and continued to regard Bossert as an archenemy. Stephenson also had another reason to oppose the bills. A protracted battle over religion could easily interfere with his primary goal during the legislative session—to seize control of the Indiana Highway Commission. Ever watchful for opportunities to make money, Stephenson hoped to restructure the commission so he would be in a position to sell patronage and influence within the state's rapidly expanding road-building program. The plan crumbled when, in a dispute over seating a new legislator, Democrats and Republicans who opposed Stephenson broke a quorum and fled across the state border to Dayton, Ohio. The anti-Stephenson insurgents refused to return until they had been satisfied that the power of the former Grand Dragon would be limited.⁵⁵

Even Walter Bossert, the official leader of the Indiana Klan, appeared only superficially interested in transforming Klan ideology into law. Like Jackson and Stephenson, Bossert's main concern was political gain. Although he supported the anti-Catholic legislation, he did not fight for its passage. Even the Klan's enemies were surprised by how quickly the order's legislative program evaporated and by the Klan's relatively small impact in the assembly.⁵⁶ Bossert later admitted that the only reason he had ever become involved with the Klan was that he thought it would be his vehicle for election to the U.S. Senate.⁵⁷

On the one issue where support from the public was assured, Indiana's Klan politicians had little difficulty acting with unanimity. The Wright "Bone Dry" bill, which had been initiated by the Indiana Anti-Saloon League to create greater barriers to Prohibition violation, easily gained Klan support. The bill passed both houses of the legislature with only one dissenting vote and represented the only real accomplishment of an elected body that had been brought into office by a powerful wave of White Protestant nationalism but showed itself to be more devoted to political opportunism.⁵⁸

As the legislative session drew to a close in the spring, the first Klan scandal erupted, placing the lackluster assembly in the background and raising fundamental questions about the men who had ascended to the top of Indiana's Invisible Empire. D. C. Stephenson, the most renowned leader of the Indiana Klan, apparently reached the breaking point after three years of inebriating power, first in the Klan and then in state politics. One evening in April 1925, he boarded a train in Indianapolis, accompanied by one of his lieutenants and Madge Oberholtzer, a twenty-eight-year-old clerical worker. During the overnight ride to Chicago, Oberholtzer would later tell Indianapolis police, Stephenson sexually assaulted her, inflicting her in the process with numerous and severe bite wounds. The next day, Oberholtzer attempted suicide using mercuric chloride tablets. While the poison did not immediately kill her, it made her terribly sick, burning her throat and causing her to convulse and vomit blood. In spite of her condition, Stephenson refused to seek medical help, sequestering her in a hotel room until he returned her to her home in Indianapolis the next day. She died about a month later as a result of the poison and the bite wounds, which had become infected.[59]

The horrible details of Oberholtzer's assault and death, combined with Stephenson's arrogant, unremorseful statements to the press during his trial, repelled citizens throughout Indiana and badly damaged the Klan's reputation. Politicians acted quickly to distance themselves from Stephenson and the Klan movement. Governor Jackson severed all contact with Stephenson and in the newspapers downplayed his association with the former Grand Dragon. Old Guard Republicans, acting through the Indiana Republican Newspaper Association, launched a campaign in 1926 to discredit the Klan's involvement in state and party politics. Later that year, a congressional investigation of electoral corruption produced testimony linking both of Indiana's senators with the state Klan movement.[60]

Other events in 1926 added to the wave of negative publicity. In Muncie, a judge sympathetic to the Klan issued a contempt-of-court citation against George R. Dale, editor of the *Muncie Post Democrat*, and halted sale of the newspaper because Dale had run a series of articles examining the Klan's role in the Delaware County courts. A number of groups—both inside and outside Indiana—protested this attack on the press and donated money for Dale's legal fees. In the fall of 1926, a grand jury met in Indianapolis for twelve weeks to investigate more charges against Stephenson and his lieutenants. No indictments resulted, but the public perception of the Klan continued to suffer.[61]

In the following year, the Klan political machine in Indianapolis dissolved in scandal as corruption destroyed Mayor John Duvall and the Klan city council. Duvall was convicted of accepting illegal campaign contributions and was forced to resign his office. Several members of the city council were found guilty on a variety of other charges. Throughout 1927 and 1928, the Indianapolis Chamber of Commerce and the *Indianapolis News* kept up a steady campaign against the Klan school board, charging its members with misuse of public funds, corrupt practices in the awarding of construction contracts, and a number of other offenses. The negative publicity had the intended affect. In 1929, when the Citizen's School Committee regained control of the school board, it promised to cut "extravagance" in the school construction program, vote down proposed pay raises for teachers, end "free" kindergarten, and look into the possibility of repealing the mandatory school attendance law. Only George Coffin survived the counterattack by the Old Guard Republicans. Because he had maintained his ties with the political establishment throughout the Klan era, Coffin held onto his post as Republican county chairman until his death in 1938.[62]

The ultimate disgrace came when the Klan governor himself was brought before the court. Unwilling to suffer alone, and furious that Ed Jackson had not pardoned him within a few months of his conviction, D. C. Stephenson began to hint in the summer of 1927 that he was ready to release information about Jackson's political dealings. After Stephenson testified before a Marion County grand jury, Governor Jackson was indicted for bribery. At the trial in September, Stephenson revealed that he had given illegal campaign contributions to Jackson and that, together, the two men had tried to bribe former governor Warren McCray.[63] Jackson escaped conviction and completed his gubernatorial term, but by that time, Indiana, which had once represented the Klan's greatest success, now symbolized its most embarrassing failure.

7. Conclusion

Many Hoosiers were deeply troubled by the ability of the Ku Klux Klan to influence state and local politics. Blacks, Catholics, Jews, immigrants, and numerous white Protestants expressed amazement, outrage, and frustration that the Klan had come so far. They also worried, of course, that Klan-dominated government would produce undesirable changes in Indiana. After the Klan's victory in the 1924 primary, the state's leading black newspaper concluded that "the Republican party exists in Indiana today only in name," having been turned into "an agency for the promotion of religious and social hate." The *Indiana Catholic and Record*, after struggling against the Klan throughout the spring and fall campaigns, could not bring itself even to mention the outcome of the November election.[1]

Fears that Indiana had embarked on a new and perhaps dangerous political course, however, were not realized. By mid-1925, the Klan movement had lost much of its momentum. Active membership had declined; the Klan-controlled state legislature had adjourned, leaving behind a generally insignificant record; and the organization's former Grand Dragon was serving a life sentence for murder. The election of 1924 had been not a beginning but a climax.

Success in the statewide campaign actually contributed to some extent to the Klan's decline by providing an obvious demonstration of continued white Protestant hegemony in Indiana. After all, the central issue of the campaign had been the Klan itself, not Prohibition, the Catholic threat, racial fears, or immigration. Even when these issues were raised, the electorate regarded them primarily as symbols of a wide range of commonly felt concerns, anxieties, and indignations. On one level, the Klan's political victory resulted not from a strong attachment to a specific agenda, but from the need of a huge section of the population to express its frustration arising from a complex, often ambiguous array of social and cultural conditions. In this regard, the election of 1924 had been extremely successful—so successful, in fact, that it seemed to begin dissipating the energy behind the Klan movement. The election proved that Klansmen could be elected to all levels of public office and affirmed that Indiana's white Protestant majority was still in command. Men and women who had believed that the foundation of their way of life might be crumbling beneath their feet could feel an uncommon sense of satisfaction. Deeply held traditional values, a common ethnic bond, and a sense of community seemed to have been upheld.

Of course, the Indiana Klan did not immediately disappear after 1924. The Indianapolis city election of 1925 represented one example of the order's continued popularity in some places. Many klaverns held meetings and scheduled holiday social activities just as they had in previous years, even though they sparked much less interest. Klan political candidates continued to be elected in other communities as well, and a brief Klan rejuvenation occurred in response to Al Smith's presidential campaign in 1928.[2] But the movement never again stimulated the wild excitement of 1923 and 1924, and, given the enormous following it attracted in that brief time, the speed with which it appeared to lose significance was remarkable indeed.

Clearly, the shameful scandals involving the leaders of the Indiana Klan played a major role in the decline of the statewide movement. The ugly details of Stephenson's assault and murder of Madge Oberholtzer; his obvious contempt for the judicial system that tried him and his smug belief that he would escape punishment; the association of the governor of the state and the mayor of its largest city with Stephenson, or even with the organization that had allowed such a man to be its leader—all of these events violated the moral standards that the Klan had claimed to champion. Surely, thousands of Klansmen abandoned the movement as a direct result of the scandals. One Lake County Klansman probably spoke for many disenchanted members when he explained in his letter of resignation that he still supported the Klan's ideals but could no longer follow its corrupt leaders.[3]

It may also have been inevitable that the Klan would begin to lose momentum once the building phase of the movement was complete and the onus fell—for the first time—on the order's inept leaders to produce something tangible with their newfound political influence. Stephenson and the other salesmen and office seekers who maneuvered for control of Indiana's Invisible Empire lacked both the ability and the desire to use the political system to carry out the Klan's stated goals. They were disinterested in, or perhaps even unaware of, grass roots concerns within the movement. For them, the Klan had been nothing more than a means for gaining wealth and power. These marginal men had risen to the top of the hooded order because, until it became a political force, the Klan had never required strong, dedicated leadership. More established and experienced politicians who endorsed the Klan—even those who did not but felt pressure to pursue some of the interests of their Klan constituents—also accomplished little. Factionalism created one barrier, but many politicians had supported the Klan simply out of expedience. When charges of crime and corruption began to taint the movement, those concerned about their political futures had even less reason to work on the Klan's behalf.

Even if the Klan had not been undermined by corruption and weak leadership, the movement could not have survived long as a viable political force. Klan organizations inspired constant, dedicated opposition by black, Catholic, Jewish, and immigrant groups. In many of the nation's major urban centers, these groups were so powerful that the Klan could not hope to sustain any lasting momentum. Even in Indiana, spokespersons for ethnic minority groups helped thwart the Klan with persistent reminders that democratic institutions were not well served by an organization that had a reputation for secrecy, violence, and bigotry. At the same time, none of the social ills that had stimulated support for the Klan showed any sign of disappearing and very quickly the order proved to be useless as a vehicle for change or reform. The problem of Prohibition violation, for example, was not made any less intractable by the Bone Dry bill, Ed Jackson, or other Klan politicians at the state and local level. Illegal alcohol continued to flow, and by the mid-1920s few white Protestants entertained hope that anyone or any movement could succeed in stopping it.[4] Even more significant, the vast array of social changes that had undermined traditional values, altered the structure of community life, and concentrated more authority into the hands of elites was also resistant to the Klan's unfocused efforts. In fact, business leaders and Old Guard politicians who had been displaced by the movement stood ready to counterattack at the first opportunity.

D. C. Stephenson, Ed Jackson, and John Duvall provided perfect openings for Indiana's Republican establishment. Once the scandals erupted, Old Guard leaders began a two-year campaign to distance the party from the Klan movement and to explain the order's political influence as a particularly insidious episode of corruption. In 1926, an unidentified group of wealthy Republican businessmen financed a "secret investigation to find out on whose front door the crookedness could be hung." Concurrently, the editors of fifteen Republican newspapers around the state agreed to take up the same task, publishing a series of investigative reports on the Klan's political corruption. One of the leaders of this effort was Thomas H. Adams, of the *Vincennes Commercial*, who initially had been receptive to the local Klan chapter. Edward H. Harris of the *Richmond Palladium*, a business booster and longtime opponent of the Klan, was also deeply involved, attacking state and local Klan politicians in a series of reports appearing from 1926 to 1928. The anti-Klan *Indianapolis Times*, while not as closely linked with the Republican establishment as other newspapers, gained the widest reputation for its assault on political corruption within the Invisible Empire; in 1928, it won the Pulitzer Prize for a two-year series of articles.[5]

Soon after the scandals began, the Republican establishment was back in control of the party and the politicians who had been elected with Klan support in 1924 or 1925 could no longer count on the Klan voting bloc. Those who remained in office for more than a few years had no choice but to accept the power of the Old Guard. The Republican establishment would not be successfully challenged again until after 1929, when the Great Depression transformed state and national politics.[6]

Still, the Indiana Klan movement was extremely powerful, albeit for a short time. On the surface, the movement symbolized ethnic chauvinism and political corruption. But beneath the outer layers of racial and religious bigotry and venal leadership, both of which hardly distinguished the Klan movement from America in general during the 1920s, there existed a more complex and fundamental explanation for the Klan's popularity. Indiana's Invisible Empire was molded out of populist energies representing a broad spectrum of concerns. It became a kind of interest group for average white Protestants who believed that their values should be dominant in their community and state as well as in American society. Those who joined the Klan did so because it stood for the most organized means of resisting the social and economic forces that had transformed community life, undermined traditional values, and made average citizens feel more isolated from one another and more powerless in their relationships with the major institutions that governed their lives.

A number of recent works on the Klan have drawn similar, if not exactly the same conclusions. Taken together, these works along with this book provide some justification for making several new generalizations about the Ku Klux Klan of the 1920s.

First, historians should abandon the notion that the Klan movement was driven simply by a sense of conflict between white Protestant America and urban-immigrant America. Although white Protestants had been aroused, and Catholics, Jews, and blacks represented convenient, time-honored targets for the expression of their pent-up frustrations, the real source of white Protestant discontent was more deeply rooted in a broader process of social change. Previous interpretations of the Klan were flawed because they began with the premise of ethnic conflict and built their arguments around the Klan's rhetoric rather than around its activities. According to the oldest explanation, the conflict was between rural, small-town white Protestants and the ethnically diverse cities. Later, Kenneth Jackson argued that the site of the struggle actually lay within the nation's large cities, where ethnic minorities encroached on native white Protestant hegemony. In Orange County, California, however, the Klan took over local government, completely ignoring the small population of Mexican-Americans that resided there. And in Colorado, where the Klan was powerful enough to assume control of state government, Robert Goldberg found that ethnic minorities constituted an insignificant threat to white Protestant authority and were not the main focus of the Klan movement. Even in Youngstown, Ohio, where the immigrant and black populations had made native-born white Protestants a numerical minority, the Klan's success resulted from widespread support for traditional moral values and law enforcement, not from problems of residential competition or economic marginality among white Protestants.[7]

In Indiana, direct ethnic conflict also played only a minor role in the success of the Klan movement. Patterns in statewide Klan membership showed no significant relationship with the geographic distribution of the state's relatively small number of ethnic minorities. The Klan thrived in cities, but it demonstrated equal strength in many rural areas where immigrants and blacks represented only a miniscule proportion of the population. In fact, regression analysis shows that residents of communities with populations of less than 2,500 were no more likely to join the Klan than residents of communities with 25,000 or 250,000 inhabitants. For the most part, individual Klan chapters paid little attention to local neighborhoods of Catholics, Jews, or blacks where they existed. Given the insignificant threat these groups represented to white Protestant dominance and the fact that numerous means already existed to control them if it appeared necessary, Klan chapters generally had little reason to concern themselves with harassing ethnic minorities.

Klan activities and membership patterns demonstrate that the main stimulus of the Klan movement had been the deterioration of a sense of cohesion, order, and shared power in community life, a process in which Indiana's ethnic minorities played only a small role. While the Klan was popular throughout the state, membership was highest in regions where economic growth had done the most to alter the traditional sense of community. These regions naturally included the cities, both large and small, that had been transformed by industrial expansion. They also included the mining counties of southwestern Indiana and a large number of rural counties, particularly those with the most successful and most modern commercial farms. The most popular Klan activities were those that engendered a sense of community, that drew together disparate social groups through a powerful appeal to white Protestant ethnic identity. These comprised not only massive demonstrations, picnics, and parades and well-supported efforts to bring about civic improvements; they also included political campaigns that challenged economic and political elites for the control of community affairs.

Related to the idea that the outpouring of ethnic consciousness resulted from the decline of community rather than conflicts with ethnic minorities per se is a second general conclusion having to do with where the national Klan movement was centered. The views that the Klan owed its strength to rural and small-town America or that the nation's large cities constituted the core of the Klan movement are both incorrect. Goldberg found equal enthusiasm for the hooded order in small Colorado towns and in Denver, concluding that, in this state, at least, "the urban-rural dichotomy proved useless as a guide to understanding the secret society."[8] This was also true of Indiana. Taken together, the cases of these two states suggest that the heart of the national Klan movement lay in those regions of the country, both urban and rural, where white Protestants represented an overwhelming majority and where an awakened sense of white Protestant ethnic identity could be used to gain greater popular control over community affairs. This would explain why the Klan achieved nationwide popularity in the 1920s and why it reached its greatest strength in states such as Colorado, Indiana, Kansas, Oklahoma, Oregon, and Texas, and in individual communities like Orange County, California, where white Protestants were particularly dominant. It also would explain why the Klan was doomed to fail in large cities such as Chicago and New York, where the influence of ethnic minorities matched or surpassed that of white Protestants.[9]

A third idea supported by this and other studies relates to the timing of the national Klan movement. After all, the hooded order had been active since 1915 and the strains on community cohesion had much deeper roots. Why, then, did the Klan erupt when it did? Traditionally, scholars have cited the residual effects of World War I: leftover nationalist passions, anxiety about renewed mass immigration from Europe, fear of internal subversion from political radicals, and postwar economic difficulties. By feeding the notion of a besieged America, these forces did contribute to the power of the Klan, just as they had helped spark the postwar race riots and the Red Scare.[10] Another common explanation, however, has been that the Klan epitomized the desire of Americans to "return to normalcy," to abandon the crusades of the Progressive Era.[11] This view now appears to be incorrect. In Indiana, Colorado, and Orange County, California, the Klan represented a desire to carry on many of the goals and ideals of those crusades, not reject them. The Klan movement was triggered, in good part, not by disillusionment with progressivism, but by a yearning to fill the void left by its demise. The great symbol of that desire was Prohibition. Support for Prohibition represented the single most important bond between Klansmen throughout the nation. The crisis created in communities throughout the United States by the ban on alcohol provided the greatest catalyst for the Klan movement, and during the early 1920s, the Klan became the most popular means of expressing support for the Noble Experiment.[12]

The pattern of confrontation between Klan groups and community elites represents another justification for the populist interpretation. At a time when organizations like the Rotary club, Chambers of Commerce, and the Indiana Farm Bureau had emerged to advocate a definition of community based almost exclusively on the idea of business success, the Klan drew together a powerful cross section of community social groups that were devoted to the primacy of a more traditional value system. Through massive demonstrations, parades, and holiday celebrations—many of them the largest ever to occur in individual towns and cities—Klan chapters forcefully asserted the notion that the essence of community was its shared ethnic culture, not simply its ability to generate profit. To members of the business elite, who generally shunned the Klan and, in many communities, led the fight against it, such populist energies constituted a grave threat, one that eventually was manifested in a wave of Klan political victories over established party organizations.

Appendix. Documentation

ll of the Klan membership documents used in this study were made available by the Indiana Historical Society with the stipulation that I not reveal the names of individual Klansmen. Accordingly, the names of Klansmen mentioned in this study were disclosed by another source. The identities of the Wayne County Klansmen I interviewed for this book are not exposed. No one I interviewed and identified by name was a member of the Klan.

Occupational samples for Indianapolis and Richmond were made using city directories for 1922–25. For Indianapolis, the names of five hundred Klansmen were selected at random from the *Tolerance* membership list ("Complete Roll of Indianapolis Klux," Indiana Historical Society) using a random number table. Names that could not be located in the city directory were replaced by other randomly selected names from the Klan list. A random number table was then used to select the names of five hundred men directly from the directory. Occupational categories were modeled after those used in Thernstrom, *The Other Bostonians*. Thernstrom's Appendix B (pp. 289–302) provides a list of occupations for each category. The same technique was used to obtain the occupational sample for Richmond. The only difference between the Indianapolis and Richmond samples is that the Richmond sample was compared with a sample of *non-Klansmen*, rather than with a sample of all men living in Richmond.

While the occupations of Indianapolis and Richmond Klansmen could be determined from readily available public records, their religious affiliations proved much more difficult to establish. In the case of Indianapolis, it would have been almost impossible to discover the church membership status of a sample of five hundred Klansmen. This would have required obtaining the membership records of virtually all of the Protestant churches in Indianapolis during the 1920s. Even if such records existed for all churches, it is doubtful that a meaningful number of churches would have allowed their membership registers to be searched for the names of former Klansmen. Indeed, gaining the cooperation of even a small number of churches in this effort required months of work. The only reasonable way to estimate the religious affiliation of Indianapolis Klansmen was to construct a very large sample of Protestant church members from one geographic area of the city that paralleled the spectrum of Indianapolis's Protestant denominations. Each denomination and group of denominations could then be checked against the *Tolerance* membership list to establish the percentage of Klan members.

The churches selected were located in the central part of Indianapolis and generally represented the largest Protestant congregations in the city. Almost all membership records were obtained directly from the churches themselves; the balance were made available by the Manuscripts Division of the Indiana State Library and the Roy O. West Library Archives, DePauw University, Greencastle, Indiana. Indianapolis churches consulted in this study are cited in the bibliography. The names of church members for the sample were selected using a random number table. The number of names chosen for each denomination is proportional to the church membership figures for Indianapolis as reported in the U.S. Bureau of the Census, *Religious Bodies* (1926).

For the city of Richmond, I originally attempted to construct a similar sample of Protestant church members. This was not possible, however, because key Presbyterian and Baptist churches did not wish their records to be used in this study. An acceptable alternative existed thanks to Richmond's public library. The Morrisson-Reeves Library contains an extensive biographical index of newspaper articles, a very large percentage of which are obituaries. In their obituaries, the Richmond newspapers regularly listed the religious affiliation of the deceased. Using a random number table, I selected the names of more than seven hundred members of the Richmond Klan, then located obituaries for more than a third of these men. Those not linked with a church in their obituaries were counted as "not affiliated." The obituaries used in this study covered the entire period between 1927 and 1981 and did not account for changes in religious affiliation that occurred during those years. Obituaries also had the disadvantage of providing information only about Klansmen who were long-term residents of Richmond. More obscure or geographically mobile individuals were probably underrepresented in the sample.

Occupational and religious data for Crown Point Klansmen came directly from Klan membership applications located in the Crown Point Ku Klux Klan Collection, Indiana Historical Society.

The sample of residence locations for Indianapolis Klansmen and all males in Indianapolis was taken from the Indianapolis Klan membership list published in *Tolerance* and the *Indianapolis City Directory*; these locations appear on the *National Street Map of Indianapolis* (National Map Company, 1921; courtesy of the Indiana State Library). Boundary lines are as follows:

For the *North-Central* area:
Washington Street on the south; White River on the west; Thirtieth Street on the north; State, West, Windsor, Commerce, Roosevelt, and Martindale avenues on the east.

For the *South-Central* area:
Washington Street on the north; White River on the west; Morris Street on the south; State Avenue on the east.

For the *North:*
White River and Martindale Avenue on the west; Thirtieth Street and Massachusetts Avenue on the south and east.

For the *West:*
White River on the east.

For the *South:*

Morris, Ayers, and Prospect streets on the north.

For the *East:*

Morris, Ayers, and Prospect streets on the south; State, Windsor, Commerce, and Massachusetts avenues on the west and north.

Notes

Chapter 1

1. The best general history of the Klan is Chalmers, *Hooded Americanism*; see also Wade, *The Fiery Cross*. On the Reconstruction-era Klan, see Trelease, *White Terror*; on Klan organizations and leaders after 1950, see Sims, *The Klan*.

2. In addition to Chalmers's *Hooded Americanism*, the standard histories of the Klan of the 1920s are Alexander, *The Ku Klux Klan in the Southwest*; Jackson, *The Ku Klux Klan in the City*; Loucks, *The Ku Klux Klan in Pennsylvania*; Mecklin, *The Ku Klux Klan*; Rice, *The Ku Klux Klan in American Politics*. More recent studies include Gerlach, *Blazing Crosses in Zion*; Goldberg, *Hooded Empire*; Jenkins, *Steel Valley Klan*; Lay, *War, Revolution, and the Ku Klux Klan*. See also Bennett's treatment of the Klan in his recent examination of nativism and right-wing political extremism in American history, *The Party of Fear*, pp. 199–237. For an extensive analysis of the literature on the Klan movement of the twenties, see Moore, "Historical Interpretations of the 1920's Klan."

3. On the Klan's great strength in Indiana, see Alexander, *The Ku Klux Klan in the Southwest*, pp. 53, 250; Bennett, *The Party of Fear*, pp. 232–33; Chalmers, *Hooded Americanism*, p. 163; Goldberg, *Hooded Empire*, pp. xi, 178; Jackson, *The Ku Klux Klan in the City*, pp. 90, 144–60, 237; Leuchtenburg, *The Perils of Prosperity*, p. 210; Wade, *The Fiery Cross*, pp. 215–47.

4. Murray, *The 103rd Ballot*; Burner, "The Democratic Party in the Election of 1924"; White, *Politics*; Chalmers, *Hooded Americanism*, pp. 202–12; Levine, *Defender of the Faith*, pp. 307–16.

5. The Denver and Fremont County Klans are discussed in Goldberg, *Hooded Empire*, pp. 12–48, 118–48. On El Paso, see Lay, *War, Revolution, and the Ku Klux Klan*; on Anaheim and other Orange County, Calif., communities, see Cocoltchos, "The Invisible Government and the Viable Community"; on Oregon, see Chalmers, *Hooded Americanism*, pp. 88–89; on Youngstown, see Jenkins, *Steel Valley Klan*, pp. 39–54.

6. See, for example, Chalmers, *Hooded Americanism*, pp. 113–15; Jackson, *The Ku Klux Klan in the City*, pp. 18–23; Leuchtenburg, *The Perils of*

Prosperity, pp. 209–13; Hofstadter, *The Age of Reform*, pp. 293–97; Higham, *Strangers in the Land*, pp. 285–99.

7. For a recent assessment of Dixon and the meaning of his works, see "Tom Dixon and *The Leopard's Spots*" in Williamson, *The Crucible of Race*, pp. 140–79, and Cook, *Fire from the Flint*. On Griffith's film and its importance to the Klan movement, see Jackson, *The Ku Klux Klan in the City*, pp. 3–4, 70, 81, 118; Chalmers, *Hooded Americanism*, pp. 22–27; Wade, *The Fiery Cross*, pp. 119–39.

8. For an example of this interpretation, see "The Bigoted Twenties" in Lipset and Raab, *The Politics of Unreason*, pp. 110–49.

9. Moore, "Historical Interpretations of the 1920's Klan"; Mecklin, *The Ku Klux Klan*, pp. 3–51, 53–54, 99, 103; Tannenbaum, *Darker Phases of the South*, pp. 3–38; Fry, *The Modern Ku Klux Klan*; Frost, *The Challenge of the Klan*; Bohn, "The Ku Klux Klan Interpreted"; Duffus, "The Ku Klux Klan in the Middle West," pp. 363–72; Chalmers, *Hooded Americanism*, p. 113; Higham, *Strangers in the Land*, pp. 285–86, 289; Hofstadter, *The Age of Reform*, pp. 293–94; Leuchtenburg, *The Perils of Prosperity*, p. 208.

10. Moore, "Historical Interpretations of the 1920's Klan." Jackson's *Ku Klux Klan in the City* has been most responsible for establishing this view. Lipset and Raab relied heavily on Jackson's work in making their assessment of the Klan movement in *The Politics of Unreason*, pp. 110–49. For a full explanation of status anxiety theory, see Bell, *The Radical Right*, particularly the essays by Bell, Hofstadter, and Lipset. On the idea that Klansmen were nearly always fundamentalists, see Hicks, *The Republican Ascendancy*, pp. 181–82; Higham, *Strangers in the Land*, p. 293; Hofstadter, *The Age of Reform*, pp. 288–89; Leuchtenburg, *The Perils of Prosperity*, p. 209; Miller, "The Ku Klux Klan," p. 223.

11. Chalmers's *Hooded Americanism*, which includes a detailed list of southern terrorist bombings during the civil rights movement (pp. 356–65), was published in 1965. Jackson's *Ku Klux Klan in the City* was published in 1967. One of the most publicized acts of Klan violence during the civil rights era occurred in Neshoba County, Miss., in 1964, when members of the local Klan executed three civil rights workers. For an account of the murders and the public outcry that followed, see Wade, *The Fiery Cross*, pp. 333–44.

12. It must also be noted that although the Klan movements of the civil rights and Reconstruction eras had much in common, they were also different in important ways. The Klan and other Klan-like organizations of Reconstruction cut a much wider path through southern society, were far more violent, and had a more profound impact on politics. During the election year of 1868, for example, Klan groups assassinated hundreds of black Republican politicians and voters and in many states succeeded in keeping blacks away from the polls. Perhaps as many as one thousand such murders took place in Louisiana alone. See McPherson, *Ordeal by Fire*, pp. 443–45; Trelease, *White Terror*, pp. 92–136.

13. Jackson (*The Ku Klux Klan in the City*, p. 239) estimates that there were 50,000 Klansmen in Chicago and 35,000 Klansmen in Detroit during the 1920s.

14. Lipset and Raab, *The Politics of Unreason*, pp. 110–49; Hofstadter, *The Age of Reform*, pp. 293–94; Chalmers, *Hooded Americanism*, pp. 32–33, 291–94.

15. On the rise of conservative and New Right movements in post–World War II America and their relationship to earlier nativist movements, see Bennett, *The Party of Fear*, pp. 273–408.

16. Klan membership in Indiana is discussed in detail in Chapter 3. The total membership estimate is based on totals for eighty-nine of Indiana's ninety-two counties listed in Crown Point Ku Klux Klan Collection, Local Officers of the Ku Klux Klan, and Wayne County Ku Klux Klan Collection, Indiana Historical Society. Population figures are drawn from U.S. Bureau of the Census, *Fourteenth Census: Indiana Compendium*. Similar documents concerning the women's organization are not available, but newspaper accounts indicate that many women were drawn to the Klan. A recent dissertation focusing on one county in Georgia during the late 1920s found a good deal of support for the Klan by local women. The author concluded that support for traditional gender roles explains a large part of the Klan's appeal. MacLean, "Beyond the Mask of Chivalry," pp. 1–61.

17. In Richmond, the largest veterans' and fraternal organizations contained several hundred members, whereas the Klan's membership approached four thousand. In 1926, the Methodist church in Indiana had just over 288,000 members over age thirteen. See U.S. Bureau of the Census, *Religious Bodies*, 1926, 1:174.

18. The Klan's assault on local party organization is discussed in Chapter 6.

19. Stephenson's importance in the Indiana Klan and the Klan movement generally is discussed in Chalmers, *Hooded Americanism*, pp. 162–74; Jackson, *The Ku Klux Klan in the City*, pp. 144–60; Wade, *The Fiery Cross*, pp. 215–47. The best histories of the Indiana Klan are Cates, "The Ku Klux Klan in Indiana Politics"; Davis, "The Ku Klux Klan in Indiana"; Madison, *Indiana through Tradition and Change*, pp. 44–75; Weaver, "Knights of the Ku Klux Klan."

20. See "Complete Roll of Indianapolis Klux," Crown Point Ku Klux Klan Collection, Local Officers of the Ku Klux Klan, and Wayne County Ku Klux Klan Collection, Indiana Historical Society.

21. See, for example, Chalmers, *Hooded Americanism*, pp. 162–74; Leuchtenburg, *The Perils of Prosperity*, pp. 210–13; Wade, *The Fiery Cross*, pp. 215–47.

22. See Chalmers, *Hooded Americanism*, pp. 162–74; Leuchtenburg, *The Perils of Prosperity*, pp. 210–13; Wade, *The Fiery Cross*, pp. 215–47.

23. The social characteristics of Klan members throughout the state are discussed in Chapter 3.

24. Ibid.

25. For a discussion of violence and the Indiana Klan movement, see Chapter 2.

26. On the activities of Klan politicians, see Chapter 6.

27. On the origin of the term *populist*, see Hicks, *The Populist Revolt*, p. 238.

28. See Chapters 4 and 5.

Chapter 2

1. Wilson, "Long Hot Summer in Indiana"; Local Officers of the Ku Klux Klan, Indiana Historical Society, p. 4.

2. On Huffington's background, see Bennett Directory Company, *Evansville City Directory*, 1920–26; Chalmers, *Hooded Americanism*, p. 163; Jackson, *The Ku Klux Klan in the City*, p. 145; Weaver, "Knights of the Ku Klux Klan," pp. 146–47.

3. When Stephenson went to prison, an associate wrote a book defending the former Grand Dragon. It stated that Stephenson had been an Evansville businessman—a partner in a retail coal company—before he became involved with the Klan. Butler, *So They Framed Stephenson*, pp. 18–19. See also Wade, *The Fiery Cross*, p. 221.

4. Butler, *So They Framed Stephenson*, pp. 18–19; Wade, *The Fiery Cross*, p. 221. Additional information on Stephenson's background appears in the notes and reports collected by newspaper reporter Harold Feightner, Feightner Papers, Manuscripts Division, Indiana State Library.

5. See Chalmers, *Hooded Americanism*, pp. 28–32; Dinnerstein, *The Leo Frank Case* (for the Leo Frank episode); Jackson, *The Ku Klux Klan in the City*, pp. 5–8; Wade, *The Fiery Cross* pp. 140–53.

6. On the backgrounds of Clarke and Tyler, see Wade, *The Fiery Cross*, pp. 153–54.

7. Jackson, *The Ku Klux Klan in the City*, pp. 9–10; Chalmers, *Hooded Americanism*, pp. 33–35; Wade, *The Fiery Cross*, pp. 154–59.

8. *Fiery Cross*, 1922–23. On the importance of social activities in the Klan movement, see Chapter 4 of this study.

9. "Ernst and Ernst Report," D. C. Stephenson Collection, Indiana Historical Society.

10. The audit of the Indiana recruiting operations ordered by Hiram Evans in 1923 gives an indication of the autonomy Stephenson enjoyed as the movement was on the rise. In addition to the "Ernst and Ernst Report," see the financial agreement between Stephenson and Evans and various bank records in the D. C. Stephenson Papers, Manuscripts Division, Indiana

State Library. On the lack of interference from Atlanta as the Klan grew in Colorado, see Goldberg, *Hooded Empire*, pp. 10–11.

11. Wade, *The Fiery Cross*, pp. 186–92; Chalmers, *Hooded Americanism*, pp. 100–108; Jackson, *The Ku Klux Klan in the City*, pp. 12–18.

12. Wade, *The Fiery Cross*, pp. 186–92; Chalmers, *Hooded Americanism*, pp. 100–108; Jackson, *The Ku Klux Klan in the City*, pp. 12–18.

13. Coughlan, "Konklave in Kokomo," pp. 105–29. Coughlan's well-known essay, based on his recollections of Kokomo during his youth, should be read in conjunction with the recent article by Safianow, "'Konklave in Kokomo' Revisited," pp. 329–47. On the rift between Stephenson and Evans and Stephenson's removal from the office of Grand Dragon, see Chapter 3 of this study.

14. Unless otherwise indicated, all recruiting pamphlets and other Klan literature discussed in this chapter are taken from Ku Klux Klan Papers, Manuscripts Division, Indiana State Library. The first quotation is from "Ideals of the Knights of the Ku Klux Klan" (pamphlet).

15. "Fifty Reasons Why I Am a Klansman" (pamphlet); Evans, *The Attitude of the . . . Klan toward the Roman Catholic Hierarchy*.

16. "A Klansman's Obligations as a Patriot to His God, His Country, His Home, and His Fellowmen" (pamphlet); *Fiery Cross*, February 23, March 7, December 21, 1923.

17. "Ideals of the Knights of the Ku Klux Klan" (pamphlet).

18. "Fifty Reasons Why I Am a Klansman" (pamphlet); Evans, *The Attitude of the . . . Klan toward the Jew* and *The Klan of Tomorrow*.

19. Evans, "The Attitude of the Knights of the Ku Klux Klan toward Immigration" (pamphlet).

20. *Indiana Catholic and Record*, *Indiana Jewish Chronicle*, and *Indianapolis Freeman*, 1922–24.

21. On the Herrin riot, see Angle, *Bloody Williamson*, pp. 157–71. Indiana newspapers gave extensive coverage to both riots. See *Indianapolis Star*, *Kokomo Daily Tribune*, and *Muncie Morning Star*, August 31–September 1, October 31–November 2, 1924.

22. For examples of warnings about the Klan as a political force, see White, "The Ku Klux Klan in Indiana," pp. 27–28; *Indiana Jewish Chronicle*, May 2, October 31, 1924; *Indianapolis Freeman*, May 17, 1924.

23. *Greensburg Daily News*, January 17, 1924; *Fiery Cross*, September 7, 21, 1924, March 16, 1923; *Vincennes Commercial*, June 28, 1924.

24. Joseph Cartwright Ives to William A. Wirt, May 19, 1923, Wirt Papers, Lilly Library, Indiana University; *Fiery Cross*, May 4, 1923; *Indianapolis Times*, April 8, 1981; "St. Vincent de Paul Church, Shelby County, Indiana," *Criterion*, April 23, 1982.

25. *Fiery Cross*, January 5, November 23, September 14, 1923; *Indianapolis News*, *South Bend Tribune*, and *Kokomo Daily Tribune*, March 11–12, 1924; *Fiery Cross*, March 14, 1924; *Indianapolis Times* and *South*

Bend Tribune, May 17, 1924; *Fiery Cross,* May 23, October 24, February 8, November 7, 1924.

26. Davidson, *Through the Rear View Mirror,* pp. 75–79; Madison, *Indiana through Tradition and Change,* p. 53; *Western Christian Advocate,* March 7, 1923.

27. See Scharlatt, "The Hoosier Newsmen and the Hooded Order," p. 52; *Richmond Evening Item,* December 23, 1922, October 10, 1923. The *Kokomo Daily Tribune* ran Klan announcements in its front-page column, "What's Doing in Kokomo."

28. In 1923, an anti-Klan organization in Chicago published a list of Indianapolis Klan members that had been stolen from the order's headquarters; Protestant ministers in the Klan were listed separately. Copies of the list are located in the Indiana Historical Society Library and in the Archives of the Catholic Archdiocese of Indianapolis.

29. Groups divided by the Klan issue are discussed in Madison, *Indiana through Tradition and Change,* pp. 52–54.

30. On the activities of anti-Klan politicians, see Chapter 6.

31. *Christian Evangelist,* December 13, 1923.

32. See, for example, *Muncie Morning Star,* February 20, 1924.

33. *Richmond Evening Item,* April 21, 1922; Lynd and Lynd, *Middletown,* p. 316.

34. *Greensburg Daily News,* January 1, 1924; *Richmond Evening Item,* April 16, 1922.

35. *Indianapolis Star,* January 11, 1924.

36. *Indiana Baptist Convention Minutes,* 1920, p. 13; *Baptist Observer,* March 19, 1925; *Indianapolis Area Herald,* June 1924.

37. *Christian Standard,* October 8, 1921.

38. *Western Christian Advocate,* February 1, 15, 1922.

39. *Indianapolis News,* April 16, 1924; *Indianapolis Star,* April 18, 1924; *Muncie Morning Star,* April 1, 1924; *Gary Post-Tribune,* May 12, 1924.

40. *Indiana Catholic and Record,* March 23, 1923, quoted in White, "The Ku Klux Klan in Indiana," p. 29.

41. "A Klansman's Obligations as a Patriot to His God, His Country, His Home, and His Fellowmen" and "The Ideals of the Ku Klux Klan" (pamphlets); *Lake County Star,* May 1–5, October 21–30, 1924.

42. *Fiery Cross,* May 4, 1923.

43. In addition to the *Fiery Cross,* see two other Klan periodicals with large circulations in Indiana: *Dawn,* published in Chicago, and *Kourier Magazine,* a national Klan monthly. For examples of the reformist views on Prohibition, see *Dawn,* November 18, 1922; *Kourier Magazine,* February 26, 1925.

44. Harold Feightner, "Wet and Dry Legislation in Indiana," pp. 5–6, 177–81, Feightner Papers, Manuscripts Division, Indiana State Library. See also Phillips, *Indiana in Transition,* pp. 494–98.

45. *Richmond Evening Item*, January 10, 1924, April 7, 1922 (quotation).

46. Woman's Christian Temperance Union ... of Indiana, *Proceedings*, 1923, pp. 52–53.

47. *Baptist Observer*, May 3, 1923; *Kokomo Daily Tribune*, July 18, 1924.

48. *Baptist Observer*, May 1, 1924. See also similar political commentaries in *Indiana Baptist Convention Minutes*, October 1924, pp. 45–46.

49. *Richmond Evening Item*, January 10, 1924, April 7, 1922.

50. Evans, *The Public School Problem in America*, p. 11. On the U.S. Army intelligence tests, see Kevles, "Testing the Army's Intelligence," and Kennedy, *Over Here*, p. 188.

51. Evans, *The Public School Problem in America*; "Our Educational Duty," in *Fiery Cross*, May 2, 1923, and in *Dawn*, February 10, 1923.

52. Evans, *The Public School Problem in America*; "Our Educational Duty," in *Fiery Cross*, May 2, 1923, and in *Dawn*, February 10, 1923. The Klan in Oregon helped pass a state compulsory public school attendance law in 1923. See Chalmers, *Hooded Americanism*, pp. 85–91; Bennett, *The Party of Fear*, pp. 227–28; Jackson, *The Ku Klux Klan in the City*, pp. 205–7.

53. On Americanization programs in public education in the early twentieth century, see Carlson, *The Quest for Conformity*; Hartmann, *The Movement to Americanize the Immigrant*; Higham, *Strangers in the Land*, pp. 234–63; Nasaw, *Schooled to Order*, pp. 87–158. On Indiana, see Mohl and Cohen, *The Paradox of Progressive Education*.

54. See Callahan, *Education and the Cult of Efficiency*; Hawley, *The Great War and the Search for a Modern Order*, pp. 142–44; Krug, *The Shaping of the American High School*, vol. 2; Nasaw, *Schooled to Order*, pp. 161–69; Tyack, *The One Best System*.

55. Evans, *The Public School Problem in America*; Slawson, "The Attitudes and Activities of American Catholics."

56. Madison, *Indiana through Tradition and Change*, pp. 263–74.

57. On the battle over the Indianapolis school building program, see Chapter 5.

58. *Fiery Cross*, February 16, March 9, 1923.

59. See *Fiery Cross*, July 18–September 5, 1923; H. M. Evans to Dean H. C. Muldoon, August 25, 1923, Correspondence, Valparaiso University Archives.

60. "Fifty Reasons Why I Am a Klansman" and "Bramble Bush Government" (pamphlets).

61. "A Klansman's Obligations as a Patriot to His God, His Country, His Home, and His Fellowmen" and "Fifty Reasons Why I Am a Klansman" (pamphlets); Evans, *The Klan of Tomorrow*; *Fiery Cross*, December 29, 1922; MacLean, "Behind the Mask of Chivalry," pp. 263–349.

62. *Fiery Cross*, April 27, 1924; "A Klansman's Obligations as a Patriot to

His God, His Country, His Home, and His Fellowmen" (pamphlet); Evans, *The Klan of Tomorrow.*"

63. "The Ideals of the Ku Klux Klan," "A Klansman's Obligations as a Patriot to His God, His Country, His Home, and His Fellowmen," and "Fifty Reasons Why I Am a Klansman" (pamphlets).

64. Lynd and Lynd, *Middletown*, pp. 121–44, 371–409. See also Madison, *Indiana through Tradition and Change*, pp. 295–306.

65. See *Fiery Cross*, 1922–24, and the Klan recruiting literature in Ku Klux Klan Papers, Manuscripts Division, Indiana State Library.

66. *Baptist Observer*, January 6, 1921; *Indianapolis Area Herald*, June 1925.

67. *Proceedings of the Tenth Assembly*, Church of the Nazarene, District of Indiana, p. 31.

Chapter 3

1. A Klan informant told a Dublin, Ga., newspaper that William J. Simmons had managed to remove most of his papers from the Klan's Imperial Palace vault at the time he was deposed, and that one of Hiram Evans's lieutenants, L. F. Savage, had taken the remaining records to his home in Brooklyn, N.Y. *Georgia Free Lance*, December 3, 1925.

2. Jackson, *The Ku Klux Klan in the City*, pp. 237, 239. For an example of how scholars have tended to treat Jackson's figures as hard facts rather than speculative estimates, see Lipset and Raab, *The Politics of Unreason*, pp. 119–31.

3. Jackson (*The Ku Klux Klan in the City*, p. 235) argues that "the Invisible Empire did not have great appeal in every city, but neither did it attract widespread support among the farmers and townspeople of many states. Generally, whenever the secret order was strong on a statewide basis, it was more attractive to white Protestants in populous communities than in Robert Lynd's *Middletown* or along Sinclair Lewis's *Main Street.*" In the case of Indiana, this was not correct. In 1925, the Lynds' *Middletown* (Muncie, in Delaware County) contained exactly the same percentage of Klansmen among native-born white men (27 percent) as Indianapolis (Marion County). See Table 3.1 below.

4. Jackson, *The Ku Klux Klan in the City*, pp. 235–49; Lipset and Raab, *The Politics of Unreason*, pp. 110–49; Bennett, *The Party of Fear*, p. 204.

5. Wade, *The Fiery Cross*, pp. 219–21.

6. Local Officers of the Ku Klux Klan, Indiana Historical Society.

7. The Klan published a fifty-one-page pamphlet containing the testimony and documents presented against Stephenson in his banishment trial in Evansville. See Knights of the Ku Klux Klan, "Charges and Specifications

against Klansman David Curtis Stephenson" (1924), Harold Feightner Papers, Manuscripts Division, Indiana State Library.

8. For further discussion of the Stephenson trial and subsequent scandals that tarnished Klan politicians and the Klan movement in Indiana, see Chapter 6.

9. The Klan's claim to 500,000 members in Indiana appeared in the *Fiery Cross*, March 10, 1923.

10. Membership List, Wayne County Ku Klux Klan Collection, Indiana Historical Society.

11. Ku Klux Klan Reel #1, Archives Division, Indiana Commission on Public Records.

12. Despite indications that women's chapters were popular in many communities, I could not locate any surviving membership lists. The only known list—for the women's organization in Kokomo and Howard County—was destroyed in a fire several years before I began this study. For a discussion of the activities of the women's and junior organizations, see Chapter 4.

13. Local Officers of the Ku Klux Klan, Indiana Historical Society; U.S. Bureau of the Census, *Fourteenth Census: Indiana Compendium*, pp. 34–42.

14. U.S. Bureau of the Census, *Religious Bodies*, 1926, 1:605–6.

15. U.S. Bureau of the Census, *Fourteenth Census: Indiana Compendium*, pp. 49–50.

16. See the last section of this chapter, "Religion."

17. It should be noted that not only do the 1925 figures represent a fraction of the total membership for the period, but also they may give a somewhat distorted picture of the membership. In other words, the kinds of people who had dropped out of the movement by 1925 may have been different from those who were still active at that time.

18. Weaver, "Knights of the Ku Klux Klan," p. 153; Jackson, *The Ku Klux Klan in the City*, pp. 144–60.

19. Elmer Davis, "Have Faith in Indiana," *Harpers Magazine* 153 (1926), p. 621, quoted in Madison, *Indiana through Tradition and Change*, p. 45.

20. *Indianapolis Freeman*, May 17, 1924.

21. With 5,000 members in 1925, Lake County probably also had a high proportion of Klansmen among the local population of white Protestant men. The same could be said of St. Joseph County. The high number of Catholics and Jews in these counties makes the percentage of Klansmen among native-born white men particularly deceptive.

22. Ecological regression is a powerful, widely used statistical tool. Its great benefit to historians is that, if used correctly, it can estimate the behavior of individual members of population groups based only on "aggregate data," such as county-level population totals listed in census documents. Regression can make accurate estimates of such things as the tendency of eth-

nic groups to support a given political candidate, the percentage of those who supported a political party in one election who will support that party in the next election, or, in other areas, the relationship between education and occupational status or tractor ownership and agricultural production. Because aggregate data (Klan membership totals for every county) are available, regression can be used here to determine if members of specific social groups were likely to have been Klan members. The regression technique is explained in Lewis-Beck, *Applied Regression*, and Achen, *Interpreting and Using Regression*; see also Langbein and Lichtman, *Ecological Inference*. On the use of regression in historical research, see Kousser, "Ecological Regression" and "The 'New Political History'"; Lichtman, "Correlation, Regression, and the Ecological Fallacy" and "Political Realignment and 'Ethnocultural' Voting"; Lichtman and Longbein, "Ecological Regression vs. Homogeneous Units"; Waterhouse, "The Estimation of Voting Behavior from Aggregated Data." Examples of the use of regression in historical studies include Baum, *The Civil War Party System*; Gienapp, *The Origins of the Republican Party*; Goodman, *Towards a Christian Republic*; Kousser, *The Shaping of Southern Politics*; Lichtman, *Prejudice and the Old Politics*. Unless otherwise indicated, all percentages used in constructing the regression equations for this study are based on the number of voting-age adults listed in the census.

23. For example, if one wanted to estimate the degree to which Catholics supported a political candidate and regressed that variable alone against the vote for the candidate, the results would leave important questions unanswered. If the results showed that Catholics tended to support the candidate, one could not be sure if the support stemmed from social factors other than religion. Perhaps Catholics supported the candidate because they were predominately the working or middle class, or because they tended to be residents of urban rather than rural communities. In a multiple regression equation, individual variables can be evaluated independent of the influence exerted by other variables in the equation. For a more detailed explanation of the multiple regression technique, see Lewis-Beck, *Applied Regression*, pp. 47–74.

24. It should be noted that the "South" variable used here and in subsequent regressions is a dummy variable. Variables used in this study generally measure the percentage of individuals within counties having certain characteristics—the percentage of Catholics, home owners, or Republican voters among all voting-age adults, for example. A dummy variable is used here to examine the independent influence of a group of counties having a common trait—the fact that they are located in the southern part of the state. The counties included in this variable are Bartholomew, Brown, Clark, Crawford, Daviess, Dearborn, Decatur, Dubois, Floyd, Franklin, Gibson, Greene, Harrison, Jackson, Jefferson, Knox, Lawrence, Martin, Monroe, Ohio, Orange, Perry, Pike, Posey, Ripley, Scott, Spencer, Sullivan, Swit-

zerland, Vanderburgh, Warrick, and Washington. For further discussion of dummy variables, see ibid., pp. 66–71.

25. Indiana voting returns appear in State of Indiana, *Yearbook, 1924*.
26. Ibid., p. 62.
27. Ibid., pp. 17–18; *Indianapolis Star*, July 1, 1939; *Indianapolis News*, June 30, 1939.
28. Harold Feightner, "One Hundred Fifty Years of Brewing in Indiana," pt. 13, p. 1, Feightner Papers, Manuscripts Division, Indiana State Library; Madison, *Indiana through Tradition and Change*, pp. 40–44.
29. Harold Feightner, "The People Vote Wet," pp. 2–8, and map, "Historic Positions of Indiana Counties on the Sale of Alcoholic Beverages," Feightner Papers, Manuscripts Division, Indiana State Library. The counties that consistently voted wet can be divided into two types: (1) those that contained major urban populations, including Allen, Cass, Lake, Marion, St. Joseph, Tippecanoe, Vanderburgh, Vigo, and Wayne; and (2) those that were predominantly rural, including La Porte and Porter (both of which had relatively high foreign-born populations) in the north and Clark, Dearborn, Dubois, Floyd, Franklin, Knox, Perry, Posey, Ripley, and Spencer in the south.
30. Harold Feightner, "The People Vote Wet," pp. 2–8, and map, "Historic Positions of Indiana Counties on the Sale of Alcoholic Beverages," Feightner Papers, Manuscripts Division, Indiana State Library. Counties that consistently voted dry included Boone, Carroll, Clinton, Hamilton, Lagrange, Owen, Putnam, Randolph, Tipton, Union, and Wells in northern and central Indiana and Lawrence, Pike, Scott, Switzerland, and Washington in the south. Feightner's interest in the history of Prohibition stemmed from his work during the 1940s and 1950s as a lobbyist for the Indiana brewing industry. His conclusions about counties not listed above are less reliable. Feightner did not state clearly his criteria for identifying counties as "leaning wet" or "leaning dry." He concluded that forty-two counties tended to be wet, while twelve tended to be dry.
31. Phillips, *Indiana in Transition*, pp. 271–322.
32. Jackson, *The Ku Klux Klan in the City*, pp. 86–87; Chalmers, *Hooded Americanism*, p. 154.
33. Local Officers of the Ku Klux Klan, Indiana Historical Society, pp. 9, 43. See also Map 3.1 above.
34. Local Officers of the Ku Klux Klan, Indiana Historical Society, p. 12.
35. Ibid., p. 41.
36. *Fort Wayne Journal Gazette*, May 8, 1924.
37. Total Klan membership in these counties was 79,912, which equaled 48.2 percent of the total for the state in 1925.
38. Cities with populations between 10,000 and 20,000 included Bloomington, Clinton, Crawfordsville, Elwood, Frankfort, Huntington, Jeffersonville, La Porte, Michigan City, Mishawaka, New Castle, Peru, Vincennes, and

Whiting. See U.S. Bureau of the Census, *Fourteenth Census: Indiana Compendium*, pp. 44–45. The total number of Klansmen in counties represented by these cities (excluding Lake, Madison, and St. Joseph, which were already counted among the fifteen largest urban counties) was 18,186 in 1925. Local Officers of the Indiana Ku Klux Klan, Indiana Historical Society.

39. "Complete Roll of Indianapolis Klux," Indiana Historical Society.

40. Local Officers of the Indiana Ku Klux Klan, Indiana Historical Society, p. 25.

41. Jackson (*The Ku Klux Klan in the City*, p. 235) believes that the Klan was much stronger in large cities such as Indianapolis rather than in smaller cities such as Muncie.

42. U.S. Bureau of the Census, *Fourteenth Census: Indiana Compendium*, p. 25. See also Map 3.1 above.

43. In 1920, the U.S. Bureau of the Census defined the term *urban* as any community with a population greater than 2,500. Units of data used here are county census and Klan membership figures for 1925. For similar evidence showing greater continuity between urban and rural groups than has previously been assumed for the 1920s, see Lichtman, *Prejudice and the Old Politics*, pp. 122–43, 236–37.

44. Local Officers of the Ku Klux Klan, Indiana Historical Society, p. 19; Polk's *Terre Haute City Directory*, 1924.

45. Indiana Historical Society: Crown Point Ku Klux Klan Collection; Wayne County Ku Klux Klan Collection; "Complete Roll of Indianapolis Klux."

46. Madison, *Indiana through Tradition and Change*, pp. 192–96, 210–19.

47. Lynd and Lynd, *Middletown*, p. 86.

48. U.S. Bureau of the Census, *Fourteenth Census: Indiana Compendium*, p. 43.

49. On the methods used to analyze these data, see Appendix.

50. In Indianapolis, 8.8 percent of all dentists and 5.1 percent of all physicians listed in the city directory appear on the Indianapolis Klan list. Officers of the fifty-two incorporated companies (incorporated with at least $500,000 in capital) and bank presidents were listed in Polk's *Indianapolis City Directory*, 1924.

51. *Indiana Catholic and Record*, July 13, 1923; Polk's *Indianapolis City Directory*, 1923–24.

52. Goldberg, *Hooded Empire*, p. 46.

53. Wayne County Ku Klux Klan Collection, Indiana Historical Society; U.S. Bureau of the Census, *Fourteenth Census: Indiana Compendium*, p. 43. In a sample of five hundred Richmond Klansmen, seventy-one—or approximately 14 percent—were listed in the *Clevenger's Directory of Farmers and Breeders, Wayne County* rather than in the city directory. For a discussion of the sampling techniques used in this study, see Appendix.

54. On the methods used to analyze these data, see Appendix.

55. Crown Point Ku Klux Klan Collection, Indiana Historical Society; U.S. Bureau of the Census, *Fourteenth Census: Indiana Compendium*, p. 46.

56. On the methods used to analyze these data, see Appendix.

57. See Goldberg, *Hooded Empire*, pp. 45–48. On Richmond, see Chapter 5 of this study.

58. The 1920 census indicates that 44 percent of the homes in Indiana were rented and 56 percent were owned. See U.S. Bureau of the Census, *Fourteenth Census: Indiana Compendium*, p. 62. Regression analysis of the influence of wage earners and southern residence on home ownership shows: wage earners, $b = .27$, standard error (SE) $= .20$, and southern residence, $b = .02$, SE $= .001$; with the equation controlling for percentage urban, Klan, and Catholic, $R^2 = .23$. A regression for the influence of wage earners and southern residence on renting reveals: wage earners, $b = .07$, SE $= .12$, and southern residence, $b = -.01$, SE $= .01$; with the equation controlling for percentage urban, Klan, and Catholic, $R^2 = .37$.

59. See the discussion of anti-Klan views in Chapter 2.

60. Pietist and liturgical differences between Protestant denominations have been shown to have had less effect on voting behavior than was thought previously, especially during the 1920s. See Lichtman, *Prejudice and the Old Politics*, pp. 233–35, and "Political Realignment and 'Ethnocultural' Voting," pp. 55–82.

61. A detailed explanation of how this sample was conducted is provided in the Appendix. Church membership records came either from archival collections or from the churches themselves. The sample was constructed to represent the spectrum of Protestant denominations in Indianapolis during the 1920s and to be large enough to make the findings statistically significant.

62. The often unclear line between fundamentalist and nonfundamentalist urban churches in the 1920s is discussed in Singleton, "Fundamentalism and Urbanization."

63. Because of the size of the samples in the nonevangelical category, it is difficult to draw conclusions about these specific denominations. The total in this category should be considered the significant figure. The samples in the evangelical category are generally much larger; therefore, the results for specific denominations are significant.

64. This is consistent with the 46.8 percent of men with no religious affiliation that was listed in a similar sample of non-Klansmen.

65. U.S. Bureau of the Census, *Religious Bodies*, 1926, 1:531.

66. The Quaker publication, *American Friend*, was published in Richmond. Its pacifist views during the war seem to have had little influence on local Friends; only a few sought exemptions from the draft. See Phillips, *Indiana in Transition*, pp. 591, 604n.

67. In a recent study of the Klan in Youngstown, Ohio, Jenkins (*Steel*

Valley Klan, pp. 88–90) found that Klan membership cut a wide path across Protestant denominational lines. Just as in Richmond and Indianapolis, large numbers of Lutherans joined the order in Youngstown, although Jenkins concludes that those members were split between pietistic and more traditional liturgical branches of the denomination. He sees a strong relationship between "what Richard Jensen and Paul Kleppner have described as pietistic politics." The findings for Indiana appear to be more in line with Allan J. Lichtman's conclusions about religion and politics during the 1920s. In analyzing the votes for Al Smith and Herbert Hoover in 1928, Lichtman (*Prejudice and the Old Politics*, pp. 40–76, 233–35) found that both pietistic and liturgical Protestants were inclined to vote against Smith. The ethnocultural thesis, he concluded, did not seem to explain religious political divisions during the twenties.

Chapter 4

1. See Wade, *The Fiery Cross*, p. 215; Coughlan, "Konklave in Kokomo"; Safianow, "Konklave in Kokomo Revisited."
2. *Kokomo Daily Tribune*, July 4–5, 1923.
3. Ibid., July 1–5, 1924.
4. Ibid.
5. Local Officers of the Ku Klux Klan, Indiana Historical Society, p. 34; U.S. Bureau of the Census, *Fourteenth Census: Indiana Compendium*, pp. 34–35.
6. Phillips, *Indiana in Transition*, pp. 363–67; U.S. Bureau of the Census, *Fourteenth Census: Indiana Compendium*, p. 8.
7. Phillips, *Indiana in Transition*, pp. 361–62; Lynd and Lynd, *Middletown*.
8. U.S. Bureau of the Census, *Fourteenth Census*, 2:47.
9. Phillips, *Indiana in Transition*, pp. 276–79.
10. U.S. Bureau of the Census, *Fourteenth Census*, 2:40–41, 47.
11. U.S. Bureau of the Census, *Fourteenth Census: Indiana Compendium*, p. 43. Jeffersonville and New Albany represented exceptions. Like Evansville, these Ohio River cities had always had a larger number of black residents. See Phillips, *Indiana in Transition*, pp. 276–77.
12. On the friction between urban and rural areas in the Midwest during the 1920s, see Kirschner, *City and Country*, pp. 33–56.
13. Madison, *Indiana through Tradition and Change*, p. 5.
14. Ibid.
15. U.S. Bureau of the Census, *Fourteenth Census*, 2:47.
16. Phillips, *Indiana in Transition*, pp. 271–322; Madison, *Indiana through Tradition and Change*, pp. 205–21.
17. On the impact of widening class differences on culture and commu-

nity in late nineteenth-century America, see Bender, *Community and Social Change in America*, pp. 108–22; Gutman, *Work, Culture, and Society in the Gilded Age*; and Tractenberg, *The Incorporation of America*, pp. 78–79. Community studies that demonstrate this process include Dawley, *Class and Community*; Frisch, *Town into City*; and Griffen and Griffen, *Natives and Newcomers*. On the general topic of elite political control in communities, see Rose, *The Power Structure*. Elite dominance in Muncie, Indiana, is discussed in Lynd and Lynd, *Middletown*.

18. Salvatore, *Eugene V. Debs*, pp. 16–17.
19. Ibid.
20. Lynd and Lynd, *Middletown*, pp. 22, 222, 419–22, 427–28, 492.
21. Frank, "Who Governed *Middletown*?"
22. Lynd and Lynd, *Middletown*, pp. 88–89.
23. Ibid., pp. 478–79, 491–502.
24. Phillips, *Indiana in Transition*, p. 382.
25. The Indianapolis Chamber of Commerce, for example, exerted great influence over the politics of education in that city. See Madison, *Indiana through Tradition and Change*, p. 281. The Lynds noted that while top businessmen no longer ran for office themselves, it was "good business" to be a member of the Republican party in Muncie. The Lynds also mentioned the leading role of businessmen in reforming city government. See *Middletown*, pp. 415, 421–22, 427.
26. Hyneman, Hofstetter, and O'Connor, *Voting in Indiana*, pp. 26–27; Lynd and Lynd, *Middletown*, pp. 413–21 (quotations, pp. 417, 416).
27. Lynd and Lynd, *Middletown*, pp. 459–63, 62–70.
28. Jensen ("The Lynds Revisited") has pointed out that the ethnic composition of Muncie was not at all typical of American industrial cities in the early twentieth century. But its nearly homogeneous white Protestant population was only one aspect of the city that attracted the Lynds. They also were interested in evaluating the impact of industrialization on traditional American culture—meaning, in their view, native, white, Protestant culture—without having to evaluate the complications of race. See *Middletown*, p. 8. If Muncie differed fundamentally from other American industrial cities because of its ethnic composition, it did not differ from other Indiana cities. Almost all towns and cities in Indiana were also overwhelmingly white Protestant.
29. Madison, *Indiana through Tradition and Change*, pp. 21–22.
30. Phillips, *Indiana in Transition*, pp. 132–48; Madison, *Indiana through Tradition and Change*, pp. 155–71.
31. Phillips, *Indiana in Transition*, pp. 132–48; Madison, *Indiana through Tradition and Change*, pp. 155–71.
32. Madison, *Indiana through Tradition and Change*, pp. 170–72; U.S. Bureau of the Census, *Fourteenth Census: Indiana Compendium*, pp. 82–90.

33. Madison, *Indiana through Tradition and Change*, pp. 172–77.

34. Ibid., pp. 7–9, 134–35, 142, 184–85, 211–22, 253–71.

35. Political corruption in Lake County is discussed in Chapter 4.

36. Harold Feightner, "150 Years of Brewing in Indiana," Feightner Papers, Manuscripts Division, Indiana State Library, pt. 13, p. 2; *Indianapolis Star*, July 16, 19, 22, 30, 1924.

37. *Indianapolis Star*, April 28, 1938; Feightner, "150 Years of Brewing," pt. 13, pp. 2–6.

38. Feightner, "150 Years of Brewing," pt. 13, pp. 2–5; pt. 14, p. 2.

39. Ibid., pp. 50, 70–71; Phillips, *Indiana in Transition*, pp. 127–31; Madison, *Indiana through Tradition and Change*, p. 75 (quotation).

40. Of the $10.00 paid by each new Klan member, $2.50 went to the recruiting agent or kleagle, $2.50 went to Stephenson, and $5.00 went to the national organization. From July 1922 to July 1923, Stephenson made more than $250,000 under this arrangement alone. "Ernst and Ernst Report," D. C. Stephenson Collection, Indiana Historical Society. For other evidence of Stephenson's financial dealings, see the agreement between Stephenson and Hiram Evans included in the same collection. See also Weaver, "Knights of the Ku Klux Klan," pp. 147–54, 169–75; Jackson, *The Ku Klux Klan in the City*, pp. 155–56; Various financial documents in D. C. Stephenson Papers, Manuscripts Division, Indiana State Library.

41. For an assessment of the limits of Stephenson's power within the state Republican party, see Madison, *Indiana through Tradition and Change*, p. 59. Catholic leaders all but ignored the TWK campaign. See *Indiana Catholic and Record*, 1922–24; White, "The Ku Klux Klan in Indiana," pp. 27–52. The Klan's threatened boycotts of Jewish-owned businesses in Indianapolis had little impact on the city's Jewish community. See Endelman, *The Jewish Community of Indianapolis*, pp. 125–26.

42. The Klan published a fifty-one-page pamphlet containing the testimony and documents presented against Stephenson at his banishment trial in Evansville. See in particular the testimony of Joseph S. Bell in Knights of the Ku Klux Klan, *Charges and Specifications against Klansman David Curtis Stephenson*, Harold Feightner Papers, Manuscripts Division, Indiana State Library.

43. Stephenson's downfall is discussed in Chapter 6.

44. Local Officers of the Ku Klux Klan, p. 39, Indiana Historical Society. The Kokomo and Terre Haute chapters, for example, held outdoor meetings.

45. Knights of the Ku Klux Klan, *Kloran* (Atlanta, 1916). During the 1920s, the *Kloran* was reprinted every year in essentially the same form.

46. Richmond Klansman #2 interview; *Kokomo Daily Tribune*, January–July 1924. The newspaper discontinued the practice of printing Klan announcements in July 1924.

47. *Kokomo Daily Tribune*, May 21, June 16, July 28, September 12, 19, 1924.

48. *Indianapolis News*, July 4, 1924; *Indianapolis Times*, June 2, 1924; *Fiery Cross*, June 13, July 11, 1924.

49. *Indianapolis Times*, June 2, 1924.

50. *Fiery Cross*, August 29, 31, 1924;; *Vincennes Sun, Indianapolis Times*, and *Indianapolis Star*, February 1, 1924.

51. *Vincennes Sun*, August 23, September 2, 1924.

52. *Vincennes Commercial*, June 6, 1924. After the Stephenson scandal in 1925, Adams led an investigation of the Klan's role in state politics. His findings greatly disturbed members of his own party, who felt he had gone too far in attacking the Klan and dragging the state Republican party through the mud. See Madison, *Indiana through Tradition and Change*, p. 69.

53. *Vincennes Commercial*, June 20, 1924.

54. *Fiery Cross*, September 21, 1924. Durgan battled the local order throughout the Klan period, intervening when possible to halt its demonstrations and parades. His actions caused considerable controversy in Lafayette. In 1924, Durgan ran as an anti-Klan candidate in the Democratic gubernatorial primary. Although he did not win the nomination, his candidacy attracted enough support to force the party machine to adopt an openly anti-Klan position.

55. *Kokomo Daily Tribune*, May 5, 1924; *Fiery Cross*, May 9, 1924.

56. *Fiery Cross*, July 6, August 17, May 17, 1923.

57. Ibid., June 1, July 6, 20, August 18, September 7, 23, 1923, May 9, June 13, July 11, 1924; *Kokomo Daily Tribue*, May 5, June 16, July 28, 30, August 25, September 19, 1924; *Indianapolis Times*, June 2, 1924.

58. *Indianapolis News*, May 10, 1924; *Indianapolis Star*, May 24–25, 1924; *Indianapolis News*, May 26, 1924; *Indianapolis Times*, May 23, 26, September 5, 1924.

59. Membership lists for Women of the Ku Klux Klan chapters have not surfaced. I encountered only one report of such a list, which had been kept for several decades in the records of a Kokomo Catholic church but was destroyed in a fire. See Rev. Francis J. Niesen to Richard A. Kastl, March 13, 1981, Records, Howard County Museum, Kokomo.

60. The *Fiery Cross*, on July 6, 1923, claimed that a crowd of 60,000 attended the convention and that 5,000 men and women marched in the parade.

61. For example, the women's order in Muncie became involved in two lawsuits with recruiting agents as a result of disputes over membership and robe fees. *Greensburg Daily News*, January 4, 1924; *Muncie Morning Star*, June 3, 1924. An organizer for the women's chapter in New Albany was poisoned by candy sent to her through the mail. *Muncie Morning Star*, September 14, 1924.

62. See, for example, *Fiery Cross*, March 2, July 6, September 7, 1923, May 9, 1924; *Kokomo Daily Tribune*, April 28, July 2, 28, August 25, 1924.

63. On Junior Klan activities in Kokomo, see *Kokomo Daily Tribune*, September 14, 1924; on the basketball tournament, see *Fiery Cross*, March 8, 1924.

64. *Fiery Cross*, March 23, 1923.

65. Ibid., July 20, 1923, January 11, 1924.

66. *Vincennes Commercial*, October 28, 1924.

67. *Fiery Cross*, March 14, 1924; *Vincennes Sun*, February 21, 1924. Other instances of the Klan exerting political pressure and collecting information were reported in the *Fiery Cross*—see, for example, March 16, 30, 1923.

68. *Indianapolis News*, May 17, 1924.

69. The Klan's assault on local party organizations is discussed in Chapter 5.

70. There are numerous examples in the *Fiery Cross*. Gift giving was one of the most frequent activities of Klan chapters nationwide, and other major Klan publications such as *Dawn* (Chicago) and *The Imperial Nighthawk* (Atlanta) took great pleasure in pointing out the order's charitable acts.

71. See, for example, *Greensburg Daily News*, April 18, 1924.

72. *Fiery Cross*, December 29, 1922.

73. *Kokomo Daily Tribune*, July 4–5, 1923, July 1, 1924; Rev. Francis J. Niesen to Richard A. Kastl, March 13, 1981, Records, Howard County Museum, Kokomo.

74. Safianow, "Konklave in Kokomo Revisited," pp. 337–47.

Chapter 5

1. Klan membership figures were obtained from the Wayne County Ku Klux Klan Collection, Indiana Historical Society; population figures were taken from the U.S. Bureau of the Census, *Fourteenth Census: Indiana Compendium*, p. 43.

2. Phillips, *Indiana in Transition*, p. 367.

3. Charles McGuire interview.

4. Polk's *Richmond City Directory, 1923–24*. The production of lawn mowers had been one of Richmond's oldest and most successful businesses. Competing firms manufacturing the machines had been well established by the 1880s. Charles McGuire interview.

5. U.S. Bureau of the Census, *Fourteenth Census: Indiana Compendium*, pp. 140, 145.

6. *Richmond Daily Sun Telegram*, December 19, 1899, March 5, 1902, March 9, 11, 1903, March 2, 1904; *Richmond Palladium*, September 27, 1913.

7. *Richmond Daily Sun Telegram*, October 21, 1903.

8. *Richmond Palladium*, March 16, April 15, 1904; *Richmond Evening Item*, January 17, 1917; Richmond South Side Improvement Association to Mayor W. W. Zimmerman, June 19, 1919, City of Richmond, Richmond Planning Commission Records.

9. *Richmond Evening Item*, April 10, 1924; *Richmond Palladium*, May 2, 1957, April 5–6, 1959.

10. Minutes, 1917, and Attendance Record, Richmond Rotary Club. See also Polk's *Richmond City Directory, 1923–24*.

11. *Richmond Evening Item*, November 11, 1920. The membership total was 106.

12. See, for example, *Richmond Palladium*, January 1, 3, 1924. Rotary club members played a large role in forming a "Merchant's Division" of the city's Welfare League in order to increase funds for the Community Chest. On the dissolution of the Commercial Club, see *Richmond Evening Item*, April 4, 1920.

13. *Richmond Daily Sun Telegram*, December 19, 1899; Charter Members, Richmond Lions Club; Charles McGuire interview.

14. Lichtman, *Prejudice and the Old Politics*, pp. 176–79.

15. See occupational data for Richmond in Chapter 3; Lynd and Lynd, *Middletown*, pp. 73–89; U.S. Bureau of the Census: *Thirteenth Census*, 1:1357, *Fourteenth Census: Indiana Compendium*, p. 63, and *Fifteenth Census*, 6:425.

16. Polk's *Richmond City Directory, 1903–4* and *1923–24*.

17. Richmond's only Baptist church chose not to make its records available for this study, but interviews with Richmond residents indicate that the First Baptist Church generally attracted a working-class membership. Charles McGuire, Argus Ogborn, and Richmond Klansman #1 interviews.

18. According to the U.S. Bureau of the Census, *Religious Bodies*, 1926, 16 percent of Richmond's citizens were members of the Catholic church. If 16 percent of the city's native white men were Catholics, Klan membership represented 49 percent of Richmond's native white non-Catholic men.

19. Argus Ogborn interview; Local Officers of the Ku Klux Klan, p. 22, and Wayne County Ku Klux Klan Collection, Indiana Historical Society; Annual Reports and Minutes, 1922, Reid Memorial United Presbyterian Church, Richmond.

20. Local Officers of the Ku Klux Klan, p. 22, Indiana Historical Society; Richmond Klansman #1 interview.

21. Early members included the first five hundred men to join the Richmond Klan. The order of membership was determined by membership number, listed in the Wayne County Ku Klux Klan Collection, Indiana Historical Society.

22. Ibid.; Polk's *Richmond City Directory, 1923–24*.

23. Goldberg (*Hooded Empire*, p. 46) found that earlier joiners in the

Denver Klan also were more inclined to be from the middle class than those who joined later. In Orange County, Calif., there appeared to be no relationship between early membership and economic status. See Cocoltchos, "The Invisible Government and the Viable Community," p. 152.

24. See Chapter 3, "Occupation" and "Religion."

25. The Richmond Kiwanis Club did not retain early membership records, so a complete list of members during the time of the Klan is not available. The list of members for 1920, which appeared in a special Kiwanis edition of the *Richmond Evening Item* (its editor was a member), included the names of only 106 members, probably less than half the number of men who had joined by 1924. Of the members in 1920, 42 later joined the Klan. *Richmond Evening Item*, November 20, 1920. For Rotary club membership, see Minutes, Richmond Rotary Club, 1924.

26. For examples of Klan-related articles appearing in the *Richmond Palladium*, see the editions for January 2–3, February 1, May 7–8, 1924. The papers of Edward H. Harris, editor of the *Palladium* from 1910 until the early 1930s, leave no doubt about his opposition to the Klan. See Harris to F. J. Prince, November 11, 1926, Herbert K. Heil to Harris, September 12, 1927, Harris to Herbert K. Heil, September 20, 1927, and biographical sketch, Harris Collection, Regional History Archives, Indiana University East, Richmond.

27. *Richmond Palladium-Item*, November 6, 1979.

28. Transcripts, John S. Robinson interview, pp. 10–11, and Russell A. Bennett interview, p. 4.

29. In *The Ku Klux Klan in the City*, pp. 243–44, Jackson emphasized the role of ethnic residential competition. But Goldberg (*Hooded Empire*, pp. 43–44) found that this interpretation could not be substantiated in the case of Denver. See also Jackson's review of Goldberg's study in the *American Historical Review* 87 (December 1982): 1486–87.

30. Local Officers of the Ku Klux Klan in Indiana, 1925, p. 22; Richmond Klansman #1 and Richmond Klansman #2 interviews.

31. Wayne County Ku Klux Klan Collection, Indiana Historical Society; Richmond Klansman #1 interview.

32. *Richmond Evening Item*, May 24, 26, 1923.

33. Ibid., October 4, 6, 1923.

34. Ibid. See also *Fiery Cross*, October 19, 1923.

35. *Richmond Evening Item*, May 30, 1908, March 24, 1914.

36. Wayne County Ku Klux Klan Collection, Indiana Historical Society; *Richmond Palladium-Item*, November 6, 1979; *Richmond Evening Item*, October 3, 1923.

37. *Richmond Evening Item*, December 23, 1923, October 3, 19, 1923; December 21, 23, 1922.

38. Ibid., February 6, 1924.

39. Biographical sketches, Rudolph Garr Leeds Collection and Edward H.

Harris Collection, Regional History Archives, Indiana University East, Richmond; *Richmond Palladium*, January 15, 19, 1924.

40. *Richmond Palladium*, January 6, February 1, 1924.

41. Minutes of the Common Council, City of Richmond, pp. 528–29; *Richmond Evening Item*, January 22, 1924; Wayne County Ku Klux Klan Collection, Indiana Historical Society.

42. *Richmond Evening Item*, January 19, 1924.

43. Ibid., January 22–23, 1924.

44. Ibid., January 19, 26, 1924.

45. *Richmond Evening Item* and *Richmond Palladium*, February 5, 1924; *Richmond Evening Item*, February 6, 1924.

46. Of the seven Klansmen on the Richmond City Council, four did not seek reelection. Of those four, two had favored annexation and two had opposed it. Of the three Klansmen who sought reelection, one had supported annexation; all were reelected. The annexation issue also had no impact on the political careers of the five non-Klansmen on the city council. See *Richmond Palladium*, November 4, 1925.

47. U.S. Bureau of the Census, *Fourteenth Census: Indiana Compendium*, pp. 20–23, 90; Membership List, Wayne County Ku Klux Klan Collection, and Local Officers of the Ku Klux Klan, p. 22, Indiana Historical Society.

48. U.S. Bureau of the Census, *Fourteenth Census: Indiana Compendium*, pp. 20–23, 90.

49. *Clevenger's Directory of Farmers and Breeders, Wayne County*. For a directory of tractor and automobile owners, see pp. 139–57. Telephone ownership was estimated from a random sample of 1,000 farmers. In that group, 731 owned telephones.

50. U.S. Department of the Interior, *Eleventh Census*, 5:138–39, and *Twelfth Census*, 5:78–79; U.S. Bureau of the Census, *Thirteenth Census*, 6:482, and *Fourteenth Census: Indiana Compendium*, p. 90.

51. U.S. Bureau of the Census, *Fourteenth Census: Indiana Compendium*, p. 90, and *Fifteenth Census*, 7:490.

52. Membership List, Wayne County Ku Klux Klan Collection, and Local Officers of the Ku Klux Klan, p. 22, Indiana Historical Society.

53. Membership List, Wayne County Ku Klux Klan Collection, Indiana Historical Society; *Clevenger's Directory of Farmers and Breeders, Wayne County*, pp. 17–115.

54. Membership List, Wayne County Ku Klux Klan Collection, Indiana Historical Society; *Clevenger's Directory of Farmers and Breeders, Wayne County*, pp. 17–115.

55. Membership List, Wayne County Ku Klux Klan Collection, Indiana Historical Society; *Clevenger's Directory of Farmers and Breeders, Wayne County*, pp. 17–115.

56. Estimates of the adult male populations for each of the six commu-

nities were obtained by multiplying the population of each town by the overall percentage (0.33) of adult men in Wayne County in 1920. Percentages of Klansmen among the estimated adult male populations were Boston, 44 percent; Centerville, 38 percent; Fountain City, 33 percent; Greenfork, 43 percent; Hagerstown, 14 percent; and Milton, 6 percent.

57. Robert Pierce, Donald McKinney, Wayne County Klansman #1, and Wayne County Klansman #2 interviews.

58. Robert Pierce, Donald McKinney, Wayne County Klansman #1, and Wayne County Klansman #2 interviews. Hagerstown's one black citizen resided there during the years between World War I and World War II. He was single, lived in a room at the edge of town, and made a living shining shoes. Robert Pierce interview.

59. Wayne County Klansman #1, Wayne County Klansman #2, and Richmond Klansman #1 interviews.

60. Wayne County Klansman #1, Wayne County Klansman #2, and Richmond Klansman #1 interviews; *Richmond Item*, May 30, 1908, March 24, 1914; Robert Pierce interview.

61. Robert Pierce, Donald McKinney, Wayne County Klansman #1, and Wayne County Klansman #2 interviews.

62. U.S. Bureau of the Census, *Fourteenth Census: Indiana Compendium*, pp. 31, 43.

63. Ibid. See also Thornbrough, *The Negro in Indiana before 1900*, pp. 260–68, and "Segregation in Indiana," pp. 594–618.

64. Occupational patterns are discussed in detail in Chapter 3.

65. Boundary lines for the north central area included Washington Avenue on the south, the White River on the west, Thirtieth Street on the north, and State, West, Windsor, Commerce, Roosevelt, and Martindale streets on the east. For boundary lines of other areas in Table 5.5, see Appendix.

66. See Thornbrough, "Segregation in Indiana." On the Indianapolis Jewish community during the 1920s, see Endelman, *The Jewish Community of Indianapolis*, pp. 111–27.

67. Endelman, *The Jewish Community of Indianapolis*, pp. 111–27 (quotations, pp. 126, 125).

68. A recent study of ethnic Germans in Missouri found that World War I accelerated the process of assimilation, which was well under way to begin with. Detjen, *The Germans in Missouri*, pp. 177–86.

69. Each of the six new city councilmen—all Republicans—had enrolled in the Klan by early 1923. Three councilmen—two Democrats and one Republican—remained from the previous term. None could be located on the 1923 Klan list. For an account of the election results, see *Indianapolis Times, Indianapolis News*, and *Indianapolis Star*, November 3, 1925. The segregation ordinance was passed by a vote of five to one. All five of the affirmative votes were cast by the newly elected Klansmen. The *no* vote was cast by one of the Democrats. Three council members—two Republicans

and one Democrat—were absent. See *Times, Star,* and *News,* March 16, 1926. The ordinance required that before a black individual took up residence in a home purchased from a white individual, he or she must first receive the written consent of all white home owners living within three hundred feet of the residence. For further discussion of the ordinance, see Thornbrough, "Segregation in Indiana," pp. 597–601.

70. Thornbrough, "Segregation in Indiana," pp. 597–601. The black community of Indianapolis, led by the local branch of the NAACP, led the fight against the ordinance and succeeded in having it overturned by the courts. Ibid.

71. For biographical information on Duvall and Coffin, see *Indianapolis News,* February 2, 1962, and *Indianapolis Star,* April 11–12, 1938. Both men were listed as Klan members on the 1923 Indianapolis list and as officers of the Marion County chapter on the 1925 list.

72. *Indianapolis Times,* November 2, 4, 7, 9–16, 21, 1925; *Indianapolis News,* November 8–18, 1925; *Indianapolis Star,* November 10, 14, 16, 1925; *Indianapolis Times,* November 9, 1925 (quotation).

73. For an account of Elliot's condemnation of Coffin, see *Indianapolis Times,* November 2, 1925. For a summary of the struggle for patronage between the Republican Old Guard, Coffin, and Duvall factions, see *Indianapolis Times,* November 10, 1925.

74. *Indianapolis Star,* April 11–12, 1938.

75. On the problems in the city's schools and the bond issues passed in 1921 and 1923, see *Indianapolis Star,* February 24, June 17, July 13, September 30, November 2, 6, 8–9, 1921; *Indianapolis Times,* February 2–3, March 5–10, 1923. On the Citizen's School Committee, the election of the school board in 1921, and the subsequent campaign to block the building program, see *Indianapolis Star,* November 21, 1921; *Indianapolis News,* February 2, 17, 1923; *Indianapolis Times,* February 2–3, 5, 16, 1923, September 8–10, 1924.

76. While the Citizen's School Committee had elected enough commissioners in 1921 to hold a majority, the rules governing the board required that the terms of commissioners be staggered. For two years after the election, two of the commissioners were holdover members from the previously elected board. Two of the citizen's committee candidates who were elected in 1921 did not assume office until two years into the four-year term. Before the final members of the citizen's slate began serving on the board, two of the citizen's committee commissioners had defected and joined forces with one of the holdover commissioners to form a majority that threatened to proceed with the building program. See *Indianapolis Times,* February 16, 1923.

77. Ibid., February 2–3, 16, 1923.

78. Ibid., February 16, 1923; *Indianapolis Star,* February 2–3, 16, 1923.

79. *Fiery Cross,* December 21, 1923, March 2, 9, 1923.

80. The Klan's school board candidates were Charles S. Kern, Mrs. Lillian Sedwick, Theodore F. Vonnegut, Fred Kepner, and Lewis E. Whiteman. Kern (a labor leader), Sedwick (an officer in the Indianapolis branch of the WCTU), and Vonnegut (a member of a well-know Indianapolis family and the owner of a hardware store) were the first to serve on the board. The first major project was to begin construction on the new Shortridge High School. The Indiana Taxpayers Association attempted further delays by calling for a remonstrance election, filing a law suit, and unearthing the old charges of extravagance and waste. Nevertheless, the new school, located north of downtown, was completed. The new black high school, Crispus Attucks, was also finished, along with a new white high school, Washington, in West Indianapolis. See *Indianapolis Times*, October 21, 28, November 2, 5, 1925, January 2, 5, 21, 25, March 9–10, May 1, 1926; *Indianapolis Star*, November 5, 25–26, 1925, January 2, March 10, May 1, June 9, 1926; *Indianapolis News*, December 5, 25, 1925.

81. See Thornbrough, "Segregation in Indiana," pp. 602–6.

Chapter 6

1. Beveridge had endorsed a Jewish congressional candidate. Also, Governor Henry Allen of Kansas had attacked the Klan while speaking in Richmond on Beveridge's behalf. See Braeman, *Albert J. Beveridge*, pp. 287–88.

2. Harold Feightner, Indiana correspondent for the *New York Times*, relayed this conclusion to his editors in the summer of 1923. See *New York Times*, November 6, 1924.

3. The fight between Watson and the Goodrich-New faction at the Indiana GOP convention is discussed in Madison, *Indiana through Tradition and Change*, pp. 32–33.

4. Watson was careful not to become too publicly associated with the Klan. He met with Klan leaders on several occasions but consistently denied that he was a member himself or that he owed the Klan political favors. See, for example, *Indianapolis News* and *Gary Post-Tribune*, May 26, 1924. Indiana journalists and other politicians, however, had no doubt about Watson's connection with the Klan and Jackson. Albert Beveridge concluded that Watson owned Jackson "body and soul." See Braeman, *Albert J. Beveridge*, p. 302.

5. *Indianapolis Star*, April 4, 28, 1924; *Greensburg Daily News*, April 4, 1924; Weaver, "Knights of the Ku Klux Klan," pp. 196–212; Madison, *Indiana through Tradition and Change*, pp. 56–58; Indiana *Yearbook, 1924*, pp. 15–16. For an example of one of Stephenson's letters, see *Indiana Catholic and Record*, April 18, 1924. Most of the information available on the "military machine" came from a dubious source—Stephenson himself. He gave details about its operation during legal proceedings from 1925 to

1927. See Deposition of D. C. Stephenson, State of Indiana, State of Indiana v. the Knights of the Ku Klux Klan; Weaver, "Knights of the Ku Klux Klan," pp. 212–21. Stephenson claimed that his organization divided each Klan chapter into political units as small as four Klansmen each, all monitored by a hierarchy of sergeants, lieutenants, majors, and colonels. But given the Klan's massive membership and the fact that only a tiny fraction of each klavern's members participated even in weekly meetings, in many communities such apparatuses probably existed only on paper, if at all. Most chapters probably saw little need to do more than distribute Klan voting slates.

6. *Fiery Cross*, May 9, 1924; *Kokomo Daily Tribune*, May 8, 22, 1924; *Indianapolis News*, May 7, 1924; *Indianapolis Star*, May 8, 1924; *Gary Post-Tribune*, May 6, 1924; *Richmond Palladium* and *Vincennes Sun*, May 7,1924; *Indiana Catholic and Record*, May 9, 1924; *Indianapolis Times*, May 8, 1924.

7. *Indianapolis Star*, May 10, 1924. The week after the election was a time of high emotion and tension for Stephenson. Jackson's victory had opened new political doors, but it had created new pressures as well, adding to those created by increasing trouble with the national Klan. Stephenson responded with a spate of erratic and reckless behavior that revealed his deep personal insecurity and his obsession with defeating the national organization. Two days after the election, he was arrested in Ohio after destroying a hotel room in a "drunken fit." *Winchester Democrat*, May 8, 1924. Early the next week, he became involved in a fistfight with Bossert, then announced plans to sue Bossert, Evans, and the national organization. *Gary Post-Tribune* and *Muncie Morning Star*, May 14, 1924. All of this occurred the same week that Stephenson attempted to depose the national order in Indiana and prepare his military machine for the opening of the GOP state convention.

8. *Indianapolis Star* and *Indianapolis News*, May 13, 1924; *Indianapolis Times*, May 16, 1924; *Indianapolis News*, May 19, 12, 1924; *Indianapolis Star*, *Kokomo Daily Tribune*, and *Muncie Morning Star*, June 19, 1924; *Winchester Democrat*, June 26, 1924. Stephenson's resignation from the Klan coincided with his official banishment from the order as well as with the conflict between Hiram Evans and Senator Watson, to whom Stephenson was politically indebted.

9. McCray declined the offer. These events were made public in 1928 when Jackson went on trial for bribery. Furious that Jackson had not pardoned him after his murder conviction, D. C. Stephenson eventually released information that led to Jackson's indictment. At the trial, Stephenson produced a canceled check to Jackson for $2,500 that the governor had failed to report as a campaign contribution. Former governor McCray, who himself had just completed a prison term, testified about the bribery attempt. Despite overwhelming evidence, Jackson escaped conviction due to the statute of limitations. Jackson's indictment, accompanied by proof of his

association with Stephenson, received a great deal of national publicity. See Taylor, "What the Klan Did in Indiana"; Budenz, "Scandals of 1927—Indiana." Jackson's trial is discussed in Madison, *Indiana through Tradition and Change*, pp. 70–71.

10. *Gary Post-Tribune*, May 23, 1924; *Richmond Palladium*, May 8, 1924; *Indianapolis Times*, May 20, 1924; *Indianapolis News*, May 22, 1924; *Indianapolis Star* and *Gary Post-Tribune*, May 23, 1924; *Muncie Morning Star*, May 25, 1924. Historians have generally concluded that Stephenson continued to command the loyalty of rank-and-file Klansmen. See Chalmers, *Hooded Americanism*, pp. 169–71; Davis, "The Ku Klux Klan in Indiana," p. 187; Jackson, *The Ku Klux Klan in the City*, pp. 154–56. Madison (*Indiana through Tradition and Change*, pp. 58–59) concludes that Jackson shared power with James Watson.

11. In the primary election, the Bossert group had given a flaccid, last-minute endorsement to a minor candidate, Edward Toner, but afterward had quickly joined the Jackson supporters. See *Indianapolis Star*, May 8, 1924. On Bossert's role in the convention and the general uncertainty as to who represented the Klan's interests at the GOP gathering, see *Kokomo Daily Tribune*, May 8, 1924; *Vincennes Sun* and *Indianapolis Times*, May 20, 1924; *Muncie Morning Star*, May 18, 1924; *Indianapolis News*, May 15, 22, 1924; *Indianapolis Star*, May 23, 1924.

12. *Muncie Morning Star*, May 11, 1924; *Indianapolis Star*, May 24, 2, 1924; *Indianapolis News*, May 14, 19, 1924; *Richmond Palladium*, May 8, 1924; *Indianapolis Star*, May 20–21, 1924; *Indianapolis News*, May 23, 27, June 1, 1924; *Vincennes Sun* and *Gary Post-Tribune*, May 22, 1924.

13. Before the Indiana GOP convention, Watson met with Evans and Bossert in Washington, D.C. Watson did not want to be linked directly with the Klan, but he appeared anxious to demonstrate to the national party that the powerful Klan vote in the Midwest might support a Coolidge-Watson ticket, as opposed to a ticket that included Albert J. Beveridge. Evans and Bossert apparently agreed to limit their divisive activities within the party and to let it be known that the national Klan favored Watson as a vice-presidential candidate. In return, Watson seems to have promised to give Bossert a position of influence at the GOP state convention. He probably promised Evans that he would vote in favor of seating Texan Earl B. Mayfield, whose election to the U.S. Senate in 1924 had been challenged because of his connection with the Klan. Both Evans and Bossert were eventually dissatisfied with the amount of power Watson had given D. C. Stephenson at the state convention. Bossert told the press that Watson was trying to play to both sides of the Klan. See Alexander, *The Ku Klux Klan in the Southwest*, pp. 126–27; Braeman, *Albert J. Beveridge*, p. 302; *Gary Post-Tribune*, May 24, 1924; *Indianapolis News*, May 23, 26–27, June 10, 1924; *Indianapolis Star*, May 24, 1924; *Indianapolis Times*, June 9, 1924; *Kokomo Daily Tribune*, June 9–10, 1924; *Vincennes Sun*, May 14, 1924.

14. *Indianapolis News*, May 19, 1924.

15. Holt ran especially well in the Fourth Congressional District, nearly embarrassing another Democratic candidate, Joseph Craven, on his home turf. *Franklin Evening Star*, May 7, 1924.

16. *Indiana Catholic and Record*, May 16, 1924.

17. Ralston's conclusion that Indiana Democrats should remain neutral on the Klan is discussed in Madison, *Indiana through Tradition and Change*, pp. 60–63. The convention, of course, did turn to a compromise candidate, John W. Davis. On Taggart's efforts to boost Ralston during the convention, see *Indianapolis Star*, June 21, July 1, 3, 9, 1924; *Indianapolis Times*, June 21, July 4, 1924; *Muncie Morning Star*, June 25–26, July 5, 1924.

18. *Indiana Catholic and Record*, May 16, 1924; Democratic platform quoted in Madison, *Indiana through Tradition and Change*, p. 64. On the struggle between pro- and anti-Klan forces during the convention, see *Indianapolis Star*, June 1, 3, 6, 1924; *Indianapolis News*, June 4, 1924; *Muncie Morning Star*, June 5, 1924; *Indiana Catholic and Record*, June 6, 1924.

19. *Indianapolis News*, October 29, 1924. Republican leaders surely realized that few blacks would be persuaded to vote for the Klan ticket. These solicitations, no matter how lame, were undoubtedly designed to placate white voters who were suspicious of the Klan's radical reputation.

20. *Kokomo Daily Tribune*, November 1, 1924. See also Madison, *Indiana through Tradition and Change*, p. 64.

21. *Indianapolis Times*, October 11, 31, November 3, October 30–31, November 1, 1924.

22. Indiana *Yearbook, 1924*, pp. 50–51.

23. *Indianapolis Freeman*, May 17, 1924. See also Griffin, "The Political Realignment of Black Voters in Indianapolis."

24. *Indiana Catholic and Record*, November 7, 1924, quoted in White, "The Ku Klux Klan in Indiana," p. 76; Bert Morgan to Will Hays, October 24, 1924, quoted in Madison, *Indiana through Tradition and Change*, p. 65. For further discussion of the perception that the Klan disrupted traditional party loyalties, see Griffin, "The Political Realignment of Black Voters in Indianapolis," and Madison, *The Indiana Way*, p. 293.

25. Waterhouse, "The Failure of Working-Class Politics in America." A regression of the 1920 presidential vote in Indiana shows that some Klansmen crossed party lines to support Calvin Coolidge in 1924. In 1920, the Klan vote had been split: Harding, $b = .14$, $SE = .16$, $R^2 = .32$, and Cox, $b = .03$, $SE = .09$, $R^2 = .23$, the equations controlling for southern residence and percentage urban, Catholic, Protestant, and renters.

26. During the 1920s, the percentage of black voters in Indiana was too small to be successfully evaluated using the regression technique with county-level data.

27. Black churches, of course, were excluded from consideration. The

proportion of Jews in Indiana was also too small to be evaluated through regression of county-level data. The number of Catholics, however, was large enough to be evaluated. Not surprisingly, they gravitated strongly toward McCullough and did not have to cross traditional party lines to do so: Jackson, $b = -.07$, SE $= .03$, $R^2 = .14$, and McCullough, $b = .42$, SE $= .10$, $R^2 = 0.11$, the equations controlling for southern residence and percentage urban, home owners, and foreign born.

28. Because the ratio of women to men varies little from county to county, it is difficult to employ regression in determining the role of gender in the elections considered here. The difficulties in analyzing the role of gender, as well as the results of a successful regression analysis of female voting patterns in the 1920s, are discussed in Lichtman, *Prejudice and the Old Politics*, pp. 159–62.

29. The results of regression analysis expressed in the form of contingency tables show that between three-quarters and two-thirds of Indiana's foreign-born residents did not vote in the elections of 1920 and 1924.

30. *Indiana Catholic and Record*, October 31, 1924; Indiana *Yearbook, 1924*, p. 17. See also a reprint of the Klan slate for Congress appearing in the *Indianapolis Times*, October 31, 1924.

31. Moores enjoyed solid support from Indianapolis business leaders. See *Fort Wayne Journal Gazette*, May 9, 1924. Moores reported $600 in campaign expenses, while Updike spent only $150. *Indianapolis Star*, May 25, 1924. See also *Indianapolis Times*, May 8, 1924; *Indianapolis News*, May 6, 9, 1924; *Kokomo Daily Tribune*, May 9, 1924; Madison, *Indiana through Tradition and Change*, p. 58.

32. *Indiana Catholic and Record*, October 31, 1924; *Indianapolis Times*, October 30, 1924; *Indianapolis News* and *Indianapolis Star*, November 5–6, 1924.

33. *Evansville Evening Journal*, May 5, 8 (quotation), 1924; Wilson, "Long Hot Summer in Indiana"—also appearing in Gray, *The Hoosier State*, 2:231–43; *Indianapolis Times*, October 30, 1924, and *Indiana Catholic and Record*, October 31, 1924 (quotations); *Evansville Evening Journal*, November 5, 1924.

34. *Indianapolis Times*, October 30, 1924 (quotations); *Fort Wayne Journal Gazette*, November 6, 1924.

35. *Indianapolis Times*, May 8, 1924. The loss of the prosecutor's race turned out to be of special importance to the Indianapolis Klan. The winner, William H. Remy, eventually presided over the prosecution of several Klan leaders and politicians, including D. C. Stephenson.

36. *Logansport Morning Press*, May 5, 7–8, November 6, 1924; *Evansville Evening Journal*, May 8, November 5, 1924.

37. *Anderson Daily Bulletin*, November 5, 1924; *Franklin Evening Star*, November 5, 1924; *Gary Post-Tribune*, April 23–24, 1924.

38. *Fort Wayne Journal Gazette*, May 8, November 6, 1924.

39. Ibid., November 6, 1924.

40. Ibid. See also Local Officers of the Ku Klux Klan, p. 43, Indiana Historical Society.

41. As discussed in Chapter 4, the Klan actually may have been weaker in Fort Wayne than in other Indiana cities.

42. Neil Betten, "The Klan in Northern Indiana," pp. 246, 245, from Betten, "Nativism and the Klan in Town and City."

43. *Gary Post-Tribune*, May 8, 1924.

44. Ibid.

45. Ibid., May 9–10, May 12 (quotation), November 5, 1924.

46. See the discussion of the Klan and mine workers in Chapter 4.

47. See, for example, *Vincennes Sun*, May 2, September 4, 1924.

48. For Adams's support for the Klan's operation of the Knox County Fair, see Chapter 4. See also *Vincennes Commercial*, May 8–9, November 5, 1924.

49. *Vincennes Commercial*, October 24–November 4, 1924.

50. *Vincennes Sun*, October 25 (quotation), October 27–November 5, 1924; *Vincennes Commercial*, October 27, 1924; *Vincennes Sun*, November 4, 1924. The Knox County Klan met in the Knights of Pythius Hall on the first and third Monday of each month. See Local Officers of the Ku Klux Klan, p. 7, Indiana Historical Society.

51. Indianapolis journalists perceived an overwhelming Klan influence in the state's upper and lower houses. Harold Feightner remembered that the head of the Klan in Logansport would sit next to the senator from his district whenever the senate was in session. Reporters referred to him among themselves as the "Fifty-first Senator." See Feightner interview, p. 23.

52. For a discussion of the Klan's legislative program, see Madison, *Indiana through Tradition and Change*, p. 67, and Weaver, "Knights of the Ku Klux Klan," pp. 166–67.

53. Because Jackson's papers have been sanitized of almost all references to the Klan and D. C. Stephenson, it is impossible to know for certain his attitudes toward the Klan's legislative program. Documents linking Jackson with Stephenson or the Klan would have been extremely damaging to the governor when he later went on trial. See Edward L. Jackson Papers, Archives Division, Indiana Commission on Public Records.

54. Stephenson apparently had more leverage in the senate than in the assembly. Journalists covering the legislative session were convinced that Stephenson had enough followers in the senate to crush any legislation he opposed. See Feightner interview, pp. 34–36; Madison, *Indiana through Tradition and Change*, pp. 66–67; Weaver, "Knights of the Ku Klux Klan," pp. 167–69.

55. Feightner interview, p. 33. On corruption within the Indiana Highway Commission in the 1920s, see Madison, *Indiana through Tradition and Change*, pp. 93–94.

56. See, for example, *Indiana Catholic and Record*, March 13, 15, 1925.

57. Feightner interview, p. 32.

58. Ibid., pp. 33-34.

59. Madison, *Indiana through Tradition and Change*, p. 68; Weaver, "Knights of the Ku Klux Klan," pp. 169-75; Wade, *The Fiery Cross*, pp. 239-44.

60. The downfall of Klan leaders in Indiana between 1925 and 1927 received considerable national attention and has been much discussed by historians of the Klan movement. A short list of articles written at the time includes Budenz, "Scandals of 1927—Indiana"; Taylor, "What the Klan Did in Indiana"; "Indiana's Political Housecleaning"; *New York Times*, October 2, 1927, sec. 9, p. 1. Historical accounts include Chalmers, *Hooded Americanism*, pp. 172-74; Jackson, *The Ku Klux Klan in the City*, pp. 157-60; Madison, *Indiana through Tradition and Change*, pp. 69-74. Both James Watson and Arthur Robinson denied any involvement with the Indiana Klan. Robinson had been appointed by Ed Jackson to fill the seat left vacant by Samuel Ralston's death in 1925.

61. *New York Times*, July 20, 26, August 2, 1926; Interview with Thomas Adams, *New York Times*, December 11, 1926; *Indianapolis Times* and *Indianapolis News*, December 23, 1926.

62. Madison, *Indiana through Tradition and Change*, pp. 70-71, and *The Indiana Way*, pp. 293-95.

63. Madison, *Indiana through Tradition and Change*, pp. 70-71; Jackson, *The Ku Klux Klan in the City*, p. 159; Chalmers, *Hooded Americanism*, p. 174.

Chapter 7

1. *Indianapolis Freeman*, May 17, 1924 (quotation); *Indiana Catholic and Record*, November 7, 14, 1924.

2. Madison, *Indiana through Tradition and Change*, pp. 71-74.

3. R. B. Bradford to M. L. Lain, June 26, 1926, Crown Point Ku Klux Klan Collection, Indiana Historical Society.

4. For a discussion of the difficulties of Prohibition enforcement in the twenties, see Kerr, *Organized for Prohibition*, pp. 242-59, 277-83.

5. E. H. Harris to "My dear Bennett," [n.d.], Edward H. Harris Collection, box 9, file 9, "Ku Klux Klan, 1926-1928," Regional History Archives, Indiana University East (quotation); Madison, *Indiana through Tradition and Change*, p. 70.

6. For a discussion of Democratic victories in Indiana politics during the Great Depression, see Madison, *Indiana through Tradition and Change*, pp. 132-52.

7. Cocoltchos, "The Invisible Government and the Viable Community,"

pp. 4–5; Goldberg, *Hooded Empire*, pp. 13, 164–67; Jenkins, *Steel Valley Klan*, pp. 77–94. Jenkins shows that the Klan's concern with ethnic minority groups was primarily cultural. Immigrants and blacks in Youngstown, however, were more inclined to view the Klan in a different light. Local Catholics attacked one Klan demonstration just outside of Youngstown and set off the largest anti-Klan riot in the Midwest during the 1920s. See Jenkins, *Steel Valley Klan*, pp. 117–39.

8. Goldberg, *Hooded Empire*, p. 181.

9. Cocoltchos, "The Invisible Government and the Viable Community," pp. 9–19; Jackson, *The Ku Klux Klan in the City*, p. 237. The difficulties encountered by New York City and Chicago Klansmen are discussed in Coben, "The Assault on Victorianism," pp. 623–24.

10. Jackson, *The Ku Klux Klan in the City*, pp. 10–11; Chalmers, *Hooded Americanism*, pp. 2, 49, 109–11; Alexander, *The Ku Klux Klan in the Southwest*, p. 13. Cocoltchos ("The Invisible Government and the Viable Community," pp. 611–40) ignores the issue of postwar pressures, and Goldberg (*Hooded Empire*, pp. 164–65) formally rejects it as a factor in the Klan's rise. Goldberg argues that the connection between anti-German attitudes and anti-Catholic and anti-Jewish feelings in Colorado cannot be proven, and that the Klan reached its zenith in that state too long after the war for it to have been a significant factor. This argument, however, seems to go too far. In Indiana, part of the defensive ethnic consciousness of white Protestants could be traced back to postwar nationalist and antiforeign attitudes (see Chapter 2). Even if Klan chapters directed most of their energies toward local problems, one cannot discount the effect of accumulated nationalist anxieties.

11. Jackson, *The Ku Klux Klan in the City*, p. 11; Alexander, *The Ku Klux Klan in the Southwest*, p. 13.

12. Recent works on Prohibition have interpreted it as a movement that was solidly in the Progressive tradition. Kerr, *Organized for Prohibition*, pp. 1–11.

Bibliography

This bibliography is organized as follows:
 Manuscript Collections
 Oral Histories and Interviews
 Church and Voluntary Association Records
 Government Documents and Publications
 City and County Directories
 Newspapers and Journals
 Books
 Articles, Theses, and Dissertations

Manuscript Collections

Bloomington, Indiana

Lilly Library, Indiana University
 William A. Wirt Papers

Indianapolis, Indiana

Indiana Commission on Public Records, Archives Division
 Emmett R. Branch Papers
 Edward L. Jackson Papers
Indiana Historical Society
 "Complete Roll of Indianapolis Klux," *Tolerance*, June 6, 1923
 Crown Point Ku Klux Klan Collection
 Local Officers of the Ku Klux Klan in Indiana, 1925
 D. C. Stephenson Collection
 Wayne County Ku Klux Klan Collection
Indiana State Library, Manuscripts Division
 Harold Feightner Papers
 Ku Klux Klan Papers
 Richmond, Ind., Ku Klux Klan Papers
 D. C. Stephenson Papers

Kokomo, Indiana

Records, Howard County Museum

Richmond, Indiana

Indiana University East, Regional History Archives
   Luther Martin Feeger Collection
   Edward H. Harris Collection
   Rudolph Garr Leeds Collection

Valparaiso, Indiana

Valparaiso University Archives
   Correspondence of Valparaiso University, 1923

Washington, D.C.

Library of Congress
   National Association for the Advancement of Colored People Papers
   National Urban League Papers
   Everett Sanders Papers

Oral Histories and Interviews

Bennett, Russell A. Interview, May 12, 1976. Transcript, Oral History Collection, Regional History Archives, Indiana University East, Richmond.

Feightner, Harold. Interview, February 28, 1968. Transcript, Oral History Project, Indiana Division, Indiana State Library, Indianapolis.

Knollenberg, Margaret. Interview, June 6, 1978. Transcript, Oral History Collection, Regional History Archives, Indiana University East, Richmond.

McGuire, Charles. Interview with author. Richmond, Ind., January 14, 1982.

McKinney, Donald. Interview with author. Richmond, Ind., September 8, 1986.

Ogborn, Argus. Interview with author. Richmond, Ind., July 6, 1981.

Osmundsen, Annetta. Interview, April 12, 1976. Transcript, Oral History Collection, Regional History Archives, Indiana University East, Richmond.

Pierce, Robert. Interview with author. Hagerstown, Ind., September 5, 1986.

Richmond Klansman #1. Interview with author. Richmond, Ind., July 7, 1981.
Richmond Klansman #2. Interview with author. Richmond, Ind., January 16, 1982.
Robinson, John S. Interview, June 17, 1976. Transcript, Oral History Collection, Regional History Archives, Indiana University East, Richmond.
Wayne County Klansman #1. Interview with author. Richmond, Ind., March 19, 1987.
Wayne County Klansman #2. Interview with author. Richmond, Ind., March 20, 1987.

Church and Voluntary Association Records

Convention Proceedings and Reports

Church of the Nazarene, District of Indiana. Records, 1924. First Nazarene Church, Indianapolis.
Indiana Anti-Saloon League. Records, 1924–26. Manuscripts Division, Indiana State Library, Indianapolis.
Indiana Baptist Convention. Records, 1924–25. Manuscripts Division, Indiana State Library, Indianapolis.
Indiana Taxpayers Association. Records, 1924–26. Manuscripts Division, Indiana State Library, Indianapolis.
Northern Indiana Conference of the Methodist Episcopal Church. Records, 1922–26. Roy O. West Library Archives, DePauw University, Greencastle, Ind.
Richmond Kiwanis Club. Members, 1920. Morrisson-Reeves Library, Richmond, Ind.
Richmond Lions Club. Charter Members, 1924. Club records.
Richmond Rotary Club. Minutes, 1917, 1924; Attendance Record, 1924. Morrisson-Reeves Library, Richmond, Ind.
Woman's Christian Temperance Union of the State of Indiana. Records, 1922–26. Manuscripts Division, Indiana State Library, Indianapolis.

Indianapolis Churches

All Saints Episcopal Church. New Members, 1907–21. Church records.
Barth Methodist Episcopal Church. Roll of Members, 1920–24. Roy O. West Library Archives, DePauw University, Greencastle, Ind.
Central Avenue Methodist Episcopal Church. Directory, 1925. Roy O. West Library Archives, DePauw University, Greencastle, Ind.
Central Christian Church. Ninetieth Anniversary Yearbook, 1923; Women's

Organization Yearbook, 1930. Christian Theological Seminary Archives, Indianapolis.

East New York Street Church of Christ. Church records.

First Baptist Church. Ladies' Organizations, 1921–22; Women's Groups, 1923–24. Church records.

First Nazarene Church. Record of Members, 1918–30. Church records.

New York Street United Brethren Evangelical Church. Live Membership Roll, 1925. Roy O. West Library Archives, DePauw University, Greencastle, Ind.

Riverside Park Methodist Episcopal Church. Yearbook, 1929. Roy O. West Library Archives, DePauw University, Greencastle, Ind.

Roberts Park Methodist Episcopal Church. Members, 1920s. Roy O. West Library Archives, DePauw University, Greencastle, Ind.

St. Paul's Evangelical Lutheran Church. Annual Report, 1919. Church records.

Tabernacle Presbyterian Church. Membership Record, 1883–1932. Manuscripts Division, Indiana State Library, Indianapolis.

Third Christian Church. Yearbook, 1922–23. Christian Theological Seminary Archives, Indianapolis.

Richmond Churches

Earlham Heights Presbyterian Church. Membership Roll, 1908–45. Church records.

First Christian Church. Roll of Members, 1895–1930. Church records.

First English Lutheran Church. Roll of Members, 1900–1939. Church records.

First Methodist Church. Record of Members, 1915–20. Central United Methodist Church records.

First Nazarene Church. Members, 1924. Church records.

Grace Methodist Church. Record of Members, 1906–25. Central United Methodist Church records.

Reid Memorial United Presbyterian Church. Annual Reports and Minutes, 1922–23; Church Register, 1914–25. Church records.

St. John's Lutheran Church. Ladies' Society, 1921–23. Church records.

St. Paul's Episcopal Church. Communicants, 1906–33. Church records.

St. Paul's Lutheran Church. Members, 1914–28. Church records.

Government Documents and Publications

City of Richmond, Ind. Minutes of the Common Council, 1918–24.

———. Richmond Planning Commission Records. Vol. 1, 1915–51.

State of Indiana. Attorney General of the State of Indiana v. Gillion

Knights of the Ku Klux Klan. Reel 27, Archives Division, Indiana Commission on Public Records, Indianapolis.
———. State of Indiana v. the Knights of the Ku Klux Klan. Reel 200, Archives Division, Indiana Commission on Public Records, Indianapolis.
———. *Statistical Report of the Legislative Reference Bureau, 1919// 1920* (Fort Wayne, 1921), *1923//1924-1928//1929* (Indianapolis, 1930).
———. *Yearbook, 1920, 1921, 1922, 1923, 1924, 1925, 1926.*
U.S. Bureau of the Census. *Eleventh Census of the United States.* Vol. 1, Population. Vol. 5, Agriculture. Washington, D.C., 1895.
———. *Twelfth Census of the United States.* Vol. 2, Population. Washington, D.C., 1901. Vol. 5, Agriculture. Washington, D.C. 1902.
———. *Thirteenth Census of the United States.* Vol. 1, Population. Vol. 6, Agriculture. Washington, D.C., 1913.
———. *Fourteenth Census of the United States.* Vols. 2-3, Population. Washington, D.C., 1922.
———. *Fourteenth Census of the United States: Indiana Compendium.* Washington, D.C., 1922.
———. *Fifteenth Census of the United States.* Vol. 6, Population. Washington, D.C., 1933. Vol. 7, pt. I, Agriculture: The Northern States. Washington, D.C., 1932.
———. *Religious Bodies, 1916.* Washington, D.C., 1919.
———. *Religious Bodies, 1926.* Washington, D.C., 1929.
U.S. House of Representatives. *Report on the Ku Klux Klan, 1921.* New York: Arno Press, 1969.

City and County Directories

Bennett Directory Company
  Evansville City Directory, 1920-26
Clevenger Directory Company
  Clevenger's Directory of Farmers and Breeders, Wayne County, Indiana, 1919
R. L. Polk and Company
  Crawfordsville City Directory, 1924
  Gary City Directory, 1925-26
  Indianapolis City Directory, 1920-26
  Kokomo City Directory, 1921-22, 1926
  Lafayette City Directory, 1924
  Logansport City Directory, 1926
  Marion Directory, 1925-26
  New Castle City Directory, 1926-27
  Richmond City Directory, 1903-4, 1922-24

Terre Haute City Directory, 1924
Vincennes and Knox County Directory, 1926

Newspapers and Journals

American Friend
American Issue
Anderson Daily Bulletin
Baptist Observer
Christian Evangelist
Christian Standard
Criterion
Dawn
Evansville Courier
Evansville Evening Journal
Fiery Cross
Fort Wayne Journal Gazette
Franklin Evening Star
Gary Post-Tribune
Greensburg Daily News
Harpers Magazine
Imperial Nighthawk
Indiana Catholic and Record
Indiana Jewish Chronicle
Indianapolis Area Herald
Indianapolis Freeman
Indianapolis News
Indianapolis Star
Indianapolis Times
Kokomo Daily Tribune
Kokomo Dispatch
Kourier Magazine
Lake County Star
Literary Digest
Logansport Morning Press
The Message
Muncie Morning Star
Muncie Post Democrat
The Nation
The New Republic
New York Times
Richmond Blade
Richmond Evening Item
Richmond Palladium
Richmond Palladium-Item
Richmond Daily Sun Telegram
South Bend Tribune
Terre Haute Star
Tolerance
Vincennes Commercial
Vincennes Sun
Western Christian Advocate
Winchester Democrat

Books

Abramson, Harold S. *Ethnic Diversity in Catholic America*. New York: Krieger, 1973.
Achen, Christopher H. *Interpreting and Using Regression*. Beverly Hills, Calif.: Sage Publications, 1982.
Ahlstrom, Sydney E. *A Religious History of the American People*. Garden City, N.Y.: Image Books, 1975.
Alexander, Charles C. *The Ku Klux Klan in the Southwest*. Lexington: University Press of Kentucky, 1966.
Allen, Frederick Lewis. *Only Yesterday: An Informal History of the Nineteen Twenties*. New York: Harper and Row, 1931.

Allport, Gordon. *The Nature of Prejudice*. Reading, Mass.: Addison-Wesley, 1954.

Anderson, Charles H. *White Protestant Americans: From National Origins to Religious Group*. Englewood Cliffs, N.J.: Prentice-Hall, 1970.

Angle, Paul M. *Bloody Williamson: A Chapter in American Lawlessness*. New York: Knopf, 1952.

Bailey, Harry A., and Ellis Katz, eds. *Ethnic Group Politics*. Columbus: Ohio State University Press, 1969.

Baum, Dale. *The Civil War Party System: The Case of Massachusetts, 1848–1876*. Chapel Hill: University of North Carolina Press, 1984.

Bayor, Ronald H. *Neighbors in Conflict: The Irish, Germans, Jews, and Italians of New York City, 1929–1941*. Baltimore: Johns Hopkins University Press, 1978.

Bell, Daniel, ed. *The Radical Right*. Garden City, N.Y.: Anchor Books, 1964.

Bender, Thomas H. *Community and Social Change in America*. Baltimore: Johns Hopkins University Press, 1978.

Benedict, Murray R. *Farm Policies of the United States, 1790–1950*. New York: Twentieth-Century Fund, 1953.

Bennett, David H. *The Party of Fear: From Nativist Movements to the New Right in American History*. Chapel Hill: University of North Carolina Press, 1988.

Bernstein, Irving. *The Lean Years: A History of the American Worker, 1920–1932*. Boston: Houghton Mifflin, 1960.

Blau, Peter, and Otis Dudley Duncan. *The American Occupational Structure*. New York: Wiley, 1967.

Booth, Edgar Allen. *The Mad Mullah of America*. Columbus, Ohio: Boyd Ellison Publishers, 1927.

Boyer, Paul. *Urban Masses and Moral Order in America, 1820–1920*. Cambridge: Harvard University Press, 1978.

Braeman, John. *Albert J. Beveridge: American Nationalist*. Chicago: University of Chicago Press, 1971.

———, Robert Bremner, and David Brody, eds. *Change and Continuity in Twentieth-Century America: The 1920's*. Columbus: Ohio State University Press, 1968.

Brinkley, Alan. *Voices of Protest: Huey Long, Father Coughlin, and the Great Depression*. New York: Knopf, 1982.

Buenker, John D. *Urban Liberalism and Progressive Reform*. New York: Charles Scribner's Sons, 1973.

———, John C. Burnham, and Robert M. Crunden. *Progressivism*. Cambridge, Mass.: Schenkman, 1976.

Burgess, John W. *Reconstruction and the Constitution, 1866–1876*. New York: Harper and Brothers, 1902.

Burner, David. *Politics of Provincialism: The Democratic Party in Transition, 1918–1932.* New York: Knopf, 1968.

Busch, Francis X. *Guilty or Not Guilty?* Indianapolis: Bobbs-Merrill, 1952.

Butler, Robert A. *So They Framed Stephenson.* Huntington, Ind.: Robert A. Butler, 1940.

Callahan, Raymond E. *Education and the Cult of Efficiency: A Study of the Social Forces That Have Shaped the Administration of Public Schools.* Chicago: University of Chicago Press, 1962.

Cameron, William Bruce. *Modern Social Movements: A Sociological Outline.* New York: Random House, 1966.

Carlson, Robert A. *The Quest for Conformity: Americanization through Education.* New York: Wiley, 1975.

Carter, Paul A. *Another Part of the Twenties.* New York: Columbia University Press, 1977.

———. *The Decline and Revival of the Social Gospel: Social and Political Liberalism in American Protestant Churches, 1920–1940.* Ithaca, N.Y.: Cornell University Press, 1954.

———. *The Twenties in America.* 2d ed. Arlington Heights, Ill.: A. H. M. Publishing Corp., 1975.

Chalmers, David M. *Hooded Americanism: The History of the Ku Klux Klan.* 3d ed. New York: Franklin Watts, 1981.

Chambers, Clark A. *Seedtime of Reform: American Social Services and Social Action, 1918–1933.* Minneapolis: University of Minnesota Press, 1963.

Chandler, Alfred D. *The Visible Hand: The Managerial Revolution in American Business.* Cambridge: Harvard University Press, 1977.

Child, Clifton James. *The German Americans in Politics.* New York: Arno Press, 1970.

Clark, Norman H. *Deliver Us from Evil: An Interpretation of American Prohibition.* New York: Norton, 1976.

Clough, Frank C. *William Allen White of Emporia.* New York: McGraw-Hill, 1941.

Coben, Stanley. *A. Mitchell Palmer: Politician.* New York: Columbia University Press, 1963.

———, ed. *Reform, War, and Reaction, 1912–1932.* Columbia: University of South Carolina Press, 1972.

———, and Lorman Ratner, eds. *The Development of an American Culture.* 2d ed. New York: St. Martin's Press, 1983.

Cook, Raymond Allen. *Fire from the Flint: The Amazing Careers of Thomas Dixon.* Winston-Salem, N.C.: John F. Blair, 1968.

Cremin, Lawrence A. *The Transformation of the School: Progressivism in American Education, 1876–1957.* New York: Knopf, 1961.

Curry, Lerond. *Protestant-Catholic Relations in America, World War I through Vatican II.* Lexington: University of Kentucky Press, 1972.

Curry, LeRoy A. *The Ku Klux Klan under the Searchlight.* Kansas City, Mo.: Western Baptist Publishing Co., 1924.
Davidson, Frank E. *Through the Rear View Mirror.* St. Louis, Mo.: N.p., 1955.
Dawley, Alan. *Class and Community: The Industrial Revolution in Lynn.* Cambridge: Harvard University Press, 1977.
Detjen, David W. *The Germans in Missouri, 1900–1918: Prohibition, Neutrality, and Assimilation.* Columbia: University of Missouri Press, 1985.
Dinnerstein, Leonard. *The Leo Frank Case.* New York: Columbia University Press, 1968.
Divine, Robert A. *American Immigration Policy, 1924–1952.* New Haven: Yale University Press, 1957.
Dogan, Mattei, and Stein Rokkan, eds. *Quantitative Ecological Analysis in the Social Sciences.* Cambridge: M.I.T. Press, 1969.
Draper, Norman R., and H. Smith. *Applied Regression Analysis.* New York: Wiley, 1966.
Dumenil, Lynn. *Freemasonry and American Culture, 1880–1930.* Princeton: Princeton University Press, 1984.
Dunning, William A. *Reconstruction, Political and Economic, 1865–1877.* New York: Harper and Brothers, 1907.
Endelman, Judith E. *The Jewish Community of Indianapolis, 1849 to the Present.* Bloomington: Indiana University Press, 1984.
Evans, Hiram W. *The Attitude of the Knights of the Ku Klux toward the Jew.* N.p., n.d. Pamphlet located in Ku Klux Klan Papers, Manuscripts Division, Indiana State Library, Indianapolis.
———. *The Attitude of the Knights of the Ku Klux Klan toward the Roman Catholic Hierarchy.* N.p., n.d. Pamphlet located in Ku Klux Klan Papers, Manuscripts Division, Indiana State Library, Indianapolis.
———. *The Klan Answers . . . What the Klan Has Done, What the Klan Must Do, Why the Klan Is Needed, Why We Are Klansmen.* Atlanta: American Printing and Manufacturing Co., 1929.
———. *The Klan of Tomorrow.* Kansas City, Mo.: Knights of the Ku Klux Klan, Inc., 1924.
———. *The Menace of Modern Immigration.* Dallas, Tex.: N.p., 1923.
———. *The Public School Problem in America.* N.p., 1924.
Ferguson, Charles W. *Fifty Million Brothers: A Panorama of American Lodges and Clubs.* New York: Farrar and Rinehart, 1937.
Fisher, William H. *The Invisible Empire: A Bibliography of the Ku Klux Klan.* Metuchen, N.J., 1980.
Fox, Richard Wrightman, and T. J. Jackson Lears, eds. *The Culture of Consumption: Critical Essays in American History, 1880–1980.* New York: Pantheon Books, 1983.
Frederickson, George M. *White Supremacy: A Comparative Study in*

American and South African History. New York: Oxford University Press, 1981.

Frisch, Michael. *Town into City: Springfield, Massachusetts, and the Meaning of Community, 1840–1880.* Cambridge: Harvard University Press, 1972.

Frost, Stanley. *The Challenge of the Klan.* Indianapolis: Bobbs-Merrill, 1924.

Fry, Henry Peck. *The Modern Ku Klux Klan.* Boston: Small, Maynard, 1922.

Furnis, Norman F. *The Fundamentalist Controversy, 1918–1931.* Hamden, Conn.: Archon Books, 1954.

Garner, Roberta Ash. *Social Movements in America.* 2d ed. Chicago: Rand McNally, 1977.

Gerlach, Larry R. *Blazing Crosses in Zion: The Ku Klux Klan in Utah.* Logan: Utah State University Press, 1982.

Gienapp, William E. *The Origins of the Republican Party, 1852–1856.* New York: Oxford University Press, 1987.

Ginger, Ray. *The Bending Cross: The Biography of Eugene V. Debs.* New Brunswick, N.J.: Rutgers University Press, 1964.

———. *Six Days or Forever? Tennessee v. John Thomas Scopes.* New York: Oxford University Press, 1958.

Goldberg, Robert Alan. *Hooded Empire: The Ku Klux Klan in Colorado.* Urbana: University of Illinois Press, 1981.

Goodman, Paul. *Towards a Christian Republic: Antimasonry and the Great Transition in New England, 1826–1836.* New York: Oxford University Press, 1988.

Goodwyn, Lawrence. *The Populist Movement: A Short History of the Agrarian Revolt in America.* New York: Oxford University Press, 1978.

Gordon, Milton M. *Assimilation in American Life: The Role of Race, Religion, and National Origins.* New York: Oxford University Press, 1964.

Graham, Otis L., Jr. *An Encore for Reform: The Old Progressives and the New Deal.* New York: Oxford University Press, 1967.

———. *The Great Campaigns: Reform and War in America, 1900–1928.* Englewood Cliffs, N.J.: Prentice-Hall, 1971.

Gray, Ralph, ed. *The Hoosier State: Readings in Indiana History.* 2 vols. Grand Rapids, Mich.: Eerdmans, 1980.

Griffin, Clyde, and Sally Griffin. *Natives and Newcomers: The Ordering of Opportunity in Mid-Nineteenth-Century Poughkeepsie, New York, 1850–1880.* Cambridge: Harvard University Press, 1977.

Gusfield, Joseph. *Symbolic Crusade: Status Politics and the American Temperance Movement.* Urbana: University of Illinois Press, 1963.

Gutman, Herbert. *Work, Culture, and Society in the Gilded Age.* New York: Knopf, 1977.

Hahn, Steven, and Jonathan Prude, eds. *The Countryside in the Age of Capitalist Transformation: Essays in the Social History of Rural America*. Chapel Hill: University of North Carolina Press, 1985.

Hammarberg, Melvyn. *The Indiana Voter: The Historical Dynamics of Party Allegiance during the 1870's*. Chicago: University of Chicago Press, 1977.

Handlin, Oscar. *Al Smith and His America*. Boston: Little, Brown, 1958.

Handy, Robert T. *A Christian America: Protestant Hopes and Historical Realities*. New York: Oxford University Press, 1971.

Hartmann, Edward G. *The Movement to Americanize the Immigrant*. New York: Columbia University Press, 1948.

Hausknecht, Murray. *The Joiners: A Sociological Description of Voluntary Association Membership in the United States*. New York: Bedminster Press, 1962.

Hawley, Ellis W. *The Great War and the Search for a Modern Order: A History of the American People and Their Institutions, 1917–1933*. New York: St. Martin's Press, 1979.

Heiss, Willard. *Abstract of the Record of the Society of Friends in Indiana*. Vols. 1–2, 4, and 7. Indianapolis: Indiana Historical Society, 1977.

Henri, Florette. *Black Migration: Movement North, 1900–1920*. Garden City, N.Y.: Anchor Press, 1975.

Herberg, Will. *Protestant, Catholic, Jew: An Essay in Religious Sociology*. Garden City, N.Y.: Doubleday, 1955.

Hicks, John D. *The Populist Revolt*. Minneapolis: University of Minnesota Press, 1955.

———. *The Republican Ascendancy, 1921–1933*. New York: Harper and Row, 1960.

Higham, John. *Strangers in the Land: Patterns of American Nativism, 1860–1925*. New Brunswick, N.J.: Rutgers University Press, 1955.

Hofstadter, Richard. *The Age of Reform: From Bryan to F.D.R.* New York: Vintage Books, 1955.

Howe, Daniel Walker, ed. *Victorian America*. Philadelphia: University of Pennsylvania, 1976.

Hutchinson, William R. *The Modernist Impulse in American Protestantism*. Cambridge: Harvard University Press, 1976.

Hyneman, Charles S., C. Richard Hofstetter, and Patrick F. O'Connor. *Voting in Indiana: A Century of Persistence and Change*. Bloomington: Indiana University Press, 1979.

Jackson, Kenneth T. *The Ku Klux Klan in the City, 1915–1930*. New York: Oxford University Press, 1967.

Jenkins, William D. *Steel Valley Klan: The Ku Klux Klan in Ohio's Mahoning Valley*. Kent, Ohio: Kent State University Press, 1990.

Josephson, Mathew, and Hannah Josephson. *Hero of the Cities: A*

Political Portrait of Alfred E. Smith. Boston: Houghton Mifflin, 1969.
Kennedy, David M. *Over Here: The First World War and American Society*. New York: Oxford University Press, 1980.
Kerr, K. Austin. *Organized for Prohibition: A New History of the Anti-Saloon League*. New Haven: Yale University Press, 1985.
Kettleborough, Charles. *Constitution Making in Indiana*. Vol. 3, *1916–1930*. Indianapolis: Historical Bureau of the Indiana Library and Historical Department, 1930.
Kirschner, Don S. *City and Country: Rural Responses to Urbanization in the 1920's*. Westport, Conn.: Greenwood Publishing Corp., 1970.
Kousser, J. Morgan. *The Shaping of Southern Politics: Suffrage Restriction and the Establishment of the One-Party South, 1880–1910*. New Haven: Yale University Press, 1974.
Krug, Edward A. *The Shaping of the American High School, 1880–1941*. 2 vols. Madison: University of Wisconsin Press, 1969.
La Barre, Weston. *The Ghost Dance: The Origins of Religion*. New York: Doubleday, 1970.
Lane, James B. *"City of the Century": A History of Gary, Indiana*. Bloomington: Indiana University Press, 1978.
Langbein, Laura Irwin, and Allan J. Lichtman. *Ecological Inference*. Beverly Hills, Calif.: Sage Publications, 1978.
Larson, Edward J. *Trial and Error: The American Controversy over Creation and Evolution*. New York: Oxford University Press, 1985.
Lay, Shawn. *War, Revolution, and the Ku Klux Klan: A Study of Intolerance in a Border City*. El Paso: Texas Western Press, 1985.
Lears, T. J. Jackson. *No Place of Grace: Anti-Modernism and the Transformation of American Culture, 1880–1920*. New York: Pantheon Books, 1981.
Leuchtenburg, William E. *The Perils of Prosperity, 1914–1932*. Chicago: University of Chicago Press, 1958.
Levine, Lawrence W. *Defender of the Faith: William Jennings Bryan: The Last Decade, 1915–1925*. New York: Oxford University Press, 1965.
Lewis-Beck, Michael S. *Applied Regression: An Introduction*. Beverly Hills, Calif.: Sage Publications, 1980.
Lichtman, Allan J. *Prejudice and the Old Politics: The Presidential Election of 1928*. Chapel Hill: University of North Carolina Press, 1979.
Lipset, Seymour Martin, and Earl Raab. *The Politics of Unreason: Rightwing Extremism in America, 1790–1970*. New York: Harper and Row, 1970.
Loucks, Emerson H. *The Ku Klux Klan in Pennsylvania: A Study in Nativism*. New York: Telegraph Press, 1936.
Lynd, Robert S., and Helen Merrell Lynd. *Middletown: A Study in Contemporary American Culture*. New York: Harcourt, Brace and World, 1929.

McLoughlin, William G., Jr. *Billy Sunday Was His Real Name*. Chicago: University of Chicago Press, 1955.

McPherson, James M. *Ordeal by Fire: The Civil War and Reconstruction*. New York: Knopf, 1982.

Madison, James H. *Indiana through Tradition and Change: A History of the Hoosier State and Its People, 1920–1945*. Indianapolis: Indiana Historical Society, 1982.

———. *The Indiana Way: A State History*. Bloomington: Indiana University Press. Indianapolis: Indiana Historical Society. 1986.

Marchand, Roland. *Advertising the American Dream: Making Way for Modernity, 1920–1940*. Berkeley: University of California Press, 1985.

Marsden, George M. *Fundamentalism and American Culture: The Shaping of Twentieth-Century Evangelism, 1870–1925*. New York: Oxford University Press, 1980.

Martin, John Bartlow. *Indiana: An Interpretation*. New York: Knopf, 1947.

May, Henry F. *The End of American Innocence: A Study of the First Years of Our Own Time*. New York: Knopf, 1959.

Mecklin, John Moffatt. *The Ku Klux Klan: A Study of the American Mind*. New York: Harcourt, Brace and Co., 1924.

Men of Affairs in Richmond, Indiana. Richmond: The Nicholson Press, 1908.

Meyer, Donald B. *The Protestant Search for Political Realism, 1919–1941*. Berkeley: University of California Press, 1960.

Miller, Robert Moats. *American Protestantism and Social Issues, 1919–1939*. Chapel Hill: University of North Carolina Press, 1958.

Mohl, Raymond A. *Steel City: Urban and Ethnic Patterns in Gary, Indiana, 1906–1950*. New York: Holmes and Meier, 1986.

———, and Ronald H. Cohen. *The Paradox of Progressive Education: The Gary Plan and Urban Schooling*. Port Washington, N.Y.: Kennikat Press, 1979.

Moore, Powell A. *The Calumet Region: Indiana's Last Frontier*. Indianapolis: Indiana Historical Bureau, 1959.

Murray, Robert K. *The 103rd Ballot: Democrats and the Disaster in Madison Square Garden*. New York: Harper and Row, 1976.

———. *The Politics of Normalcy: Governmental Theory and Practice in the Harding-Coolidge Era*. New York: Norton, 1973.

———. *Red Scare: A Study in National Hysteria, 1919–1920*. Minneapolis: University of Minnesota Press, 1955.

Nasaw, David. *Schooled to Order: A Social History of Public Schooling in the United States*. New York: Oxford University Press, 1979.

Niblack, John. *The Life and Times of a Hoosier Judge*. N.p., 1973.

Nye, Russell B. *Midwestern Progressive Politics: A Historical Study of Its Origins and Development, 1870–1950*. East Lansing: Michigan State University Press, 1951.

Perrett, Geoffrey. *America in the Twenties: A History*. New York: Simon and Schuster, 1982.
Phillips, Clifton J. *Indiana in Transition: The Emergence of an Industrial Commonwealth, 1880–1890*. Indianapolis: Indiana Historical Society, 1968.
Preston, William, Jr. *Aliens and Dissenters: Federal Suppression of Radicals, 1903–1933*. Cambridge: Harvard University Press, 1963.
Randel, William Pierce. *The Ku Klux Klan: A Century of Infamy*. Philadelphia: Chilton Books, 1965.
Rhodes, James Ford. *History of the United States from the Compromise of 1850*. 7 vols. New York: Harper and Brothers, 1893–1906.
Ribuffo, Leo P. *The Old Christian Right: The Protestant Far Right from the Great Depression to the Cold War*. Philadelphia: Temple University Press, 1983.
Rice, Arnold S. *The Ku Klux Klan in American Politics*. Washington, D.C.: Public Affairs Press, 1962.
Rose, Arnold M. *The Power Structure: Political Process in American Society*. New York: Oxford University Press, 1967.
Saloutos, Theodore, and John D. Hicks. *Agricultural Discontent in the Middle West, 1900–1939*. Madison: University of Wisconsin Press, 1951.
Salvatore, Nick. *Eugene V. Debs: Citizen and Socialist*. Urbana: University of Illinois Press, 1982.
Sanders, James W. *The Education of an Urban Minority: Catholics in Chicago, 1833–1965*. New York: Oxford University Press, 1977.
Schlesinger, Arthur M., Jr. *The Crisis of the Old Order, 1919–1933*. Boston: Houghton Mifflin, 1957.
Shannon, David A. *Between the Wars: America, 1919–1941*. 2d ed. Boston: Houghton Mifflin, 1979.
Shideler, James H. *Farm Crisis, 1919–1923*. Berkeley: University of California Press, 1957.
Silva, Ruth. *Rum, Religion, and Votes: 1928 Reexamined*. University Park: Pennsylvania State University Press, 1962.
Sims, Patsy. *The Klan*. New York: Stein and Day, 1978.
Sinclair, Andrew. *Prohibition: The Era of Excess*. Boston: Little, Brown, 1962.
Smelser, Neil. *Theory of Collective Behavior*. New York: Free Press, 1962.
Stephenson, D. C. *Roosevelt's Unfinished Program*. Indianapolis: D. C. Stephenson, 1924.
Tannenbaum, Frank. *Darker Phases of the South*. New York and London: G. P. Putnam's Sons, 1924.
Thelen, David. *Paths of Resistance: Tradition and Dignity in Industrializing Missouri*. New York: Oxford University Press, 1986.
Thernstrom, Stephan. *The Other Bostonians: Poverty and Progress in*

the *American Metropolis, 1880–1970*. Cambridge: Harvard University Press, 1973.
Thornbrough, Emma Lou. *The Negro in Indiana before 1900*. Indianapolis: Indiana Historical Bureau, 1957.
———. *Since Emancipation: A Short History of Indiana Negroes, 1863–1963*. Indianapolis: Indiana Division, American Negro Emancipation Centennial Authority, 1963.
Timberlake, James H. *Prohibition and the Progressive Movement, 1900–1920*. Cambridge: Harvard University Press, 1963.
Tractenberg, Alan. *The Incorporation of America: Culture and Society in the Gilded Age*. New York: Hill and Wang, 1982.
Trelease, Allen W. *White Terror: The Ku Klux Klan Conspiracy and Southern Reconstruction*. New York: Harper and Row, 1971.
Turner, Ralph H., and Lewis Killian. *Collective Behavior*. 2d ed. Englewood Cliffs, N.J.: Prentice-Hall, 1972.
Tyack, David. *The One Best System: A History of American Urban Education*. Cambridge: Harvard University Press, 1974.
VanderMeer, Philip R. *The Hoosier Politician: Office Holding and Political Culture in Indiana, 1896–1920*. Urbana: University of Illinois Press, 1985.
Wade, Wyn Craig. *The Fiery Cross: The Ku Klux Klan in America*. New York: Simon and Schuster, 1987.
Weinstein, James. *The Decline of Socialism in America, 1912–1925*. New York: Monthly Review Press, 1967.
White, William Allen. *Politics: The Citizen's Business*. New York: Macmillan, 1924.
Wiebe, Robert H. *The Search for Order, 1877–1920*. New York: Hill and Wang, 1967.
Williamson, Joel. *The Crucible of Race: Black-White Relations in the American South since Emancipation*. New York: Oxford University Press, 1984.
Wilson, John. *Introduction to Social Movements*. New York: Basic Books, 1973.
Wilson, William E. *Indiana: A History*. Bloomington: Indiana University Press, 1966.
Zunz, Olivier. *The Changing Face of Inequality: Urbanization, Industrial Development, and Immigrants in Detroit, 1880–1920*. Chicago: University of Chicago Press, 1982.

Articles, Theses, and Dissertations

Barrows, Robert G. "The 1910 Census: A Note." *Indiana Magazine of History* 78 (1982): 341–45.

Betten, Neil. "The Klan in Northern Indiana." In *The Hoosier State: Readings in Indiana History*, edited by Ralph Gray, pp. 242–51. Grand Rapids, Mich.: Eerdmans, 1980.

———. "Nativism and the Klan in Town and City: Valparaiso and Gary, Indiana." *Studies in History and Society* 4 (1973): 3–13.

Bigham, Darrell E. "Work, Residence, and the Emergence of the Black Ghetto in Evansville, Indiana, 1865–1900." *Indiana Magazine of History* 76 (1980): 287–318.

Bohn, Frank. "The Ku Klux Klan Interpreted." *American Journal of Sociology* 30 (1925): 385–407.

Brownell, Blain A. "Birmingham, Alabama: New South City in the 1920's." *Journal of Southern History* 38 (February 1972): 21–48.

Budenz, Louis Francis. "Scandals of 1927—Indiana." *The Nation* 125, no. 3248 (October 5, 1927): 332–33.

Burbank, Garin. "Agrarian Radicals and Their Opponents: Political Conflict in Southern Oklahoma, 1910–1924." *Journal of American History* 58 (1971): 5–23.

Burner, David B. "The Democratic Party in the Election of 1924." *Mid-America* 46 (1964): 92–113.

Burnham, John C. "New Perspectives on the Prohibition Experiment of the 1920's." *Journal of Social History* 2 (1968): 51–68.

Cates, Frank M. "The Ku Klux Klan in Indiana Politics: 1920–1925." Ph.D. dissertation, Indiana University, 1971.

Chalmers, David. "The Ku Klux Klan in Politics in the 1920's." *Mississippi Quarterly* 18 (1965): 234–47.

———. "The Ku Klux Klan in the Sunshine State: The 1920's." *Florida Historical Quarterly* 42 (1964): 209–15.

Clark, Carter B. "A History of the Ku Klux Klan in Oklahoma." Ph.D. dissertation, University of Oklahoma, 1976.

Clark, Malcolm, Jr. "The Bigot Disclosed: Ninety Years of Nativism." *Oregon Historical Quarterly* 75 (1974): 108–90.

Clutter, Richard Morris. "The Indiana American Legion, 1919–1960." Ph.D. dissertation, Indiana University, 1974.

Coben, Stanley. "The Assault on Victorianism in the Twentieth Century." *American Quarterly* 27 (1975): 604–25.

———. "The First Years of Modern America." In *The Unfinished Century*, edited by William E. Leuchtenburg, pp. 255–353. Boston: Little, Brown, 1973.

———. "A Study in Nativism: The American Red Scare of 1919–1920." *Political Science Quarterly* 79 (1964): 52–75.

Cocoltchos, Christopher Nickolas. "The Invisible Government and the Viable Community: The Ku Klux Klan in Orange County, California, during the 1920's." Ph.D. dissertation, University of California, Los Angeles, 1979.

Coughlan, Robert. "Konklave in Kokomo." In *The Aspirin Age*, edited by Isabel Leighton, pp. 105–29. New York: Simon and Schuster, 1949.

Crownover, Donald A. "The Ku Klux Klan in Lancaster County, 1923–1924." *Journal of the Lancaster County [Pa.] Historical Society* 68 (1964): 63–77.

Curry, Richard O. "The Civil War and Reconstruction, 1861–1877: A Critical Overview of Recent Trends and Interpretation." *Civil War History* 20 (1974): 215–28.

Davis, John A. "The Ku Klux Klan in Indiana, 1920–1930: A Historical Study." Ph.D. dissertation, Northwestern University, 1966.

Degler, Carl N. "A Century of the Klans: A Review Article." *Journal of Southern History* 31 (1965): 435–43.

Dewey, Richard. "The Rural-Urban Continuum: Real but Relatively Unimportant." *American Journal of Sociology* 66 (1960): 60–66.

Du Bois, W. E. B. "The Shape of Fear." *North American Review* 223 (1926): 291–304.

Duffus, Robert L. "The Ku Klux Klan in the Middle West." *World's Work* 46 (1923): 363–72.

Eagles, Charles W. "Urban-Rural Conflict in the 1920's: A Historiographic Assessment." *The Historian* 49 (1986): 26–48.

Edmonson, Ben G. "Pat Harrison and Mississippi in the Presidential Elections of 1924–1928." *Journal of Mississippi History* 33 (1971): 333–50.

Evans, Hiram W. "The Klan's Fight for Americanism." *North American Review* 223 (1926): 33–63.

Fischer, Claude S. "Toward a Subcultural Theory of Urbanism." *American Journal of Sociology* 80 (1975): 1319–41.

Foner, Eric. "Reconstruction Revisited." In *The Promise of American History: Progress and Prospects*, edited by Stanley I. Kutler and Stanley N. Katz. Baltimore: Johns Hopkins University Press, 1982.

Frank, Carrolyle M. "Who Governed Middletown? Community Power in Muncie, Indiana, in the 1930's." *Indiana Magazine of History* 79 (1979): 322–43.

Garson, Robert A. "Political Fundamentalism and Popular Democracy in the 1920's." *South Atlantic Quarterly* 76 (1977): 219–33.

Gatewood, Willard B., Jr. "Politics and Piety in North Carolina: The Fundamentalist Crusade at High Tide, 1925–1927." *North Carolina Historical Review* 42 (1965): 275–90.

Glad, Paul W. "Progressives and the Business Culture of the 1920's." *Journal of American History* 53 (1966): 75–89.

Goldberg, Robert A. "The Ku Klux Klan in Madison, Wisconsin, 1922–1927." *Wisconsin Magazine of History* 58 (1974): 31–44.

Goodman, Leo A. "Some Alternatives to Ecological Correlation." *American Journal of Sociology* 64 (1959): 610–25.

Gordon, Milton M. "Assimilation in America: Theory and Reality." In *The Ethnic Factor in American Politics*, edited by Brett W. Hawkins and Robert A. Lorinskas, pp. 24–44. Columbus: Ohio State University Press, 1970.

Griffen, Clyde. "The Progressive Ethos." In *The Development of an American Culture*, 2d ed., edited by Stanley Coben and Lorman Ratner, pp. 144–80. New York: St. Martin's Press, 1983.

Griffin, William W. "The Political Realignment of Black Voters in Indianapolis, 1924." *Indiana Magazine of History* 79 (1983): 133–66.

Hofstadter, Richard. "Could a Protestant Have Beaten Hoover in 1928?" *Reporter* 22 (1960): 31–33.

———. "U. B. Phillips and the Plantation Legend." *Journal of Negro History* 29 (1944): 109–24.

Hoover, Dwight W. "To Be a Jew in Middletown: A Muncie Oral History Project." *Indiana Magazine of History* 81 (1985): 131–58.

Howe, Daniel Walker. "American Victorianism as a Culture." *American Quarterly* 27 (1975): 507–32.

Ibson, John. "Virgin Land or Virgin Mary? Studying the Ethnicity of White Americans." *American Quarterly* 33 (1981): 284–308.

"Indiana's Political Housecleaning." *Literary Digest* 95, no. 1 (October 1, 1927): 14.

Irwin, Laura, and Allan J. Lichtman. "Across the Great Divide: Inferring Individual Level Behavior from Aggregate Data." *Political Methodology* 4 (1976): 411–39.

Jackson, Charles O. "William J. Simmons: A Career in Ku Kluxism." *Georgia Historical Quarterly* 50 (1966): 351–65.

Jenkins, William D. "The Ku Klux Klan in Youngstown, Ohio: Moral Reform in the Twenties." *The Historian* 41 (1978): 76–93.

Jensen, Richard. "The Lynds Revisited." *Indiana Magazine of History* 75 (1979): 303–19.

Jones, E. Terrence. "Ecological Inference and Electoral Analysis." *Journal of Interdisciplinary History* 2 (1972): 249–69.

Jones, Lila L. "The Ku Klux Klan in Eastern Kansas during the 1920's." *Emporia State Research Studies* 23 (1975): 5–41.

Kelly, Darwin N. "The McNary-Haugen Bills, 1924–1928." *Agricultural History* 14 (1940): 170–80.

Kevles, Daniel J. "Testing the Army's Intelligence: Psychologists in World War I." *Journal of American History* 55 (1968): 565–81.

Kleppner, Paul. "Searching for the Indiana Voter: A Review Essay." *Indiana Magazine of History* 76 (1980): 346–66.

Kousser, J. Morgan. "Ecological Regression and the Analysis of Past Politics." *Journal of Interdisciplinary History* 4 (1973): 237–62.

———. "The 'New Political History': A Methodological Critique." *Reviews in American History* 4 (1976): 1–10.

Kyvig, David E. "Women against Prohibition." *American Quarterly* 28 (1976): 464–82.
La Barre, Weston. "Materials for a History of Studies of Crisis Cults: A Bibliographic Essay." *Current Anthropology* 12 (1971): 3–44.
Lichtman, Allan J. "Correlation, Regression, and the Ecological Fallacy: A Critique." *Journal of Interdisciplinary History* 4 (1974): 417–33.
———. "Critical Election Theory and the Reality of American Presidential Politics, 1916–1940." *American Historical Review* 81 (1976): 317–51.
———. "Political Realignment and 'Ethnocultural' Voting in Late Nineteenth-Century America." *Journal of Social History* 16 (1983): 55–82.
———, and Laura Longbein. "Across the Great Divide: Inferring Individual Behavior from Aggregate Data." *Political Methodology* 5 (1976): 411–39.
———, and Laura Longbein. "Ecological Regression vs. Homogeneous Units: A Specification Analysis." *Social Science History* 2 (1978): 172–93.
Link, Arthur S. "What Happened to the Progressive Movement in the 1920's?" *American Historical Review* 64 (1959): 833–51.
MacLean, Nancy K. "Behind the Mask of Chivalry: Gender, Race, and Class in the Making of the Ku Klux Klan of the 1920's in Georgia." Ph.D. dissertation, University of Wisconsin–Madison, 1989.
May, Henry F. "Shifting Perspectives on the 1920's." *Mississippi Valley Historical Review* 43 (1956): 405–27.
Meier, August, and Elliot Rudwick. "Early Boycotts of Segregated Schools: The Case of Springfield, Ohio." *American Quarterly* 20 (1968): 744–58.
Miller, Robert Moats. "The Ku Klux Klan." In *Change and Continuity in Twentieth-Century America: The 1920's*, edited by John Braeman, Robert Bremner, and David Brody, pp. 215–55. Columbus: Ohio State University Press, 1968.
———. "A Note on the Relationship between the Protestant Churches and the Revived Ku Klux Klan." *Journal of Southern History* 22 (1956): 355–68.
Moore, Leonard J. "Historical Interpretations of the 1920's Klan: The Traditional View and the Populist Revision." *Journal of Social History* 24 (1990): 341–57.
———. "White Protestant Nationalism in the 1920's: The Ku Klux Klan in Indiana." Ph.D. dissertation, University of California, Los Angeles, 1985.
Moore, William V. "A Sheet and a Cross: A Symbolic Analysis of the Ku Klux Klan." Ph.D. dissertation, Tulane University, 1975.
Moseley, Clement C. "Invisible Empire: A History of the Ku Klux Klan in Twentieth-Century Georgia, 1915–1965." Ph.D. dissertation, University of Georgia, 1968.
———. "The Political Influence of the Ku Klux Klan in Georgia, 1915–1925." *Georgia Historical Quarterly* 57 (1973): 235–55.

Murphy, Paul L. "The Sources and Nature of Intolerance in the 1920's." *Journal of American History* 51 (1964): 60–67.

Noggle, Burl. "The Twenties: A New Historiographic Frontier." *Journal of American History* 52 (1966): 299–324.

O'Brian, Kenneth B., Jr. "Education, Americanization, and the Supreme Court: The 1920's." *American Quarterly* 13 (1961): 161–71.

Parker, Albert C. E. "Beating the Spread: Analyzing American Election Outcomes." *Journal of American History* 61 (1980): 61–87.

Racine, Philip N. "The Ku Klux Klan, Anti-Catholicism, and Atlanta's Board of Education, 1916–1927." *Georgia Historical Quarterly* 57 (1973): 63–75.

Rambow, Charles. "The Ku Klux Klan in the 1920's: A Concentration on the Black Hills." *South Dakota History* 4 (1973): 63–81.

Robinson, William S. "Ecological Correlations and the Behavior of Individuals." *American Sociological Review* 15 (1950): 351–57.

Safianow, Allen. "'Konklave in Kokomo' Revisited." *The Historian* 50 (1988): 329–47.

Scharlatt, Bradford. "The Hoosier Newsmen and the Hooded Order." M.A. thesis, Indiana University, 1978.

Schonbach, Morris. "Native Fascism in the 1930's and 1940's: A Study of Its Roots, Its Growth, and Its Decline." Ph.D. dissertation, University of California, Los Angeles, 1958.

Shideler, James H. "*Flappers and Philosophers*, and Farmers: Rural-Urban Tensions of the Twenties." *Agricultural History* 47 (1973): 283–99.

Singleton, Gregory. "Fundamentalism and Urbanization: A Quantitative Critique of Impressionistic Interpretations." In *The New Urban History: Quantitative Explorations by American Historians*, edited by Leo F. Schnore and Eric E. Lampard, pp. 205–27. Princeton: Princeton University Press, 1975.

———. "Religion in the City of the Angels: American Protestant Culture and Urbanization, Los Angeles, 1850–1930." Ph.D. dissertation, University of California, Los Angeles, 1976.

Slawson, Douglas J. "The Attitudes and Activities of American Catholics Regarding the Proposals to Establish a Federal Department of Education between World War I and the Great Depression." Ph.D. dissertation, Catholic University of America, 1981.

Sloan, Charles W., Jr. "Kansas Battles the Invisible Empire: The Legal Ouster of the K.K.K. from Kansas, 1922–1927." *Kansas Historical Quarterly* 40 (1974): 393–409.

Smith, Norman. "The Ku Klux Klan in Rhode Island." *Rhode Island History* 37 (1978): 35–45.

Smith, William. "William Jennings Bryan and Racism." *Journal of Negro History* 54 (1969): 127–49.

Snell, William R. "Fiery Crosses in the Roaring Twenties: Activities of the Revived Klan in Alabama, 1915–1930." *Alabama Review* 23 (1970): 256–76.

Stamp, Kenneth M. "The Historian and Southern Negro Slavery." *American Historical Review* 57 (1952): 613–24.

Swart, Stanley L. "A Memo on Cross-Burning—And Its Implications." *Northwest Ohio Quarterly* 43 (1971): 70–74.

Taylor, Alva W. "What the Klan Did in Indiana," *The New Republic* 52, no. 676 (November 16, 1927): 330–32.

Thornbrough, Emma Lou. "Segregation in Indiana during the Klan Era of the 1920's." *Mississippi Valley Historical Review* 47 (1961): 594–618.

Thornton, J. Mills, III. "Alabama Politics, J. Thomas Heflin, and the Expulsion Movement of 1929." *Alabama Review* 21 (1968): 83–112.

Toll, William. "Progress and Piety: The Ku Klux Klan and Social Change in Tillamook, Oregon." *Pacific Northwest Quarterly* 69 (1978): 75–85.

Toy, Eckard V., Jr. "The Ku Klux Klan in Tillamook, Oregon." *Pacific Northwest Quarterly* 53 (1962): 60–64.

Tyack, David B. "The Perils of Pluralism: The Background of the Pierce Case." *American Historical Review* 74 (1968): 74–98.

Wald, Kenneth D. "The Visible Empire: The Ku Klux Klan as an Electoral Movement." *Journal of Interdisciplinary History* 11 (1980): 217–37.

Wallace, Anthony F. C. "Revitalization Movements." *American Anthropologist* 58 (1956): 264–81.

Waterhouse, David L. "The Estimation of Voting Behavior from Aggregated Data: A Test." *Journal of Social History* 16 (1983): 35–53.

———. "The Failure of Working-Class Politics in America: The Case of the Progressive Movement of 1924." Ph.D. dissertation, University of California, Los Angeles, 1982.

Weaver, Norman F. "The Knights of the Ku Klux Klan in Wisconsin, Indiana, Ohio, and Michigan." Ph.D. dissertation, University of Wisconsin, 1955.

Weinstein, James. "Radicalism in the Midst of Normalcy." *Journal of American History* 52 (1966): 773–90.

Weisenberger, Bernard A. "The Dark and Bloody Ground of Reconstruction Historiography." *Journal of Southern History* 25 (1959): 427–47.

White, Joseph Michael. "The Ku Klux Klan in Indiana in the 1920's as Viewed by the *Indiana Catholic and Record*." M.A. thesis, Butler University, 1974.

Wilson, William E. "Long Hot Summer in Indiana." *American Heritage* 16 (August 1965): 57–64.

Index

Abington, Indiana, 131
Adams, Thomas H., 97, 178, 187
Akron, Ohio, 14
Alabama, 2, 15
Allen County, 59, 174–76
American Issue, 179
Anaheim, California, 2
Anderson, Albert B., 90–91, 116
Anderson, Indiana, 80, 83, 96
Anderson Daily Bulletin, 173
Arkansas, 2
Armitage, William H., 146
Atlanta, Georgia, 1, 15–16
Austin, Indiana, 84

Ball Brothers Company, 84
Baptist church, 26, 34–35, 72, 74; anti-Catholicism, 29
Baptist Observer, 29, 30, 35, 42
Barry, Charles, 149
Beveridge, Albert J., 151–52, 158
Blacks, 223 (n. 19); opposition to Klan, 21–22, 25; Klan membership near black neighborhoods in Indianapolis, 142; residential segregation campaign, 144–45; and Republican party, 159–60; vote against Jackson, 160–61. *See also* Indianapolis: racial segregation; *Indianapolis Freeman*
Boone County, 53
Bossert, Walter, 154; appointed Grand Dragon, 46, 93; conflict with Stephenson, 155–58, 180–81

Boston, Indiana, 131, 136
Branch, Emmett F., 153
Bryan, William Jennings, 42
Buhler, Robert A., 175
Business elite: industrialization and expanding role in community, 82–84; in Terre Haute, 84–85; in Muncie, 85–87; control over charity and social services, 87; lack of support for Prohibition, 103–4; annexation controversy in Richmond, 124–30; conflict with Klan, 172–75. *See also* Richmond, Indiana; Whitewater Klan No. 60

California, 2
Cambridge City, Indiana, 130–31, 133
Canfield, Harry C., 171
Canon City, Colorado, 2
Cass County, 173
Catholics, 53; opposition to Klan, 21–22, 25; and anti-Catholicism, 36–37. *See also* Gary, Indiana; *Indiana Catholic and Record*; Indianapolis; Ku Klux Klan—Indiana: anti-Catholicism; Ku Klux Klan—national movement; Richmond, Indiana
Centerville, 121, 130, 131, 136–37, 138–39
Chester, Indiana, 131
Chicago, Illinois, 6, 80, 81, 82
Christian Standard, 30

Church of the Nazarene, 42, 70
Cincinnati, Ohio, 80, 82
Citizen's School Committee, 147–49, 182. *See also* Indianapolis: school building program controversy
Clark County, 56–58
Clarke, Edward Young, 15–16, 18
Cleveland, Ohio, 80, 81, 82
Coffin, George V., 145–46, 183
Colorado, 2, 189–90
Committee of Ten, 103, 178. *See also* Vincennes, Indiana
Cook, Samuel, 172, 173
Coolidge, Calvin, 2, 151, 157, 162
Copeland, Guild A., 126–29
Craven, Joseph M., 56
Crawfordsville, Indiana, 96
Crispus Attucks High School, 149
Crittenburg, Dale J., 173
Crown Point, Indiana, 61–62, 65, 73; occupations of Klan members, 67–68; Klan membership in Protestant churches, 72–73

Dale, George R., 182
Dalton, Indiana, 131
Davis, John, 162
Dayton, Ohio, 180
Delaware County, 47
Democratic party, 2, 12, 27, 53, 55; Klan influence in 1924 election, 152; defections to Republican party in 1924, 161. *See also* Election, 1924
Denver, Colorado, 65, 142
Detroit, Michigan, 6
Disciples of Christ, 26, 72, 74; anti-Catholicism, 30. *See also* Indiana: anti-Catholicism
Dixon, Thomas, 3
Durgan, George R., 24, 25, 98, 159
Duvall, John L., 145–46, 182, 187

Earlham College, 108
East Chicago, Indiana, 80, 176
Economic conditions in Indiana: differences between northern and southern Indiana, 57; industrial development (1890–1920), 79–91; centralization and modernization of industry, 83–84; rural, 87–89; declining rural population, 88; farm consolidation and tenancy, 88–89; modernization of agriculture, 88–89; rural decline in southern Indiana, 89
Economy, Indiana, 131
Election, 1924: "anti-Klan" variables, 162; party alignment (1920–24), 162–64; religious affiliation, 164–67; urban/rural status, 167; economic status, 167, 169; women and immigrants, 168–69; continued Republican control, 169–70; local party organizations disrupted by Klan, 170–79
Eliot, George, 146
Elliott, Richard N., 171
El Paso, Texas, 2
Elwood, Indiana, 96, 98
Endelman, Judith E., 143
Episcopal church, 72, 75
Evans, Hiram, 13, 14, 36, 46, 155; takes over national Klan, 18; appoints Stephenson Grand Dragon, 19; conflict with Stephenson, 93; weakens and divides Indiana Klan, 93
Evansville, Indiana, 13–16, 57, 80, 81, 84, 98, 172, 173
Evansville Evening Journal, 172

Fairfield, Lewis, 172–73
Feightner, Harold, 46

Fiery Cross, 16, 25, 32, 35, 36, 38, 92, 98, 149, 154
Floyd County, 57
Fort Wayne, Indiana, 80, 81, 102, 175–76; Klan political influence, 57–59
Fort Wayne Home for the Feeble Minded, 175
Fort Wayne Journal Gazette, 175
Fountain City, Indiana, 131, 136
Franklin Evening Star, 26
Fundamentalism, 72; and Klan movement, 41–43

Gardner, Frank, 171
Gary, Indiana, 80, 81, 82, 83, 176
Gary Post-Tribune, 31, 176
Georgia, 2, 15
German immigrants, 56, 72
Goldberg, Robert, 65, 70, 189–90
Goodrich, James P., 91, 153, 156
Grayson, John M., 178
Greenfork, Indiana, 131, 136
Greensburg Daily News, 29
Greenwood, Arthur H., 26, 56, 172
Griffith, D. W.: *The Birth of a Nation*, 3, 15, 52

Hagerstown, Indiana, 131, 136–37, 138–39
Hall, Albert R., 171, 173
Halsep, Marie, 148
Hamilton, Ohio, 127
Hammond, Indiana, 80, 176
Handley, Lawrence A., 125, 126, 127, 128
Hanley, J. Frank, 91
Harris, Edward H., 125, 187
Henry County, 130
Herrin, Illinois, 24, 35
Hickey, Andrew J., 171
Hill, James W., 26

Hogg, David, 171, 173, 174, 175
Holt, Orin, 158
Horse Thief Detective Association, 123
Houston, Texas, 13
Huffington, Joseph M., 13–14, 16, 46, 93, 155

Illinois, 81, 145
Indiana: ethnic population, 10; pervasiveness of Protestant values, 28–29; anti-Catholicism, 29–31; antiforeign attitudes, 31; Prohibition enforcement, 33–36; public education, 37–38; foreign-born population and Klan membership, 47, 51–52; German population, 51–52; Catholic population, 52; Jewish population, 52; alcohol restrictions before 1917, 56; urban-rural conflict, 80–82; philanthropy, 84, 86–87; decline in voter turnout, 86–87; reactions to Jackson's election, 154. See also Economic conditions in Indiana; Election, 1924; Ku Klux Klan—Indiana
Indiana American Legion, 26
Indiana Anti-Saloon League, 26, 34, 42, 79, 178–79, 181
Indiana Catholic and Record, 21–22, 24, 32, 159, 160, 171, 184
Indiana Farm Bureau, 89, 191
Indiana Highway Commission, 180
Indiana Historical Society, 193
Indiana Jewish Chronicle, 22, 160
Indiana Republican Newspaper Association, 182
Indiana State Library, Manuscript Division, 194
Indiana Tax Board, 149
Indiana Taxpayers Association, 147
Indiana Woman's Christian Temper-

ance Union, 26, 34, 79. *See also* Halsep, Marie

Indianapolis, 7, 8, 16, 25, 61–62, 81, 82, 83, 84, 86, 100, 103, 104, 107; school building program controversy, 38, 147–50; black population, 53, 140–41; economic conditions, 62; occupations of Klansmen, 62–65; Klan membership in Protestant churches, 71–72; native white population, 82; business leaders and reform, 86; Klan demonstration, 100; "Dear Jerry" episode, 103; Klan Christmas charity drive, 104; immigrant population, 140; racial segregation, 141, 144–45, 149–50; Klan and Republican machine, 145–47; occupational, religious, and residential samples, 193–95

Indianapolis Area Herald, 30, 42

Indianapolis Board of School Commissioners, 147, 149

Indianapolis Chamber of Commerce, 86, 87, 147, 149, 182; education committee, 148; advocates fewer resources for Prohibition enforcement, 103. *See also* Business elite; Indianapolis: school building program controversy

Indianapolis City Directory, 195

Indianapolis Commercial Club, 86

Indianapolis Freeman, 22, 53, 160

Indianapolis News, 147, 148, 149, 155, 182

Indianapolis Star, 148, 155

Indianapolis Times, 24, 146, 148, 154, 155, 160, 187

International Harvester, 109

Irish immigrants, 56

Jackson, Edward, 46, 91, 151–53, 154, 156, 157, 159, 161, 178, 187; supported by Stephenson and Watson, 152–53; supported by Bossert, 156–57; campaign against McCulloch, 159–60; fails to carry Allen County, 174; refuses to support anti-Catholic legislation, 180; indicted for bribery, 183; personal papers, 225 (n. 53). *See also* Election, 1924; Stephenson, David Curtis: relationship with Jackson

Jackson, James G., 175

Jackson, Kenneth, 44, 60

Jefferson County, 56

Jeffersonville, Indiana, 57–58, 96

Jews, 21–22, 25. *See also* Indiana: Jewish population; *Indiana Jewish Chronicle*; Ku Klux Klan— Indiana: anti-Semitism; Ku Klux Klan—Indianapolis: ethnic conflict; TWK campaign

Johnson, Noble J., 171

Johnson, Roswell O., 176

Johnson County, 174

Junior Klan, 7, 47, 77, 101

Kansas, 2

Kendallville, Indiana, 96

Kimmell, Joseph, 178

Kinney, Jeremiah, 90

Kiper, Roscoe, 172

Kloran, 94, 120

Knights of Columbus, 30

Knox County, 178

Kokomo, Indiana, 77, 80, 83, 96, 105; Fourth of July Klan rally (1923), 19, 76; Fourth of July Klan rally (1924), 76–78; weekly Klan meetings and social events, 94–95; Klan County hospital campaign, 105; "Klan bank" and dredging of Wild Cat Creek, 105–6

Kokomo Daily Tribune, 26, 34, 77, 94, 98, 154

Ku Klux Klan:

—Indiana: significance in national movement, 6–8; membership documents, 7–8, 46, 62; traditional interpretation, 8–12; conflict with ethnic minority groups, 10–11; as a populist organization, 11–12; early membership campaign, 16–17; anti-Catholicism, 19–20, 36–38; anti-Semitism, 20–21; racism, 20–21; anti-foreign attitudes, 21; white Protestant nationalism as a means of articulating social and political concerns, 22–23; violence as a tactic, 23–25; opposed by groups and individuals, 25–28; ethnocentric rhetoric and mainstream values, 31; views on Prohibition, 32–33; views on public education, 36–37; support for Indianapolis school building program, 38; views on political corruption, 39; views on traditional gender roles, 39–40; views on youth culture, 40; and fundamentalism, 41–43; active state membership (1925), 46–48; foreign-born (mostly German) members, 47, 51–52; membership in southern Indiana, 52–57; membership in central and northern Indiana, 53; membership in New Albany, 57–58; membership in urban and rural areas, 57–60; membership in Fort Wayne, 58–59; membership in Marion County, 59; occupations of members, 61–65, 67–68; initiation fee, 63; business elites fail to join, 64–65; wage-earner status and Klan membership, 68–69; home owner/renter status and Klan membership, 69–70; Protestant church members and Klan membership, 70–75; community activities, 78; Prohibition enforcement, 78–79, 102–4, 175–79; ineffectiveness of leaders, 92–94; grass roots nature of movement, 93–94; weekly meetings, 94; as a social organization, 94–101; accessibility compared to other voluntary organizations, 95; and labor groups, 96–97; importance of large demonstrations in communities, 96–100; women and families in social activities, 100–101; as a civic organization, 102–6; charity works, 104–6; influence of Klan vote on 1924 state election, 161–62; influence on party alignment (1920–24), 162–64; influence on state congressional races (1924), 171–73; fails to enact anti-Catholic education program, 179–80; decline, 184–88; Stephenson murder scandal, 191–83

—Indianapolis: ethnic conflict, 139–41; characteristics of members, 141–44; residential membership patterns, 142–44; relations with Jewish community, 143–44; and German community, 144; racial conflict and segregation, 144–45, 149–50; and Republican machine, 145–47, 172–73; school building program controversy and control of school board, 148–50, 182–83; anti-Catholicism, 149; supports Bossert over Stephenson, 155; Duvall and Klan city council resign offices, 182–83

—national movement: popular perceptions of, 1, 3; traditional interpretation, 1–6; in politics, 2; regional popularity, 2; ideology, 2–3; origins, 15–16; Simmons removed from leadership, 17–18; Prohibition enforcement and violence in Herrin, Illinois, 35–36; membership records lost, 44, 204 (n. 1); problems in estimating social characteristics of members, 44–45; urban thesis, 44–45; ethnic conflict, 188–89; Prohibition as a catalyst, 190–91; as a populist movement, 190–91; distinct characteristics of three major Klan movements, 198 (n. 12)

Lafayette, Indiana, 24, 96, 98
LaFollette, Robert, 162
Lake County, 67, 81, 82, 176, 177–78; Prohibition and corruption in government, 90
LaPorte, Indiana, 59, 174
Leeds, Rudolph Garr, 125
Lilly, Eli, 86
Lipset, Seymour Martin, 45
Logansport, Indiana, 96, 98, 103
Logansport Morning Press, 173
Louisville, Kentucky, 57, 58
Lutheran church, 72, 75
Lynd, Robert, and Helen Lynd: *Middletown*, 28–29, 40–41, 80, 85, 86
Lyons, Robert, 115–16

McCray, Warren T., 24, 91, 151, 156, 162, 183, 221 (n. 9)
McCulloch, Carleton B., 27, 158, 159, 160, 161
Madison, James H., 82
Madison County, 173
Marion County, 53, 59, 94, 155
Marsall, Thomas R., 91
Men of Affairs in Richmond, Indiana, 111

Methodist church, 7, 26, 42, 72, 74; anti-Catholicism, 30
Michigan, 81
Michigan City, Indiana, 59
Middleboro, Indiana, 131
Middletown. See Lynd, Robert, and Helen Lynd
Milton, Indiana, 131
Mitchell, Indiana, 24
Montana, 2
Moores, Merrill, 172
Morgan, Bert, 90
Morgan Packing Company, 84
Morrisson-Reeves Library, 124, 194
Muncie, Indiana, 28, 40–41, 80, 81, 83, 84, 96, 103, 182; and "business class," 85–87; political conditions, 86–87; charity and social service organizations, 87; as a "typical" American city, 211 (n. 28). *See also* Lynd, Robert, and Helen Lynd
Muncie Morning Star, 31
Muncie Post-Democrat, 24, 26, 182

National Origins Act, 31
National Road, 130–31
National Street Map of Indianapolis, 195
New, Harry S., 153, 157
New Albany, Indiana, 57–58
New Castle, Indiana, 59, 83
New Jersey, 2
New York, 2
New York Times, 46
Nicholson, Meredith, 92
Niles, Ohio, 24
North Vernon, Indiana, 96

Oberholtzer, Madge, 46, 181, 185
Ohio, 2, 81
Ohio County, 56
Oklahoma, 2, 13

Orange County, California, 189, 191
Oregon, 2

Paoli, Indiana, 96
Pennsylvania, 2
Pennsylvania Railroad, 109
Peru, Indiana, 59
Presbyterian church, 72, 74
Prohibition, 3, 23, 78, 79, 92; Klan's attitude toward, 32; history in Indiana, 56; importance at local level in Klan movement, 78–79; and political corruption, 90; and impact on communities, 90–92; Klan enforcement efforts, 102–4; "Dear Jerry" episode, 103; Klan enforcement efforts in Richmond, 123; local option elections in Richmond, 123; support for enforcement in rural Wayne County Klan, 138–39; Klan support for "law enforcement" candidates, 179; vice and corruption in Lake County, 175–78; Wright "Bone Dry" bill, 181; as catalyst for Klan movement, 190–91
Protestant Episcopal church, Indianapolis Diocese, 25, 70
Protestant School Ticket, 149. *See also* Ku Klux Klan—Indianapolis: school building program controversy and control of school board
Pulaski County, 53
Purdue University, 88, 89
Purnell, Fred S., 111

Quakers, 72, 74; *See also* Richmond, Indiana; White Water Klan No. 60

Raab, Earl, 45
Ralston, Samuel, 27, 91, 158
Reed Church, 124
Reed Hospital, 124
Regression analysis, 53–54, 59, 69–70, 163–64, 205–7 (nn. 22, 23, 24)
Reid United Presbyterian Church, 116
Republican party, 12, 27, 53, 55; Klan influence in 1924 election, 151–52, 155–58. *See also* Election, 1924; Indiana Republican Newspaper Association; Jackson, Edward; Ku Klux Klan—Indiana: influence on party alignment; Ku Klux Klan—Indiana: influence on state congressional races; Ku Klux Klan—Indianapolis: and Republican machine; Stephenson, David Curtis; Watson, James E.
Richmond, Indiana, 8, 33, 61–62, 65, 81, 96, 130, 131, 138, 142; economic conditions, 66, 108–10; occupations of Klan members, 66–67; Klan membership among Quakers, 72; Klan membership in Protestant churches, 72; business elite, 108, 109–13; importance of Quaker community, 108; Klan membership, 108; population, 109; black and immigrant neighborhoods, 109, 119–20; working-class social conditions, 112–13; churches, 113; declining political participation, 113–15; Klan and black community, 119; local option elections (1908, 1914), 123; occupational and religious samples, 193–95. *See also* Whitewater Klan No. 60
Richmond City Council, 125
Richmond Commercial Club, 110–12
Richmond Evening Item, 26, 29, 121–22, 126–28
Richmond Kiwanis Club, 111, 112, 118

Richmond Lions Club, 112
Richmond Municipal Light Plant, 125, 127
Richmond Palladium, 119, 125, 126, 127–28, 187
Richmond Public Service Commission, 124
Richmond Rotary Club, 87, 111, 112, 118, 125, 139
Richmond South Side Improvement Association, 110
Roosevelt, Theodore, 115
Rowbottom, Harry E., 171–73
Roy O. West Library, 194

St. Louis, Missouri, 80, 81, 82
Salvatore, Nick, 85
Seymour, Indiana, 96
Shank, Lew, 25, 29, 145, 146, 154
Shelby County, 25
Shortridge High School, 149
Shumaker, Edward S., 34, 178
Simmons, William J., 15–16, 18
Smith, Al, 185
South Bend, Indiana, 25, 80, 81, 82, 83
South Bend Tribune, 26
Spurgeon, Silcott, 106
Standard Oil of Indiana, 83
Starke County, 53
Star Piano Company, 109
Starr, Oliver, 177
Stephenson, David Curtis (D. C.), 7, 38, 43, 46, 47, 70, 153, 116, 187; traditional interpretation, 8–9; early association with Klan, 14–15; early organizing efforts, 16–17; role in deposing Simmons, 18; appointed Grand Dragon, 19; attempts to buy Valparaiso University, 38–39; impact of murder conviction on Klan movement, 46, 185–86; life-style, 92; fails to promote Klan's ideals, 92–93; conflict with Evans, 93; organizes Richmond Klan, 116; 1924 primary campaign, 153–54; relationship with Jackson, 153–56; attempt to separate Indiana from national Klan movement, 154–58; conflict with Bossert, 154–58, 180–81; Republican state convention (1924), 156; and Indiana Highway Commission, 180–681; murder conviction, 181–83; testifies against Jackson, 183; made scapegoat for Klan's domination of Republican party, 187–88; arrested for public drunkenness, 221 (n. 7); autonomy from national leaders, 200–201 (n. 10)
Sullivan County, 53
Sunday, Billy, 28, 98
Switzerland County, 56

Taggart, Thomas, 27, 158. *See also* Democratic party
Terre Haute, Indiana, 25, 53, 60, 61, 80, 81, 84–85
Terre Haute, Indianapolis, and Eastern Traction Company, 124
Texas, 2
Thernstrom, Stephan: *The Other Bostonians*, 193
Tolerance, 193
Turk, Joseph P., 26, 172
TWK (Trade with Klansmen) campaign, 92
Tyler, Elizabeth, 16, 18

Union County, 53
United Brethren church, 72, 74
United Mine Workers of America, 96
U.S. Bureau of the Census: *Religious Bodies*, 194

U.S. Steel Corporation, 80
University of Notre Dame, 25
Updike, Ralph E., 171, 172

Valparaiso, Indiana, 96, 98
Valparaiso University: Klan's attempt to purchase, 38–39, 92, 93
Van Camp Company, 84
Vanderburgh County, 13–14, 173
Vestal, Albert H., 171
Vigo County, 61
Vincennes, Indiana, 24, 59, 84, 96, 103, 178, 179
Vincennes Commercial, 97, 178, 187
Vincennes Sun, 29, 178
Violence: employed by Indiana Klan, 23–25; employed against Klan, 25. *See also* Blacks; Catholics; Herrin, Illinois; Jews; Ku Klux Klan—Indianapolis: ethnic conflict; Ku Klux Klan—Indianapolis: racial conflict and segregation; Niles, Ohio; Whitewater Klan No. 60

Walb, Clyde, 157
Watson, James E., 153, 157, 220 (n. 4); conflict with Goodrich-New faction, 153; supports Jackson, 153; leading figure in state GOP, 157–58; makes deals with both Klan factions, 222 (n. 13)
Wayne County, 107; Klan membership records, 46–47; Irish and German immigrants in rural areas, 130–31; rural economy and population, 130–32; black population in rural areas, 131; absence of ethnic conflict in rural areas, 137; rural elites, 139
Webster, Indiana, 131
Wehrmeyer, Fred J., 175

Western Christian Advocate, 30
White County, 53, 59
Whitewater Klan No. 60 (Richmond, Wayne County): membership, 115; organized, 115–16; Anderson installed as leader, 116; characteristics of early members, 116–17; characteristics of all members, 117–18; and ethnic minorities, 118–20; weekly meetings, 120–21; social activities, 120–22; parade (October 4, 1923), 121–22; as a civic organization, 122–30; and Prohibition enforcement, 123; charitable activities, 123–24; attempts to build auditorium, 123–24; annexation controversy, 124–30; membership in rural areas, 130; characteristics of rural members, 133–37; membership among farm owners/tenants, 134–37; membership among rural town residents, 136–37; Prohibition and rural Klans, 138–39. *See also* Richmond, Indiana; Wayne County
Whiting, Indiana, 83
Williamsburg, Indiana, 131
Wilson, William E., 26, 172
Wisconsin, 81
Women of the Ku Klux Klan (Indiana), 7, 25, 47, 77, 213 (n. 59); involvement in social activities, 100–101; Kokomo membership records, 205 (n. 12). *See also* Halsep, Marie; Ku Klux Klan—Indiana
Wood, William R., 171
Wright "Bone Dry" bill, 181, 187

Young, Floyd, 178
Youngstown, Ohio, 2, 189, 209–10 (n. 67)

www.ingramcontent.com/pod-product-compliance
Lightning Source LLC
Chambersburg PA
CBHW031831180725
29815CB00001B/27